DEADPOOL

MONKEY BUSINESS

DEADPOOL MONKEY

WRITER: **DANIEL WAY**
PENCILS: **CARLO BARBERI & TAN ENG HUAT**
INKS: **JUAN VLASCO, SANDU FLOREA & TAN ENG HUAT**
COLORS: **MARTE GRACIA**
LETTERS: **VIRTUAL CALLIGRAPHY'S JOE SABINO**
COVER ARTIST: **JASON PEARSON**

ASSISTANT EDITOR: **JODY LEHEUP**
EDITOR: **AXEL ALONSO**

HIT-MONKEY #1

WRITER: **DANIEL WAY**
ART: **DALIBOR TALAJIĆ**
COLORS: **MATT HOLLINGSWORTH**
LETTERS: **JEFF ECKLEBERRY**
COVER ARTIST: **FRANK CHO**

ASSISTANT EDITOR: **SEBASTIAN GIRNER**
EDITOR: **AXEL ALONSO**
DIGITAL PRODUCTION: **TIM SMITH 3**
EDITOR: **HARRY GO**
VICE PRESIDENT, DIGITAL CONTENT: **JOHN CERILLI**

THIS COMIC ORIGINALLY APPEARED ON MARVEL DIGITAL COMICS UNLIMITED

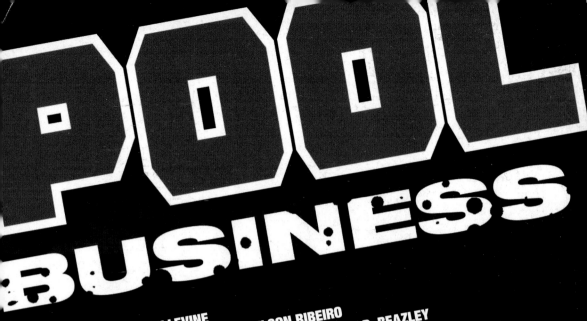

POOL BUSINESS

COLLECTION EDITOR: **CORY LEVINE**
ASSISTANT EDITORS: **ALEX STARBUCK** & **NELSON RIBEIRO**
EDITORS, SPECIAL PROJECTS: **JENNIFER GRÜNWALD** & **MARK D. BEAZLEY**
SENIOR EDITOR, SPECIAL PROJECTS: **JEFF YOUNGQUIST**
SENIOR VICE PRESIDENT OF SALES: **DAVID GABRIEL**
SVP OF BRAND PLANNING & COMMUNICATIONS: **MICHAEL PASCIULLO**
BOOK DESIGN: **RODOLFO MURAGUCHI**

EDITOR IN CHIEF: **AXEL ALONSO**
CHIEF CREATIVE OFFICER: **JOE QUESADA**
PUBLISHER: **DAN BUCKLEY**
EXECUTIVE PRODUCER: **ALAN FINE**

DEADPOOL VOL. 4: MONKEY BUSINESS. Contains material originally published in magazine form as DEADPOOL #19-22 and HIT-MONKEY #1. Second printing 2012. ISBN# 978-0-7851-4531-8. Published by MARVEL WORLDWIDE, INC., a subsidiary of MARVEL ENTERTAINMENT, LLC. OFFICE OF PUBLICATION: 135 West 50th Street, New York, NY 10020. Copyright © 2010 Marvel Characters, Inc. All rights reserved. $15.99 per copy in the U.S. and $17.99 in Canada (GST #R127032852); Canadian Agreement #40668537. All characters featured in this issue and the distinctive names and likenesses thereof, and all related indicia are trademarks of Marvel Characters, Inc. No similarity between any of the names, characters, persons, and/or institutions in this magazine with those of any living or dead person or institution is intended, and any such similarity which may exist is purely coincidental. **Printed in the U.S.A. ALAN FINE**, EVP - Office of the President, Marvel Worldwide, Inc. and EVP & CMO Marvel Characters B.V.; DAN BUCKLEY, Publisher & President - Print, Animation & Digital Divisions; JOE QUESADA, Chief Creative Officer; TOM BREVOORT, SVP of Publishing; DAVID BOGART, SVP of Operations & Procurement, Publishing; RUWAN JAYATILLEKE, SVP & Associate Publisher, Publishing; C.B. CEBULSKI, SVP of Creator & Content Development; DAVID GABRIEL, SVP of Publishing Sales & Circulation; MICHAEL PASCIULLO, SVP of Brand Planning & Communications; JIM O'KEEFE, VP of Operations & Logistics; DAN CARR, Executive Director of Publishing Technology; SUSAN CRESPI, Editorial Operations Manager; ALEX MORALES, Publishing Operations Manager; STAN LEE, Chairman Emeritus. For information regarding advertising in Marvel Comics or on Marvel.com, please contact Niza Disla, Director of Marvel Partnerships, at ndisla@marvel.com. For Marvel subscription inquiries, please call 800-217-9158. **Manufactured between 5/23/2012 and 6/11/2012 by R.R. DONNELLEY, INC., SALEM, VA, USA.**

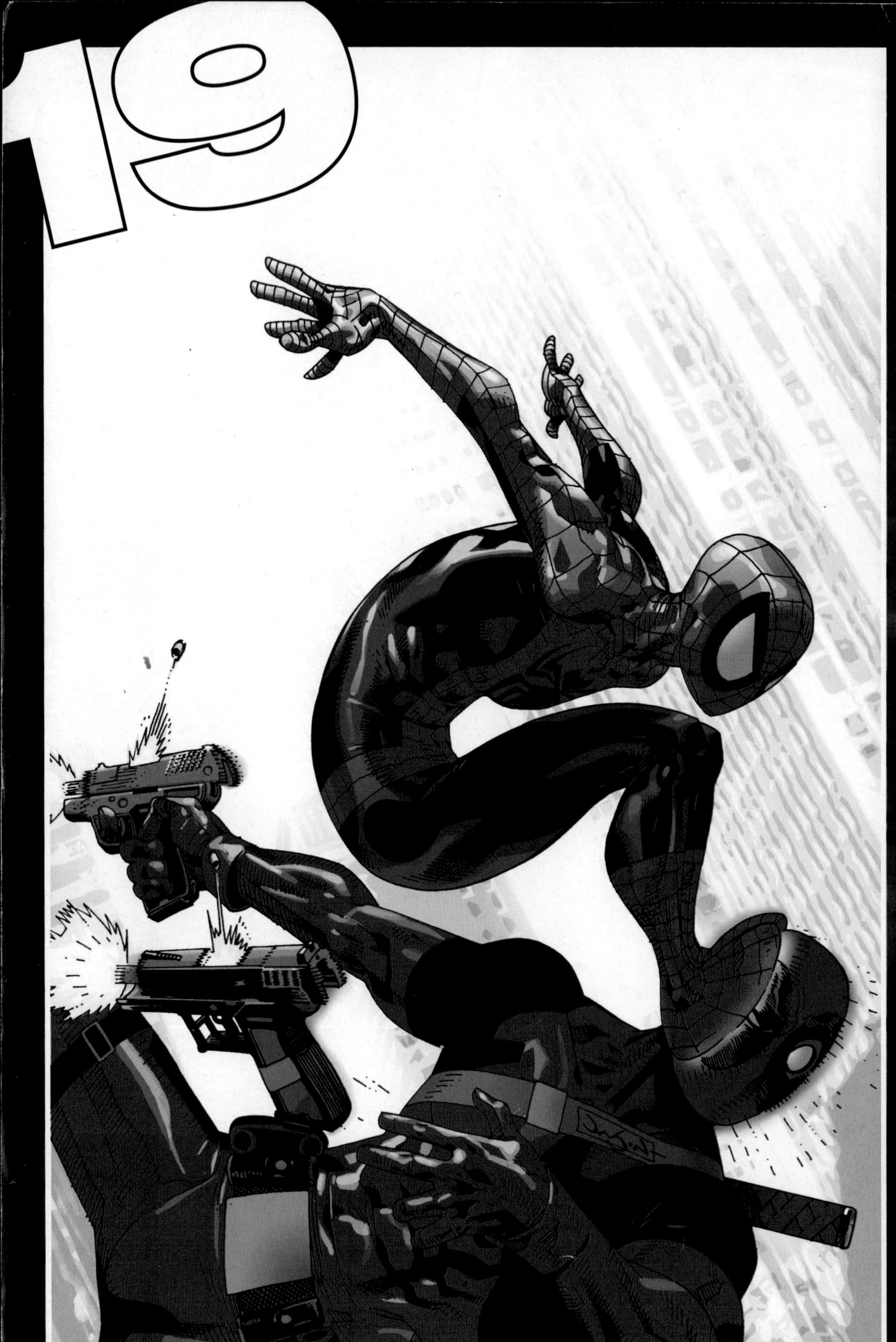
19

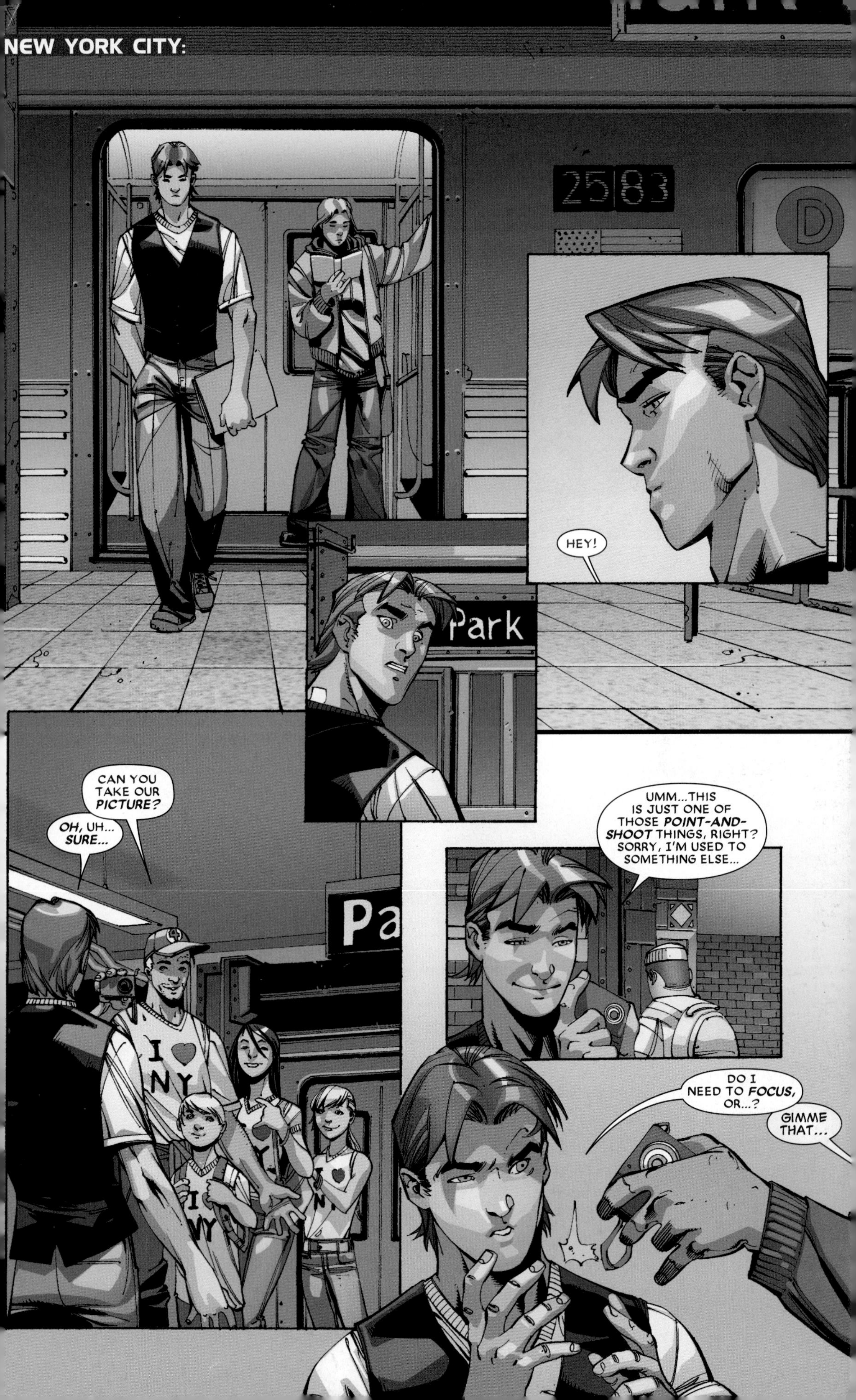
NEW YORK CITY:
2583
D
HEY!
Park
CAN YOU TAKE OUR PICTURE?
OH, UH... SURE...
Pa
I NY
UMM...THIS IS JUST ONE OF THOSE POINT-AND-SHOOT THINGS, RIGHT? SORRY, I'M USED TO SOMETHING ELSE...
DO I NEED TO FOCUS, OR...?
GIMME THAT...

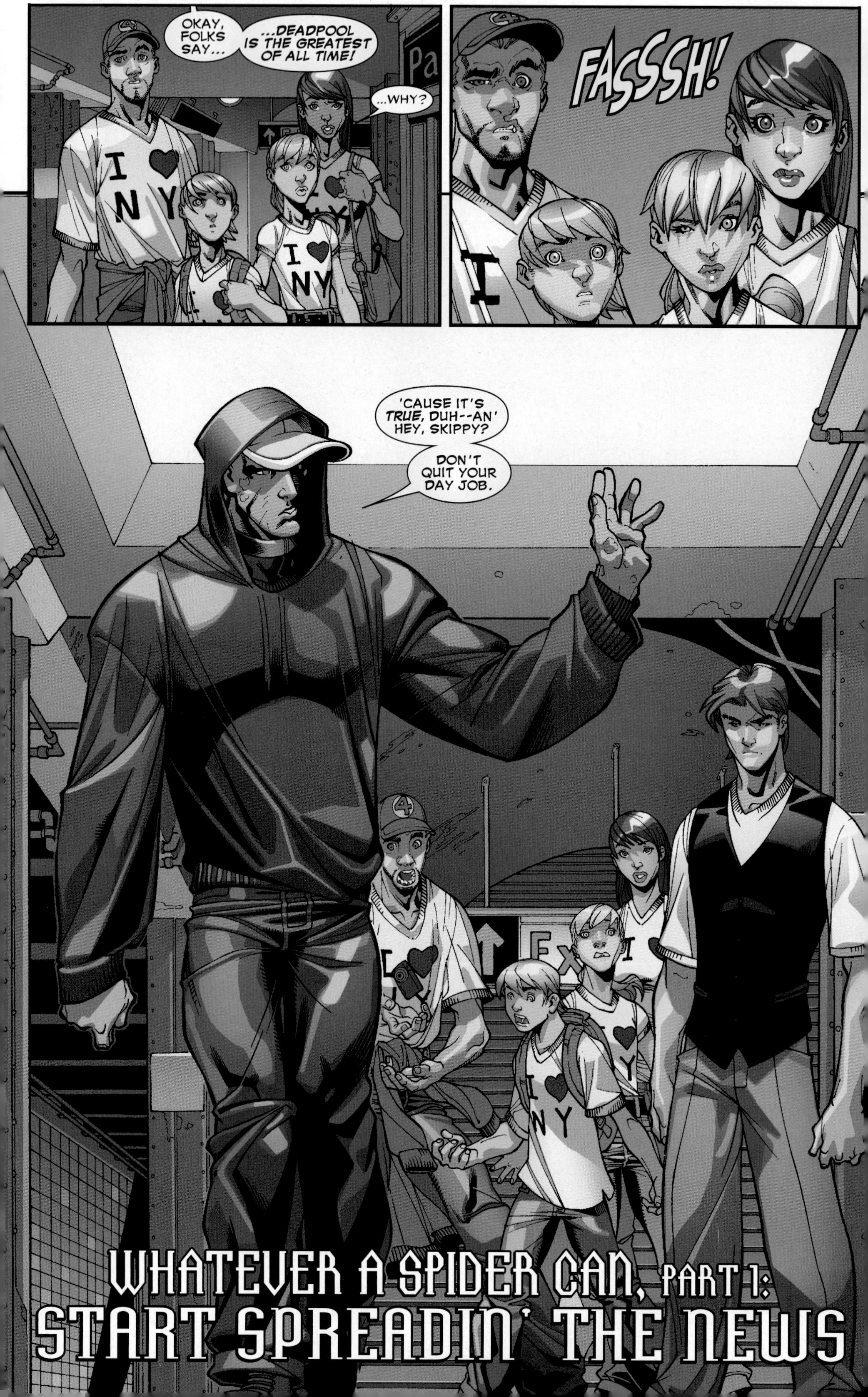
OKAY, FOLKS SAY...
...DEADPOOL IS THE GREATEST OF ALL TIME!
...WHY?
FASSSH!
'CAUSE IT'S TRUE, DUH--AN' HEY, SKIPPY?
DON'T QUIT YOUR DAY JOB.
WHATEVER A SPIDER CAN, PART 1:
START SPREADIN' THE NEWS

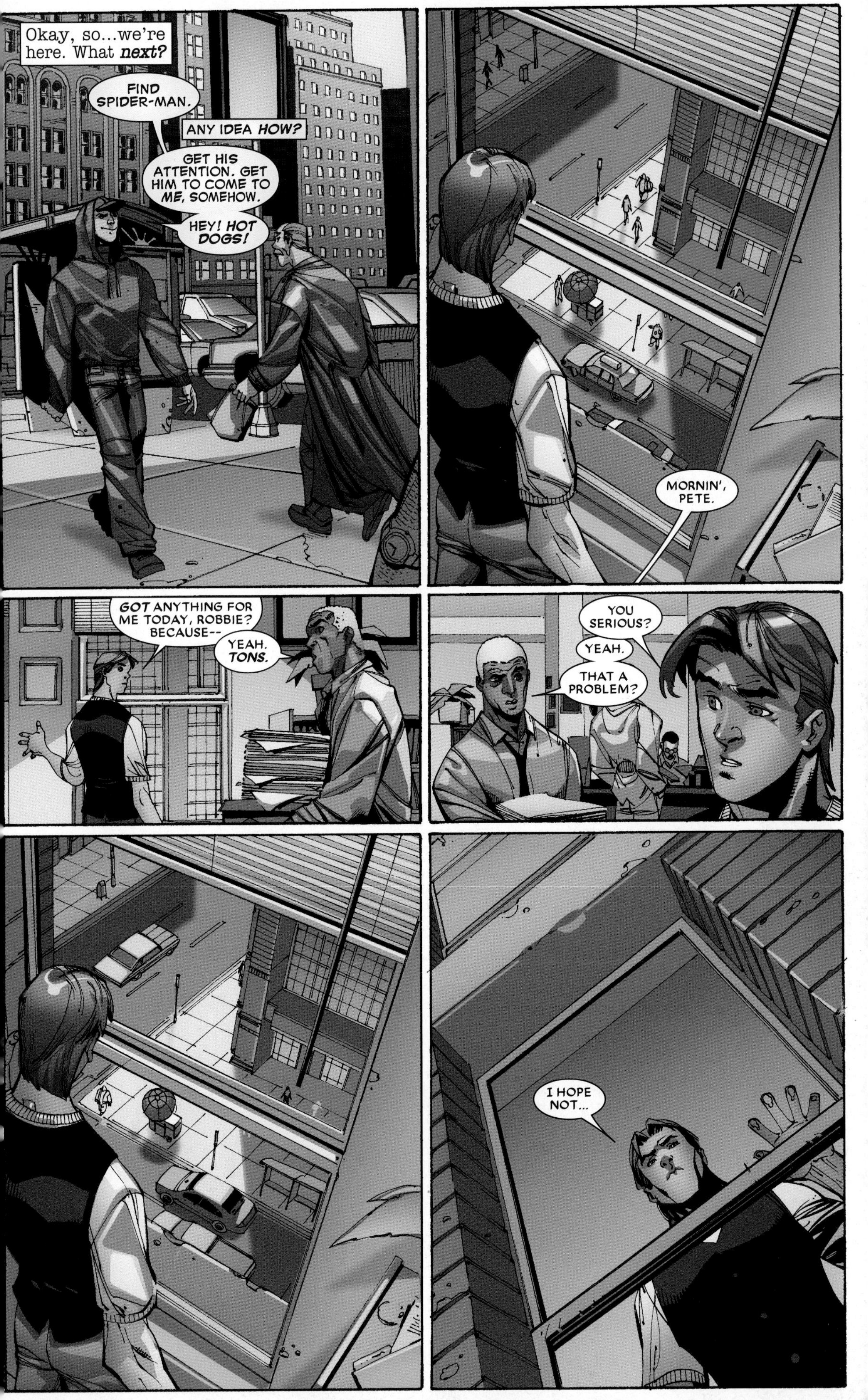
Okay, so...we're here. What *next?*
FIND SPIDER-MAN.
ANY IDEA *HOW?*
GET HIS ATTENTION. GET HIM TO COME TO *ME*, SOMEHOW.
HEY! *HOT DOGS!*
MORNIN', PETE.
GOT ANYTHING FOR ME TODAY, ROBBIE? BECAUSE--
YEAH. *TONS.*
YOU SERIOUS?
YEAH.
THAT A PROBLEM?
I HOPE NOT...

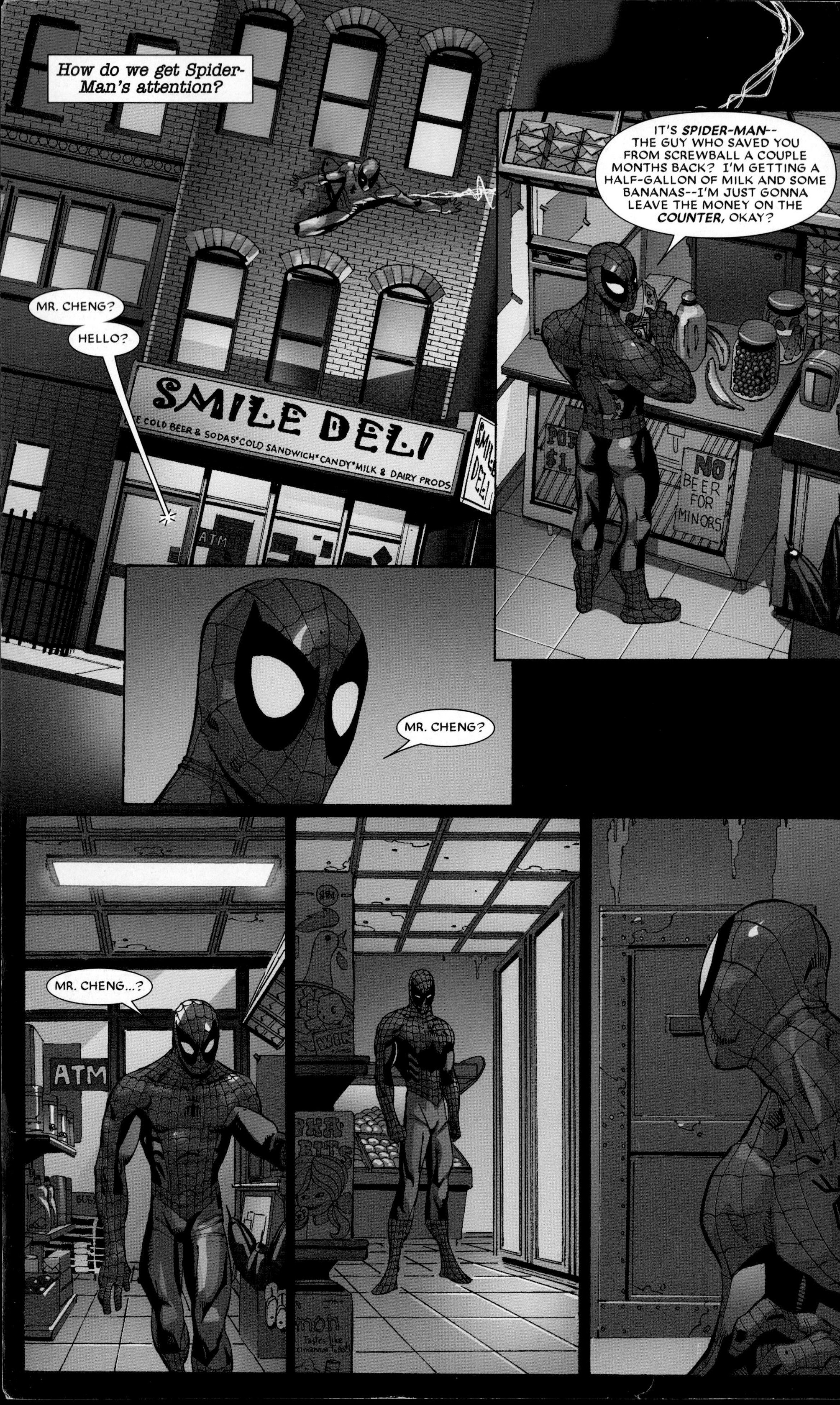
How do we get Spider-Man's attention?
MR. CHENG?
HELLO?
SMILE DELI
COLD BEER & SODAS*COLD SANDWICH*CANDY*MILK & DAIRY PRODS
SMILE DELI
ATM
IT'S SPIDER-MAN-- THE GUY WHO SAVED YOU FROM SCREWBALL A COUPLE MONTHS BACK? I'M GETTING A HALF-GALLON OF MILK AND SOME BANANAS--I'M JUST GONNA LEAVE THE MONEY ON THE COUNTER, OKAY?
NO BEER FOR MINORS
MR. CHENG?
MR. CHENG...?
ATM
Tastes like cinnamon toast

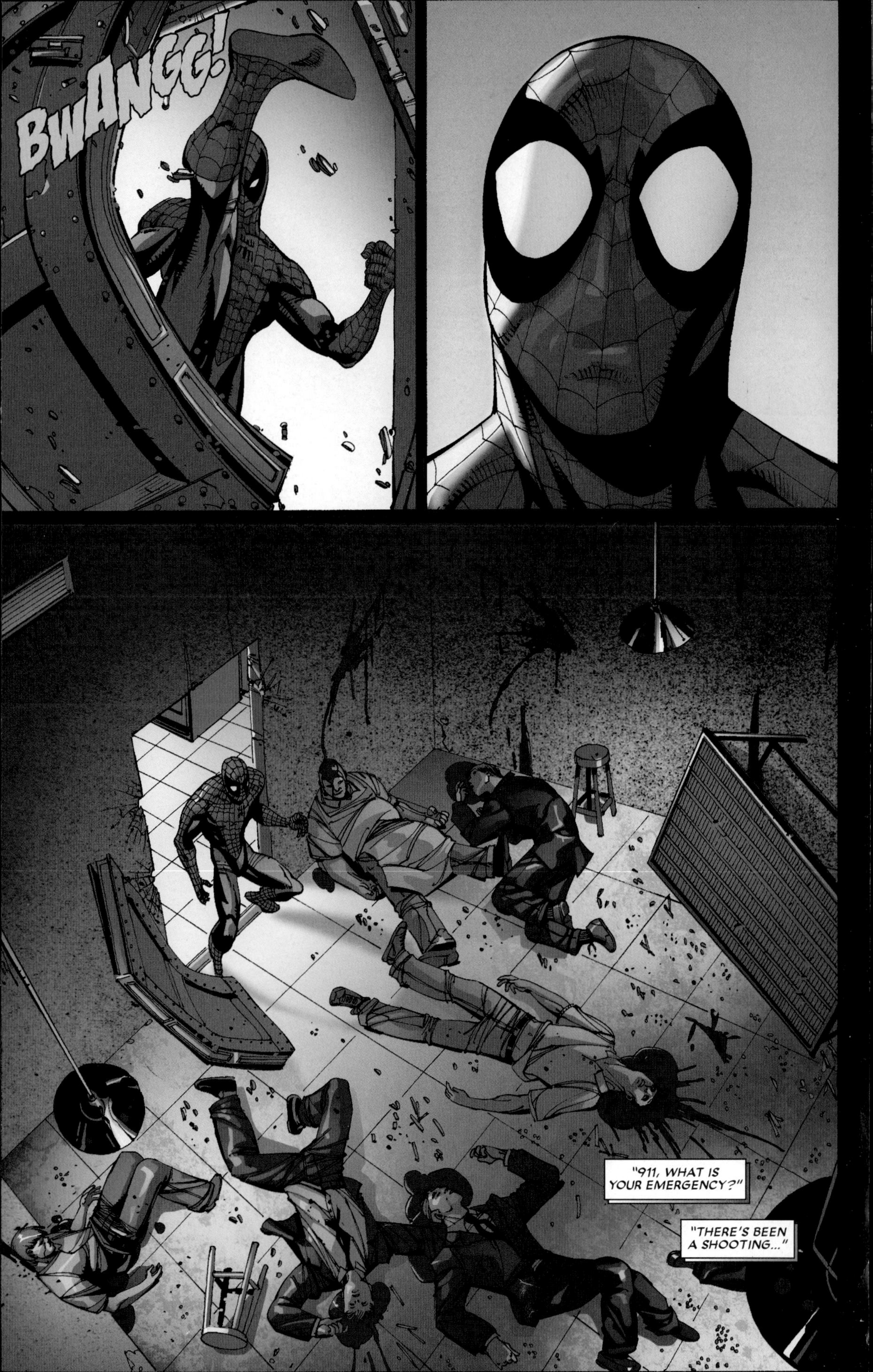
BWANGG!
"911, WHAT IS YOUR EMERGENCY?"
"THERE'S BEEN A SHOOTING..."

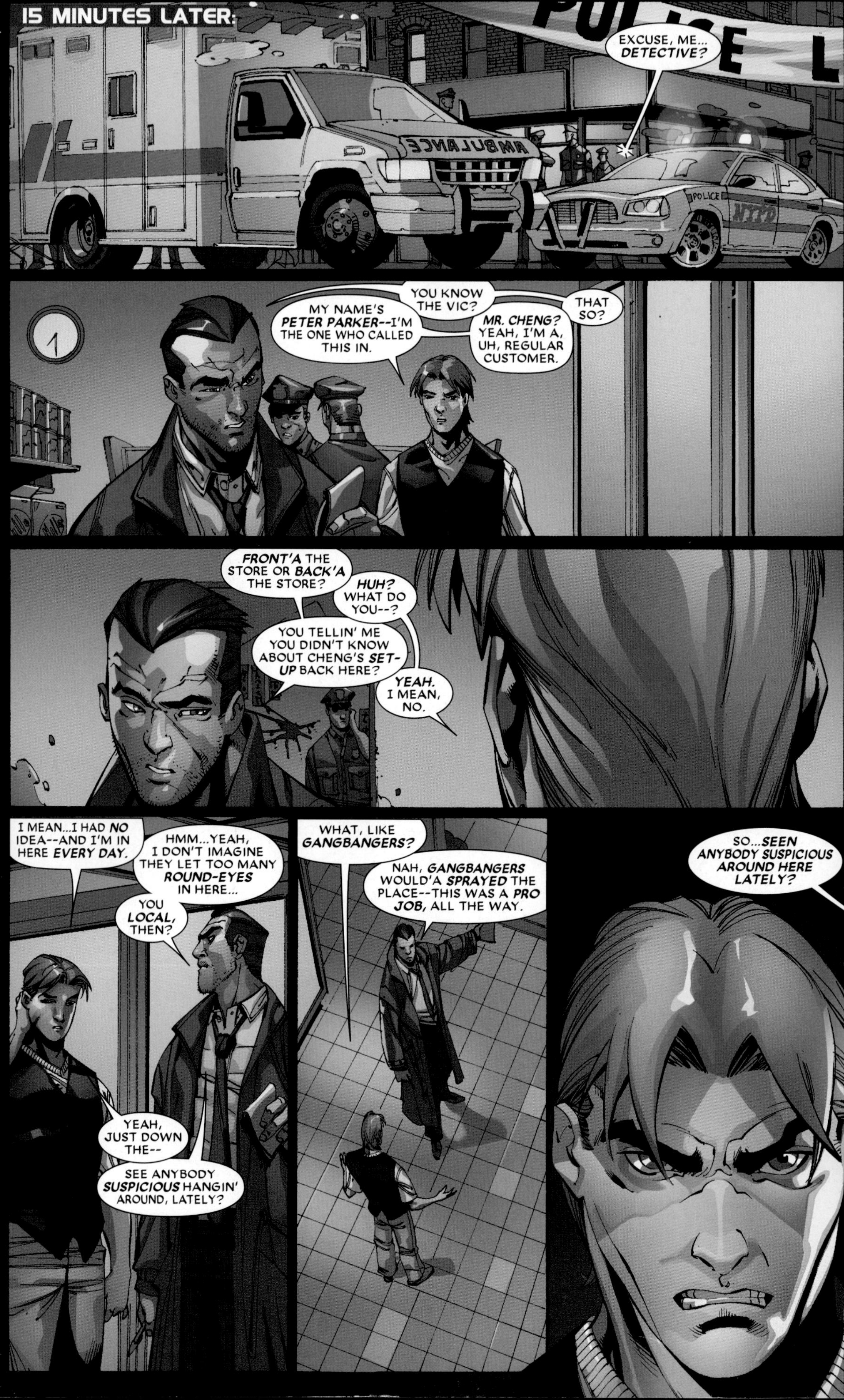
15 MINUTES LATER:
POLICE L
EXCUSE, ME... DETECTIVE?
AMBULANCE
POLICE
NYPD
MY NAME'S PETER PARKER--I'M THE ONE WHO CALLED THIS IN.
YOU KNOW THE VIC?
MR. CHENG? YEAH, I'M A, UH, REGULAR CUSTOMER.
THAT SO?
FRONT'A THE STORE OR BACK'A THE STORE?
HUH? WHAT DO YOU--?
YOU TELLIN' ME YOU DIDN'T KNOW ABOUT CHENG'S SET-UP BACK HERE?
YEAH. I MEAN, NO.
I MEAN...I HAD NO IDEA--AND I'M IN HERE EVERY DAY.
HMM...YEAH, I DON'T IMAGINE THEY LET TOO MANY ROUND-EYES IN HERE...
YOU LOCAL, THEN?
YEAH, JUST DOWN THE--
SEE ANYBODY SUSPICIOUS HANGIN' AROUND, LATELY?
WHAT, LIKE GANGBANGERS?
NAH, GANGBANGERS WOULD'A SPRAYED THE PLACE--THIS WAS A PRO JOB, ALL THE WAY.
SO...SEEN ANYBODY SUSPICIOUS AROUND HERE LATELY?

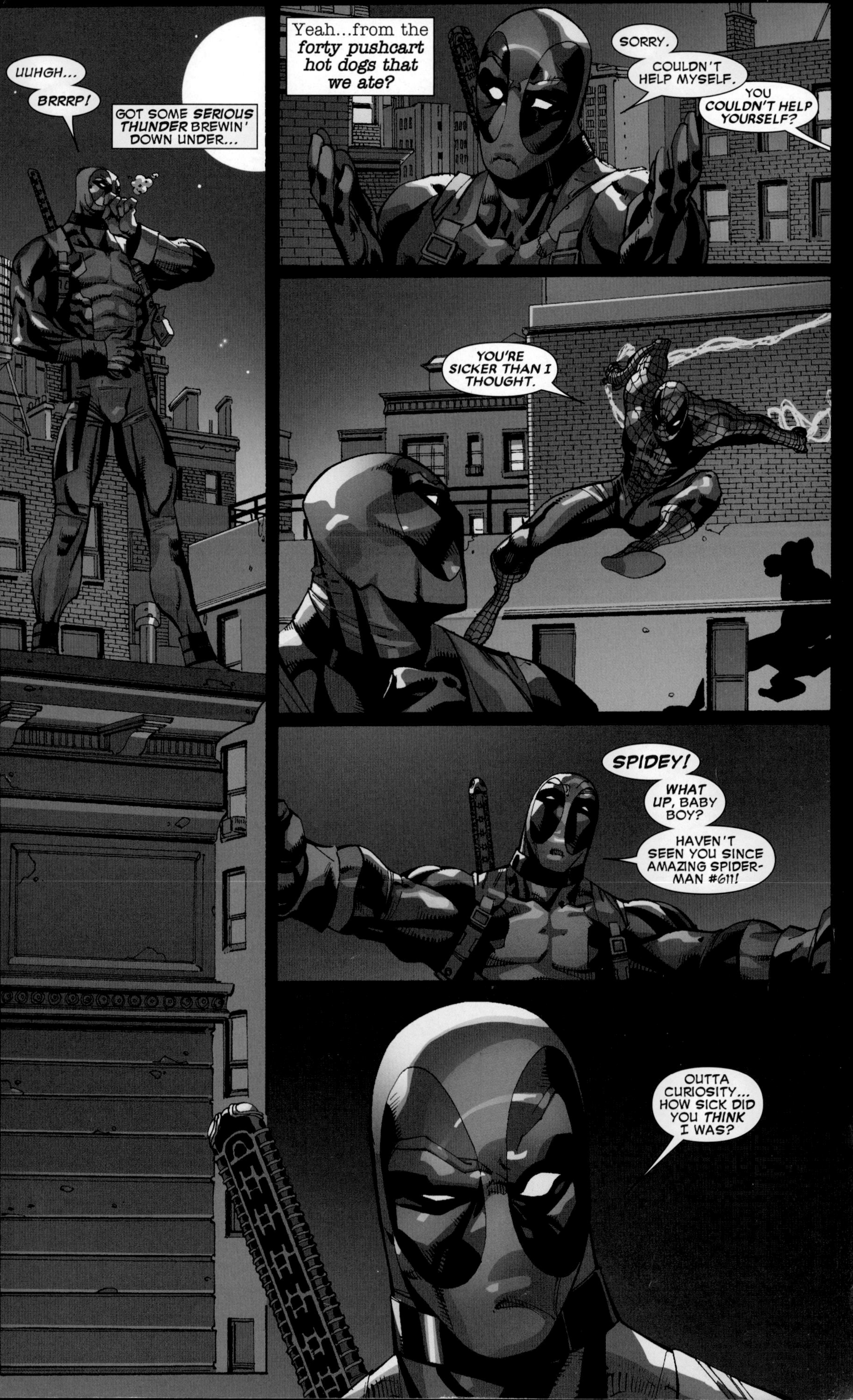
UUHGH...
BRRRP!
GOT SOME SERIOUS THUNDER BREWIN' DOWN UNDER...
Yeah...from the forty pushcart hot dogs that we ate?
SORRY.
COULDN'T HELP MYSELF.
YOU COULDN'T HELP YOURSELF?
YOU'RE SICKER THAN I THOUGHT.
SPIDEY!
WHAT UP, BABY BOY?
HAVEN'T SEEN YOU SINCE AMAZING SPIDER-MAN #611!
OUTTA CURIOSITY... HOW SICK DID YOU THINK I WAS?

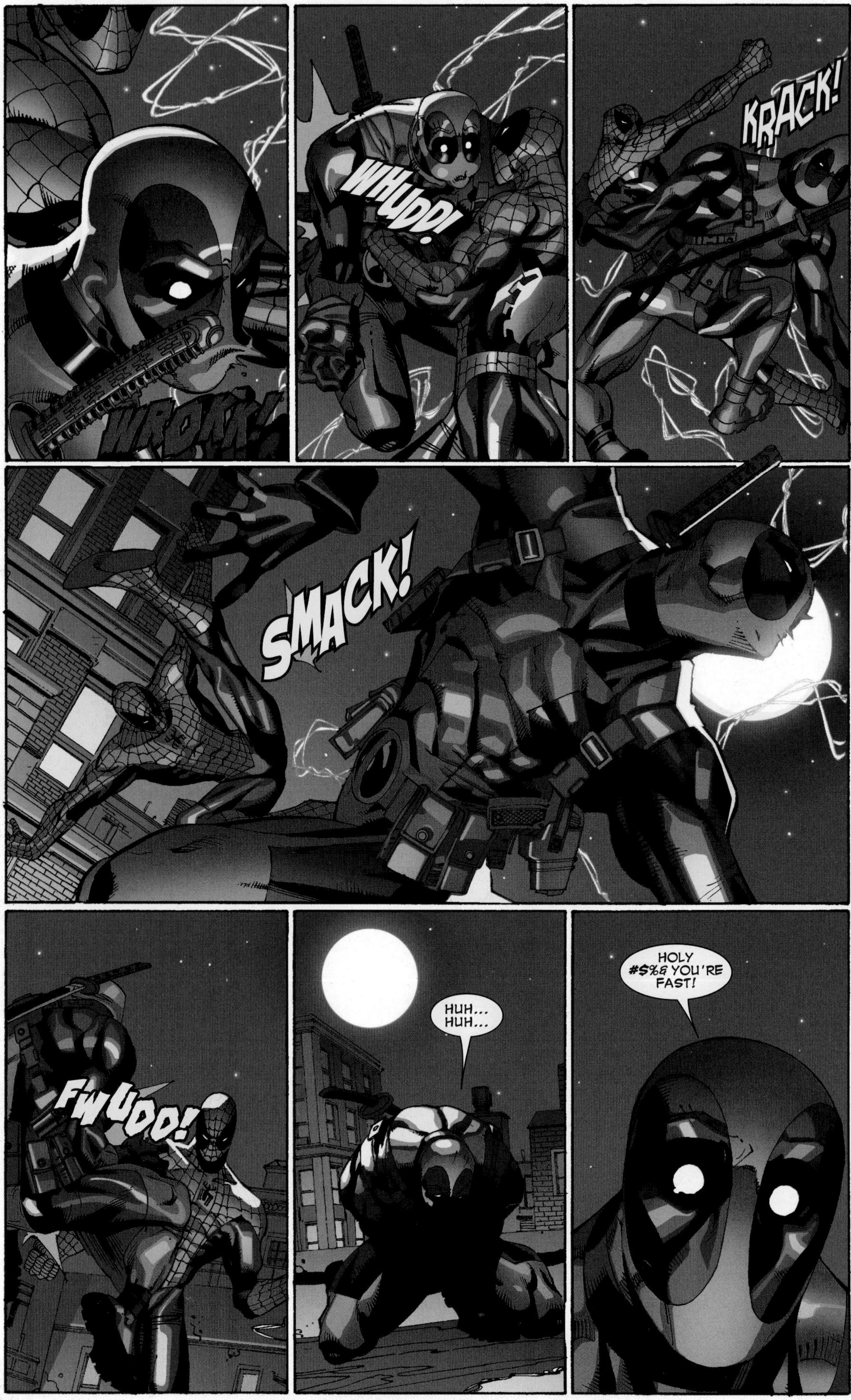
WROKK!
WHUDD!
KRACK!
SMACK!
FWUDD!
HUH...
HUH...
HOLY
#$%& YOU'RE
FAST!

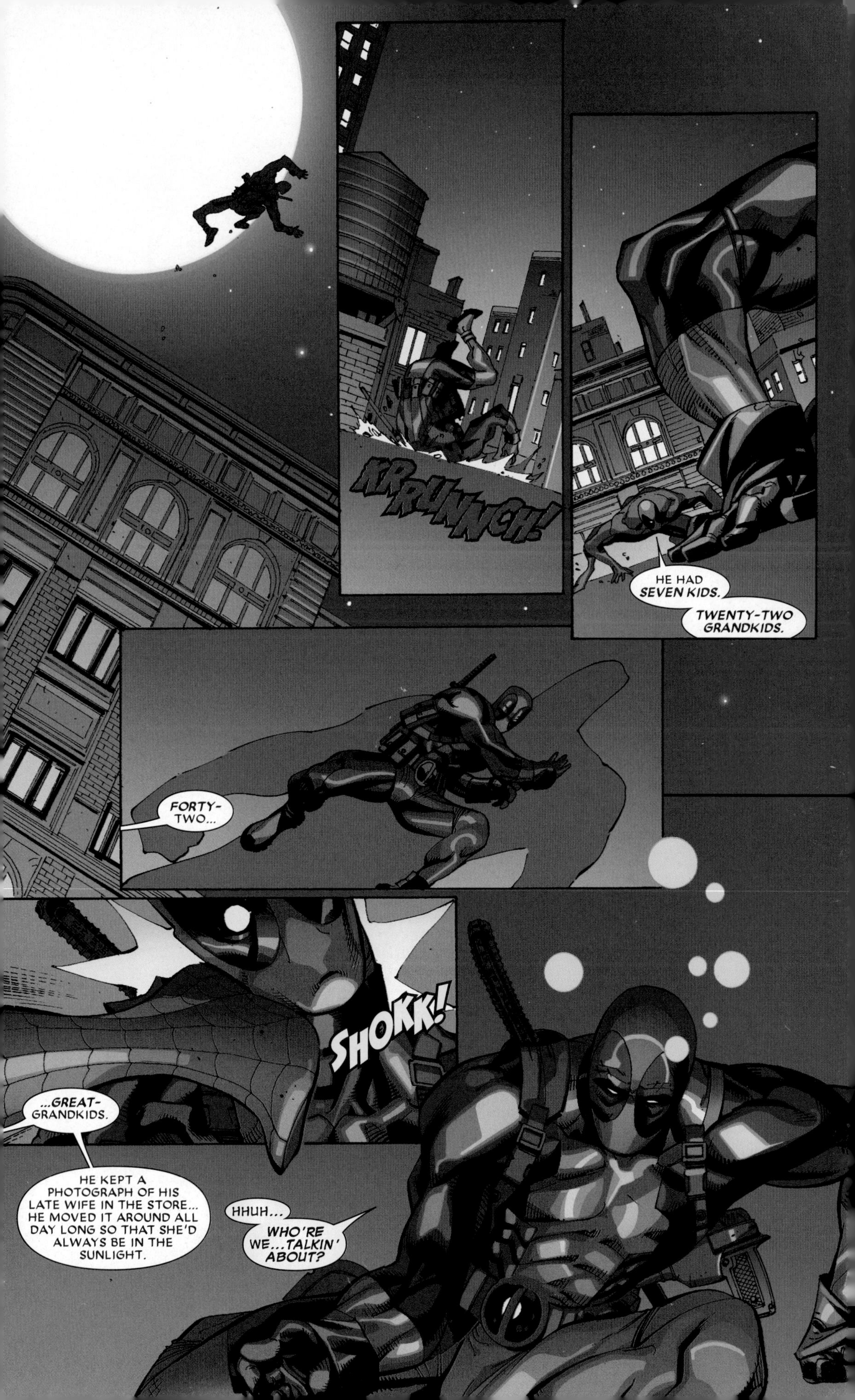
KRRUNNCH!
HE HAD SEVEN KIDS.
TWENTY-TWO GRANDKIDS.
FORTY-TWO...
SHOKK!
...GREAT-GRANDKIDS.
HE KEPT A PHOTOGRAPH OF HIS LATE WIFE IN THE STORE... HE MOVED IT AROUND ALL DAY LONG SO THAT SHE'D ALWAYS BE IN THE SUNLIGHT.
HHUH... WHO'RE WE...TALKIN' ABOUT?

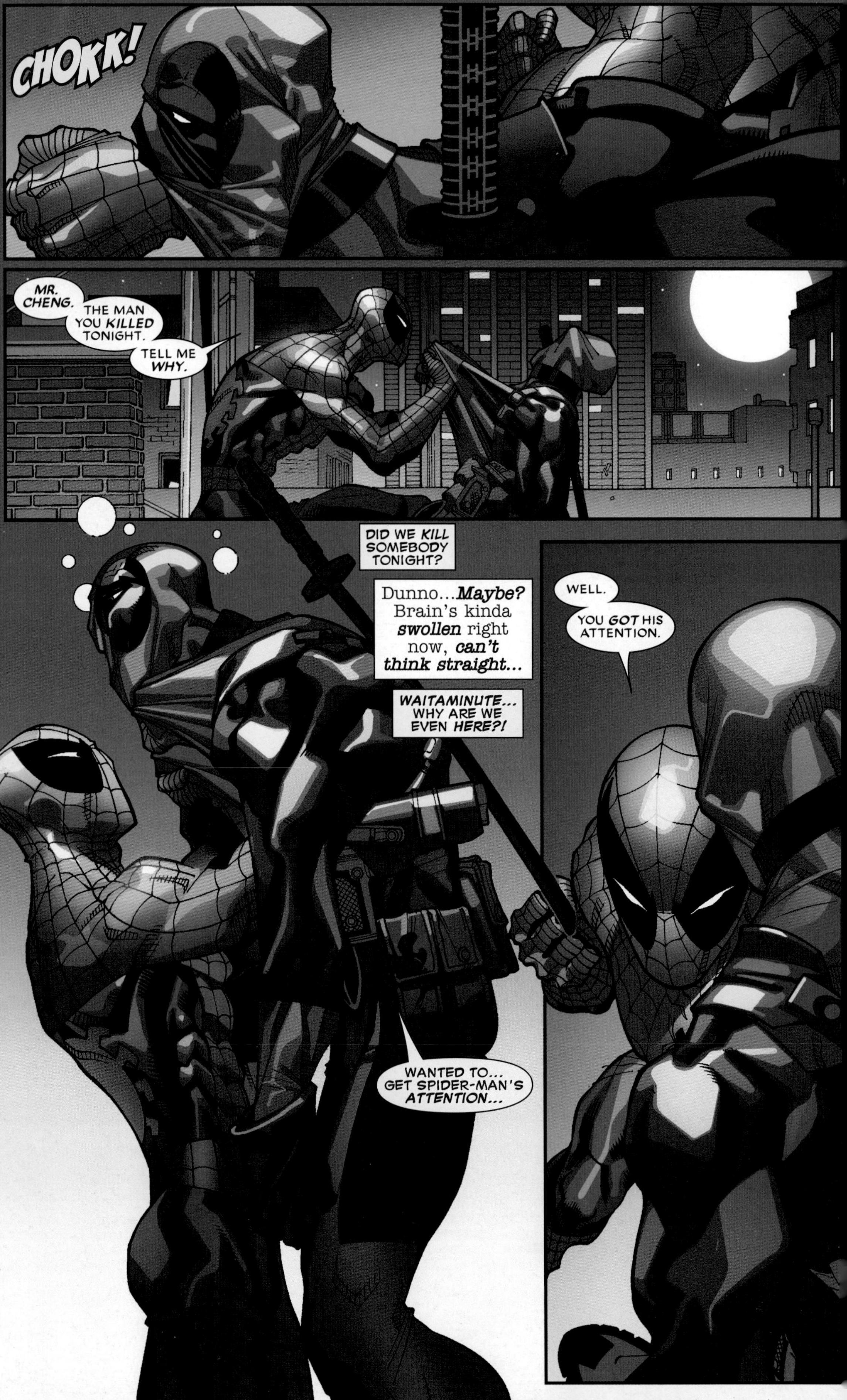
CHOKK!
MR. CHENG.
THE MAN YOU KILLED TONIGHT.
TELL ME WHY.
DID WE KILL SOMEBODY TONIGHT?
Dunno...Maybe? Brain's kinda swollen right now, can't think straight...
WAITAMINUTE... WHY ARE WE EVEN HERE?!
WANTED TO... GET SPIDER-MAN'S ATTENTION...
WELL.
YOU GOT HIS ATTENTION.

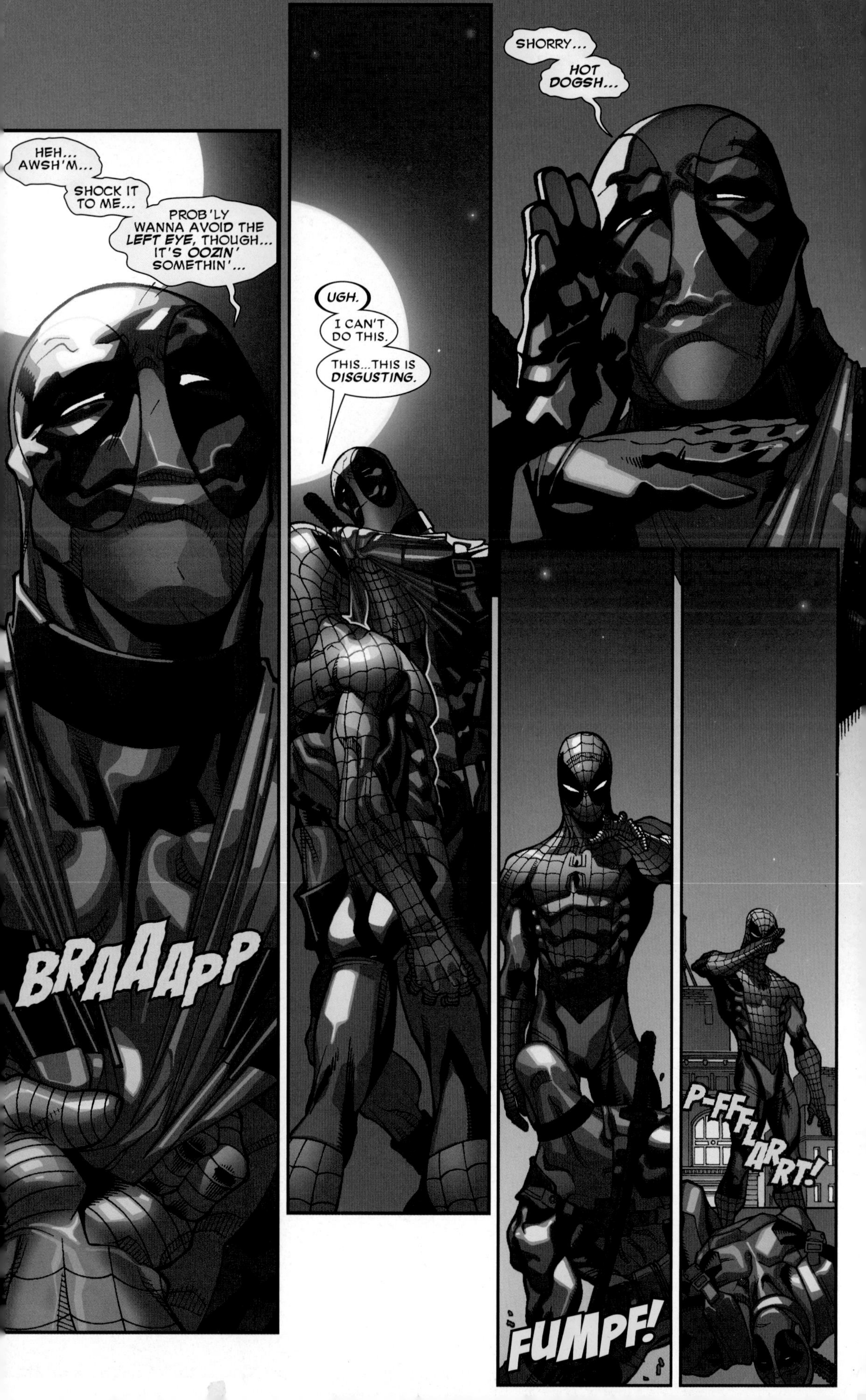
HEH... AWSH'M...
SHOCK IT TO ME...
PROB'LY WANNA AVOID THE LEFT EYE, THOUGH... IT'S OOZIN' SOMETHIN'...
BRAAAPP
UGH.
I CAN'T DO THIS.
THIS...THIS IS DISGUSTING.
SHORRY...
HOT DOGSH...
FUMPF!
P-FFFLARRT!

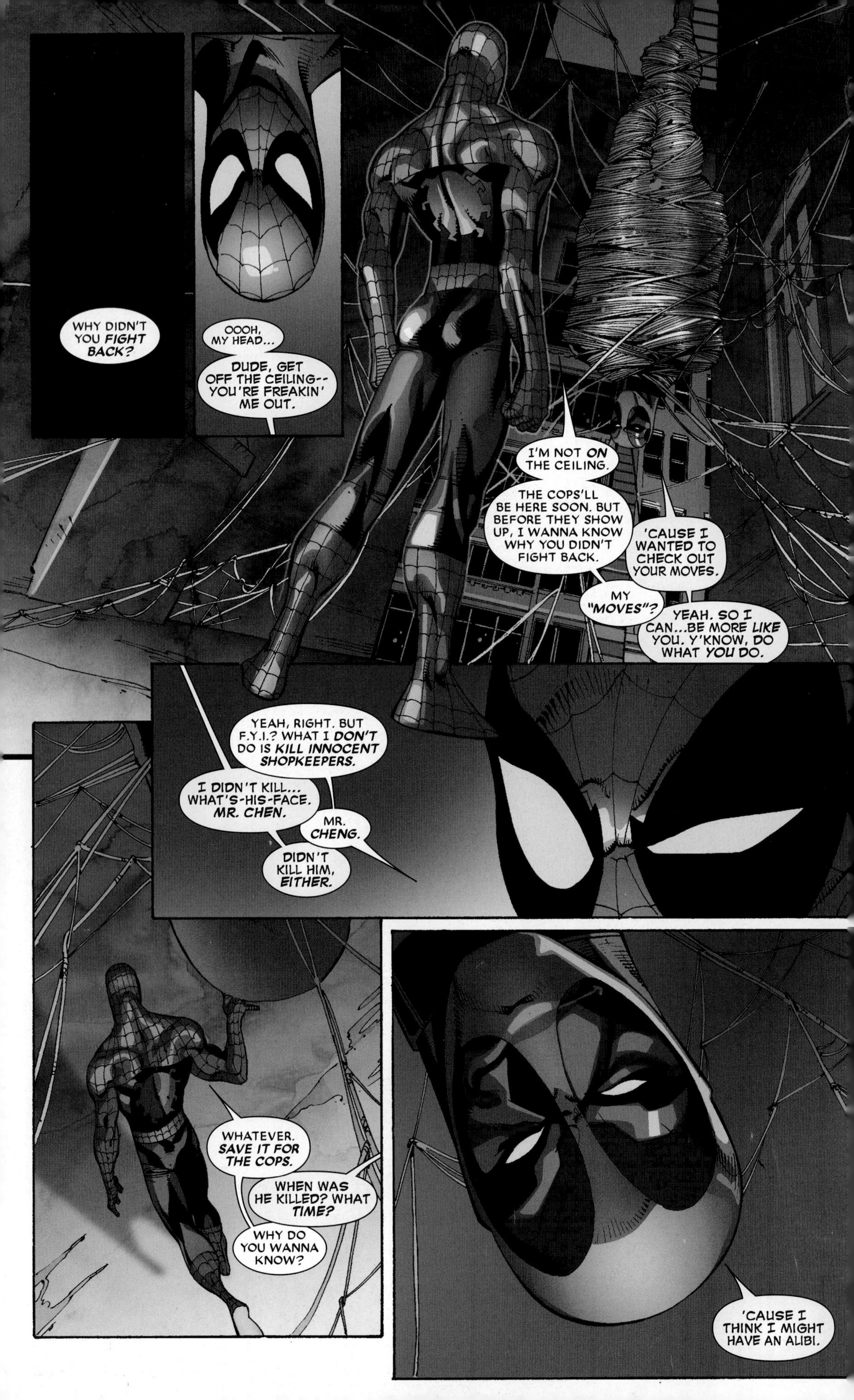

WHY DIDN'T YOU FIGHT BACK?
OOOH, MY HEAD...
DUDE, GET OFF THE CEILING-- YOU'RE FREAKIN' ME OUT.
I'M NOT ON THE CEILING.
THE COPS'LL BE HERE SOON. BUT BEFORE THEY SHOW UP, I WANNA KNOW WHY YOU DIDN'T FIGHT BACK.
'CAUSE I WANTED TO CHECK OUT YOUR MOVES.
MY "MOVES"?
YEAH. SO I CAN...BE MORE LIKE YOU. Y'KNOW, DO WHAT YOU DO.
YEAH, RIGHT. BUT F.Y.I.? WHAT I DON'T DO IS KILL INNOCENT SHOPKEEPERS.
I DIDN'T KILL... WHAT'S-HIS-FACE. MR. CHEN.
MR. CHENG.
DIDN'T KILL HIM, EITHER.
WHATEVER. SAVE IT FOR THE COPS.
WHEN WAS HE KILLED? WHAT TIME?
WHY DO YOU WANNA KNOW?
'CAUSE I THINK I MIGHT HAVE AN ALIBI.

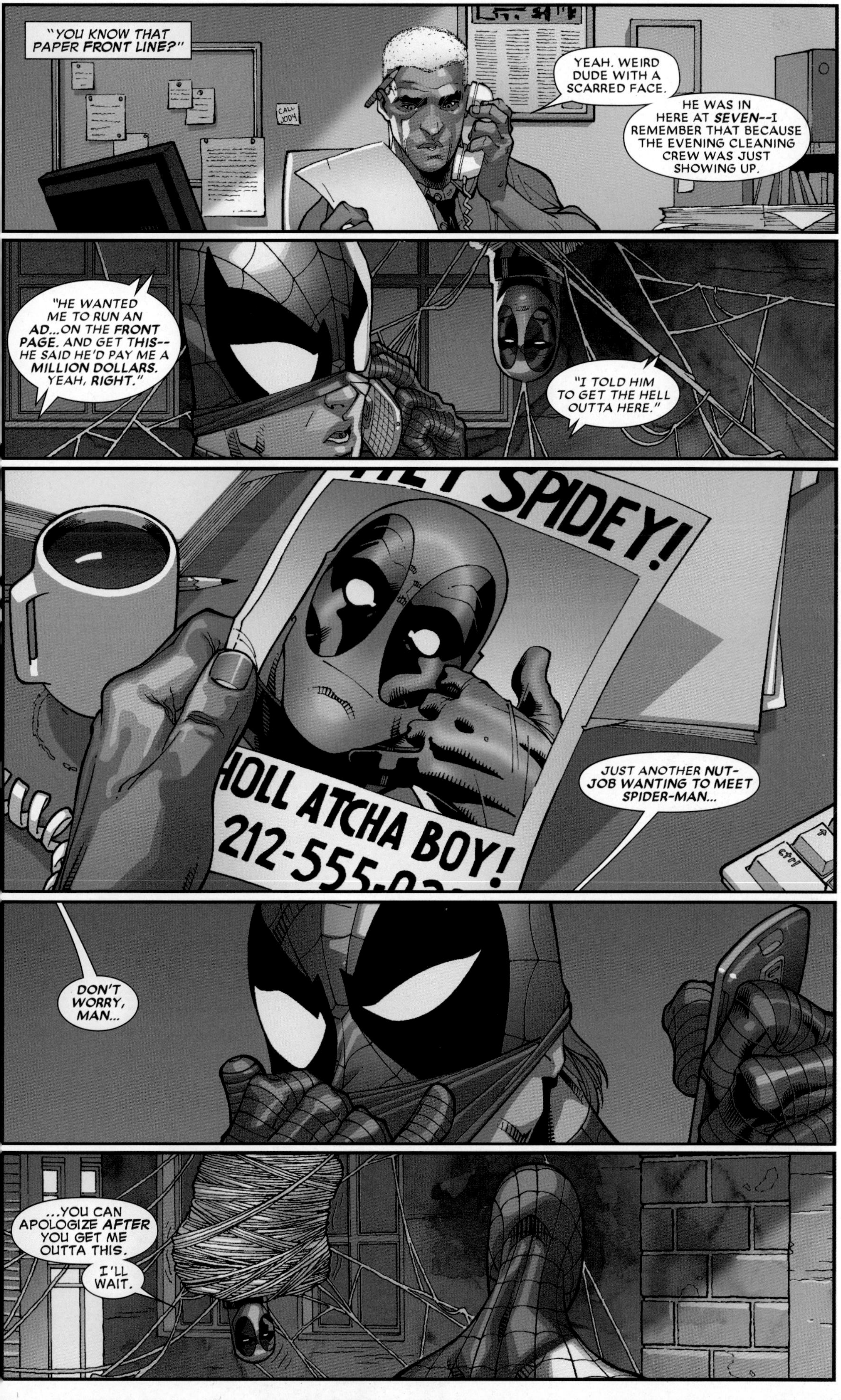
"YOU KNOW THAT PAPER FRONT LINE?"
YEAH. WEIRD DUDE WITH A SCARRED FACE.
HE WAS IN HERE AT SEVEN--I REMEMBER THAT BECAUSE THE EVENING CLEANING CREW WAS JUST SHOWING UP.
"HE WANTED ME TO RUN AN AD...ON THE FRONT PAGE. AND GET THIS--HE SAID HE'D PAY ME A MILLION DOLLARS. YEAH, RIGHT."
"I TOLD HIM TO GET THE HELL OUTTA HERE."
SPIDEY!
HOLL ATCHA BOY!
212-555-
JUST ANOTHER NUT-JOB WANTING TO MEET SPIDER-MAN...
DON'T WORRY, MAN...
...YOU CAN APOLOGIZE AFTER YOU GET ME OUTTA THIS.
I'LL WAIT.

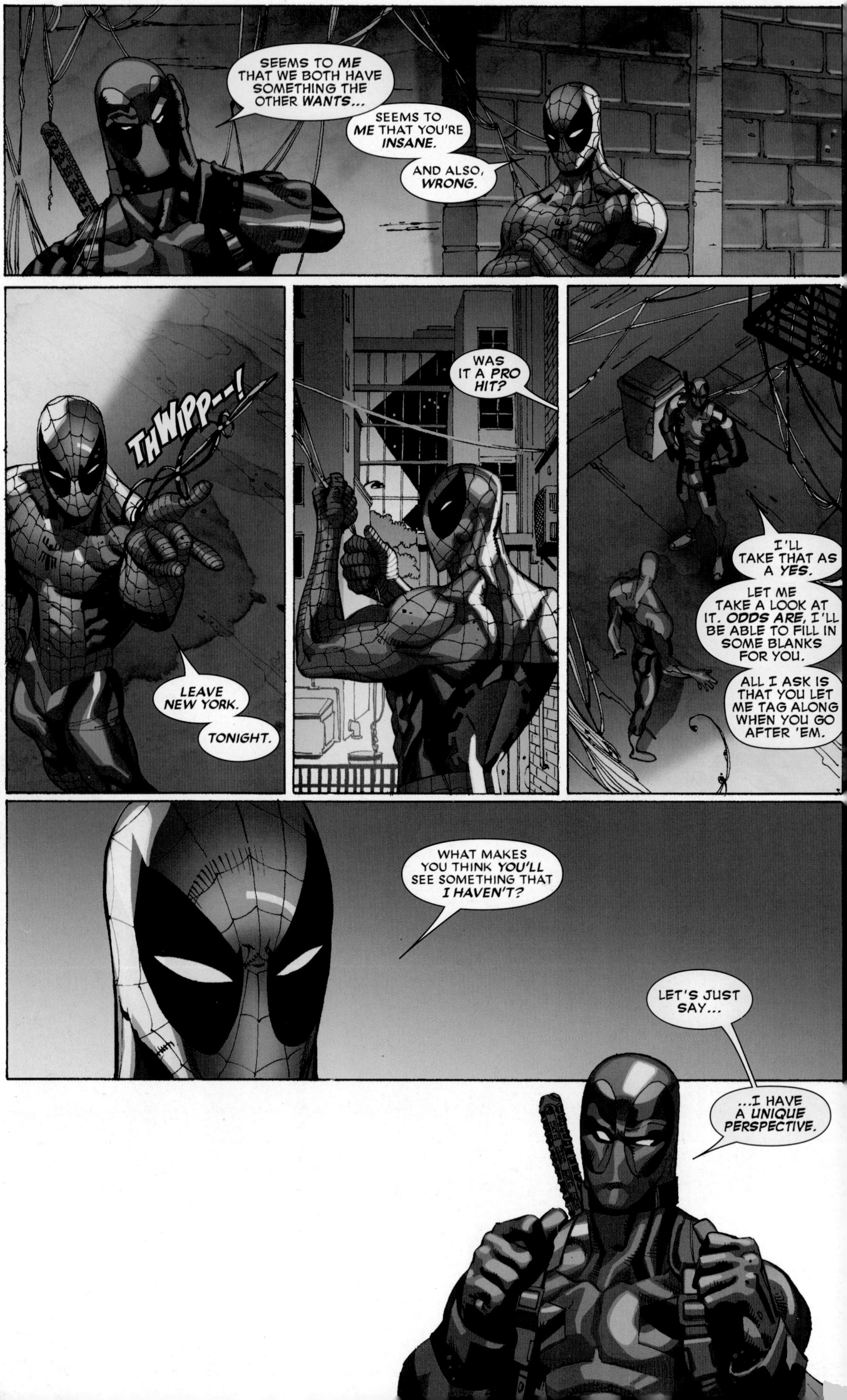
SEEMS TO ME THAT WE BOTH HAVE SOMETHING THE OTHER WANTS...
SEEMS TO ME THAT YOU'RE INSANE.
AND ALSO, WRONG.
THWIPP--!
LEAVE NEW YORK.
TONIGHT.
WAS IT A PRO HIT?
I'LL TAKE THAT AS A YES.
LET ME TAKE A LOOK AT IT. ODDS ARE, I'LL BE ABLE TO FILL IN SOME BLANKS FOR YOU.
ALL I ASK IS THAT YOU LET ME TAG ALONG WHEN YOU GO AFTER 'EM.
WHAT MAKES YOU THINK YOU'LL SEE SOMETHING THAT I HAVEN'T?
LET'S JUST SAY...
...I HAVE A UNIQUE PERSPECTIVE.

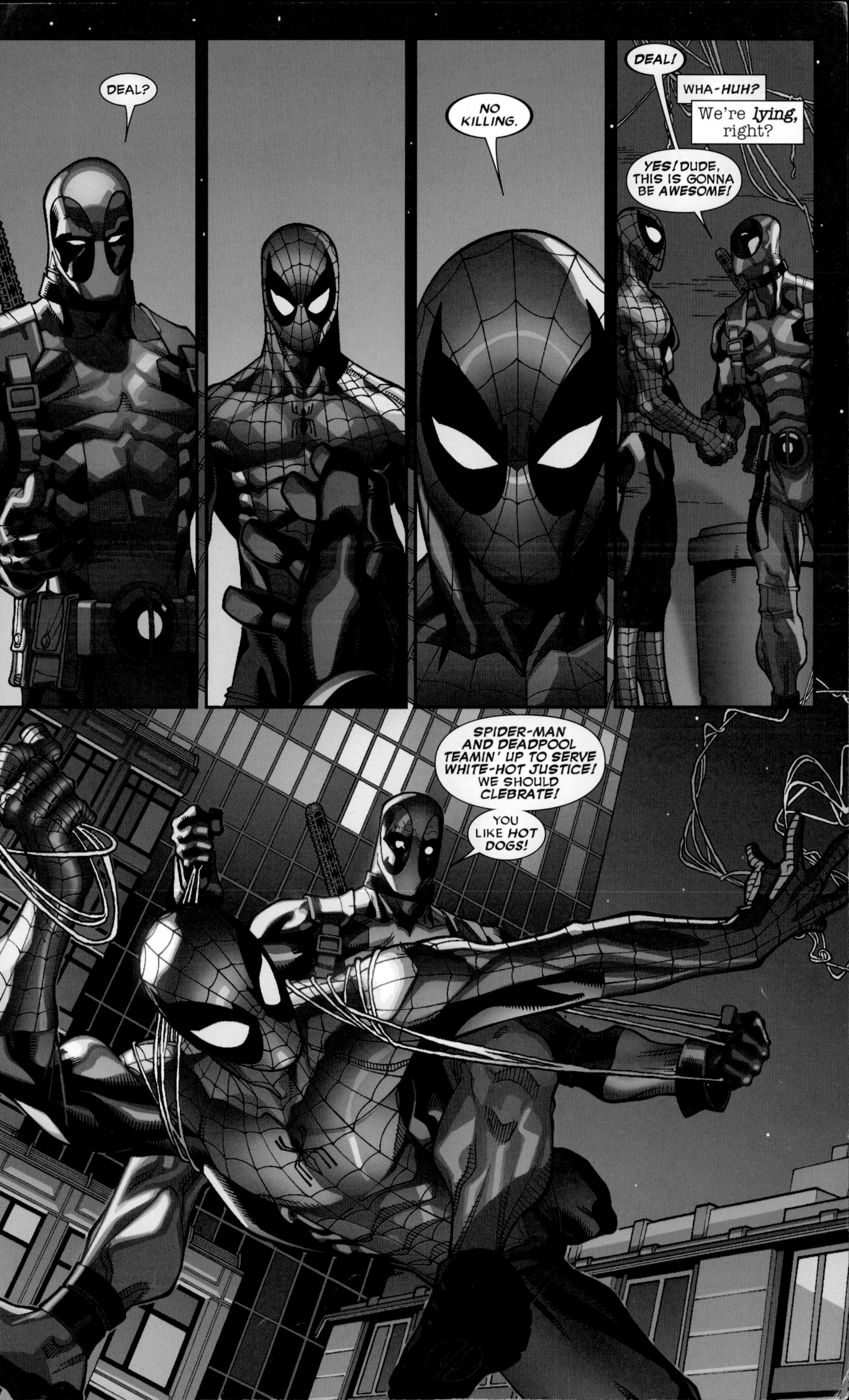
DEAL?
NO KILLING.
DEAL!
WHA-HUH?
We're lying, right?
YES! DUDE, THIS IS GONNA BE AWESOME!
SPIDER-MAN AND DEADPOOL TEAMIN' UP TO SERVE WHITE-HOT JUSTICE! WE SHOULD CLEBRATE!
YOU LIKE HOT DOGS!

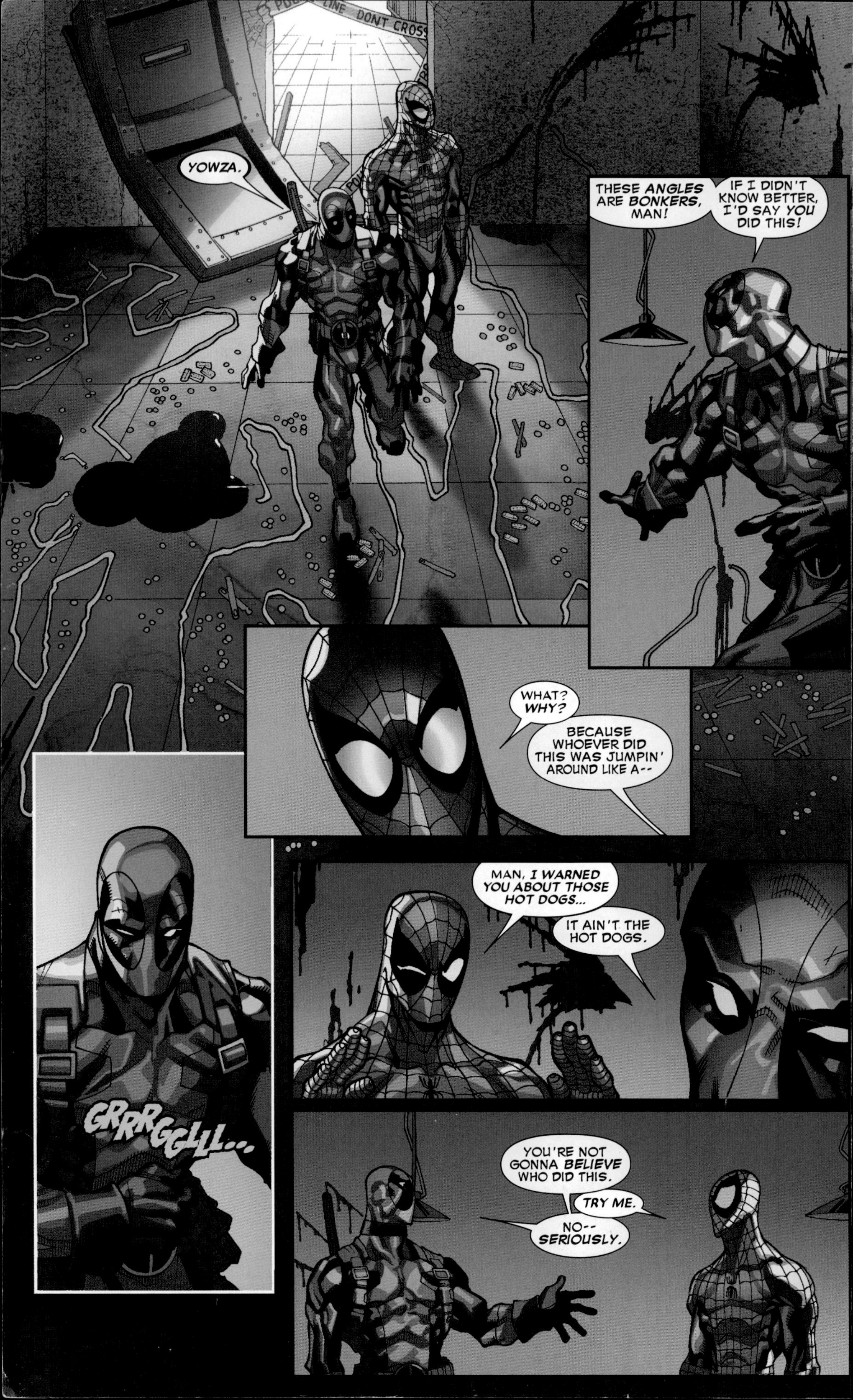

POLICE LINE DONT CROSS
YOWZA.
THESE ANGLES ARE BONKERS, MAN!
IF I DIDN'T KNOW BETTER, I'D SAY YOU DID THIS!
WHAT? WHY?
BECAUSE WHOEVER DID THIS WAS JUMPIN' AROUND LIKE A--
GRRRGGLLL...
MAN, I WARNED YOU ABOUT THOSE HOT DOGS...
IT AIN'T THE HOT DOGS.
YOU'RE NOT GONNA BELIEVE WHO DID THIS.
TRY ME.
NO-- SERIOUSLY.

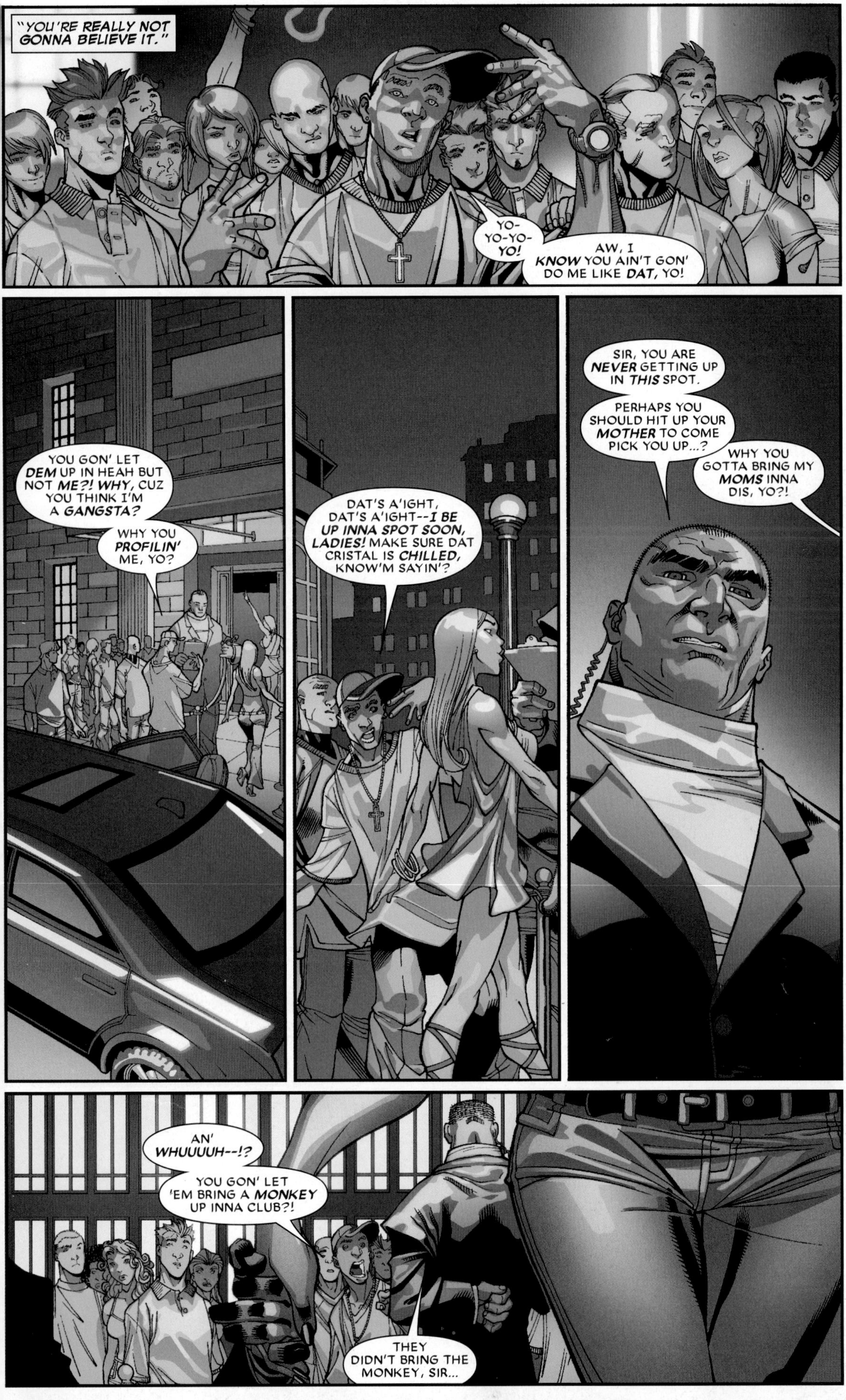
"YOU'RE REALLY NOT GONNA BELIEVE IT."
YO-YO-YO-YO!
AW, I KNOW YOU AIN'T GON' DO ME LIKE DAT, YO!
YOU GON' LET DEM UP IN HEAH BUT NOT ME?! WHY, CUZ YOU THINK I'M A GANGSTA?
WHY YOU PROFILIN' ME, YO?
DAT'S A'IGHT, DAT'S A'IGHT--I BE UP INNA SPOT SOON, LADIES! MAKE SURE DAT CRISTAL IS CHILLED, KNOW'M SAYIN'?
SIR, YOU ARE NEVER GETTING UP IN THIS SPOT.
PERHAPS YOU SHOULD HIT UP YOUR MOTHER TO COME PICK YOU UP...?
WHY YOU GOTTA BRING MY MOMS INNA DIS, YO?!
AN' WHUUUUH--!?
YOU GON' LET 'EM BRING A MONKEY UP INNA CLUB?!
THEY DIDN'T BRING THE MONKEY, SIR...

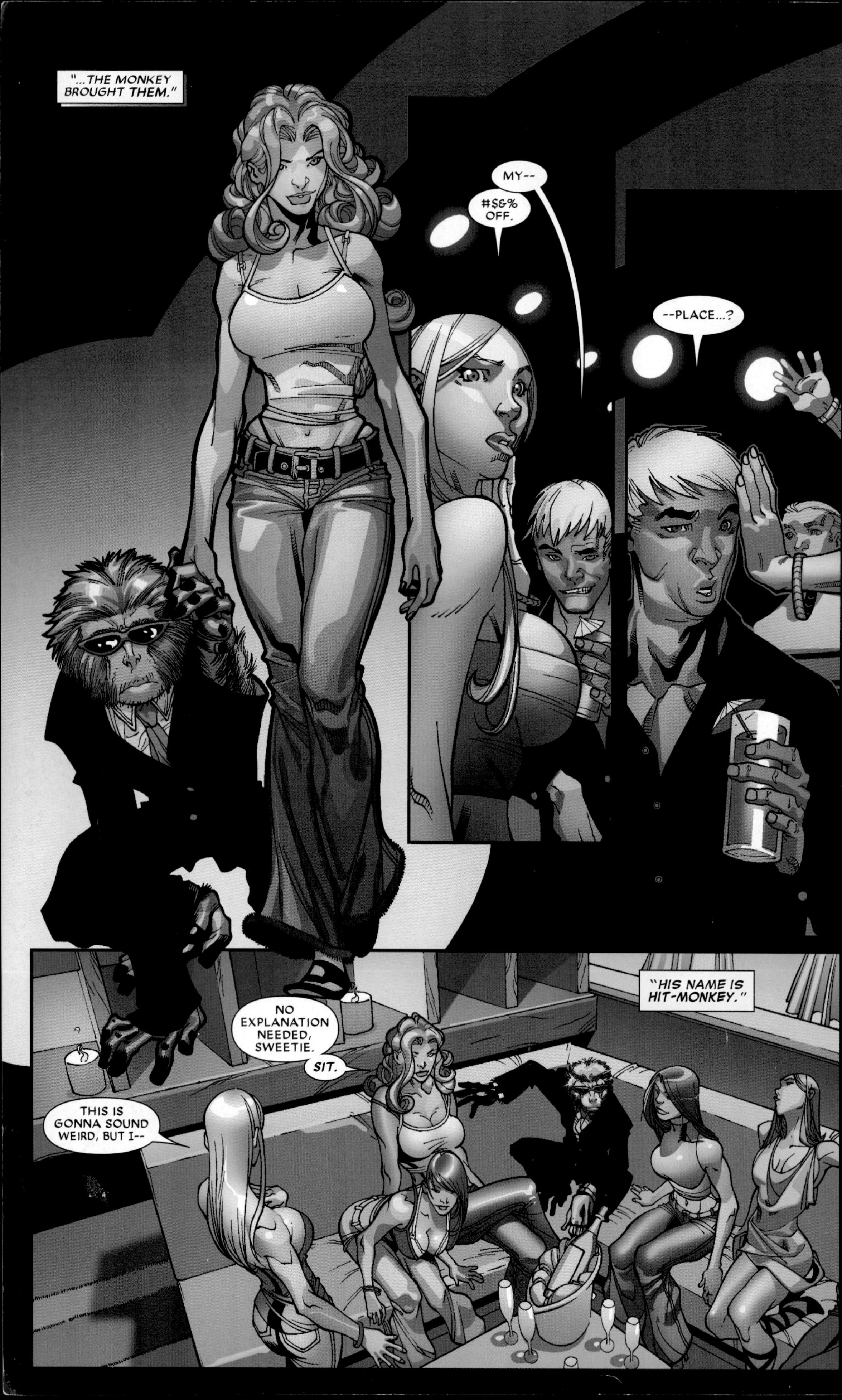
"...THE MONKEY BROUGHT THEM."
MY--
#$&% OFF.
--PLACE...?
"HIS NAME IS HIT-MONKEY."
NO EXPLANATION NEEDED, SWEETIE.
SIT.
THIS IS GONNA SOUND WEIRD, BUT I--

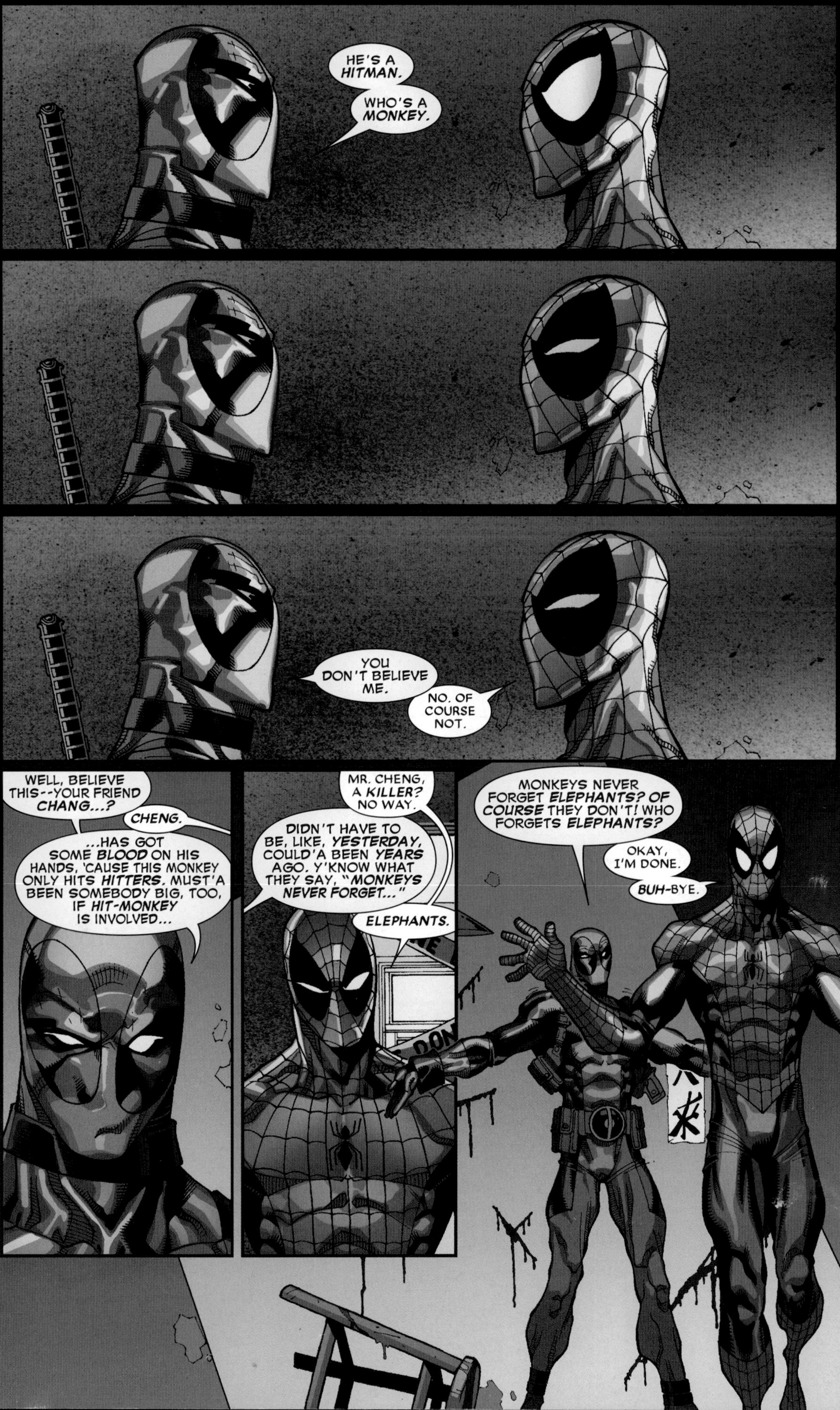
HE'S A HITMAN.
WHO'S A MONKEY.
YOU DON'T BELIEVE ME.
NO. OF COURSE NOT.
WELL, BELIEVE THIS--YOUR FRIEND CHANG...?
CHENG.
...HAS GOT SOME BLOOD ON HIS HANDS, 'CAUSE THIS MONKEY ONLY HITS HITTERS. MUST'A BEEN SOMEBODY BIG, TOO, IF HIT-MONKEY IS INVOLVED...
MR. CHENG, A KILLER? NO WAY.
DIDN'T HAVE TO BE, LIKE, YESTERDAY, COULD'A BEEN YEARS AGO. Y'KNOW WHAT THEY SAY, "MONKEYS NEVER FORGET..."
ELEPHANTS.
MONKEYS NEVER FORGET ELEPHANTS? OF COURSE THEY DON'T! WHO FORGETS ELEPHANTS?
OKAY, I'M DONE.
BUH-BYE.

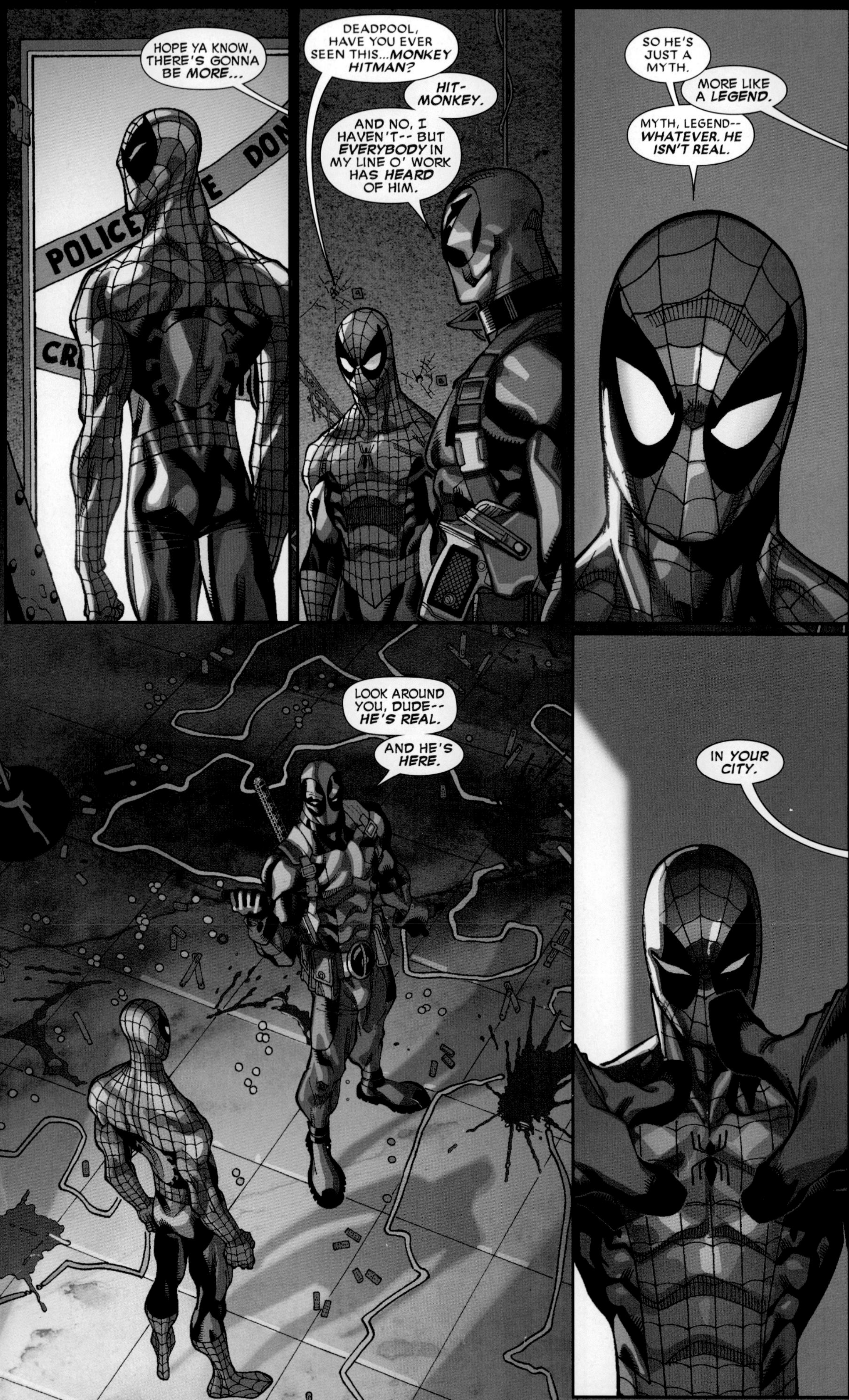
HOPE YA KNOW, THERE'S GONNA BE MORE...
POLICE
CR
E
DO
DEADPOOL, HAVE YOU EVER SEEN THIS...MONKEY HITMAN?
HIT-MONKEY.
AND NO, I HAVEN'T-- BUT EVERYBODY IN MY LINE O' WORK HAS HEARD OF HIM.
SO HE'S JUST A MYTH.
MORE LIKE A LEGEND.
MYTH, LEGEND-- WHATEVER. HE ISN'T REAL.
LOOK AROUND YOU, DUDE-- HE'S REAL.
AND HE'S HERE.
IN YOUR CITY.

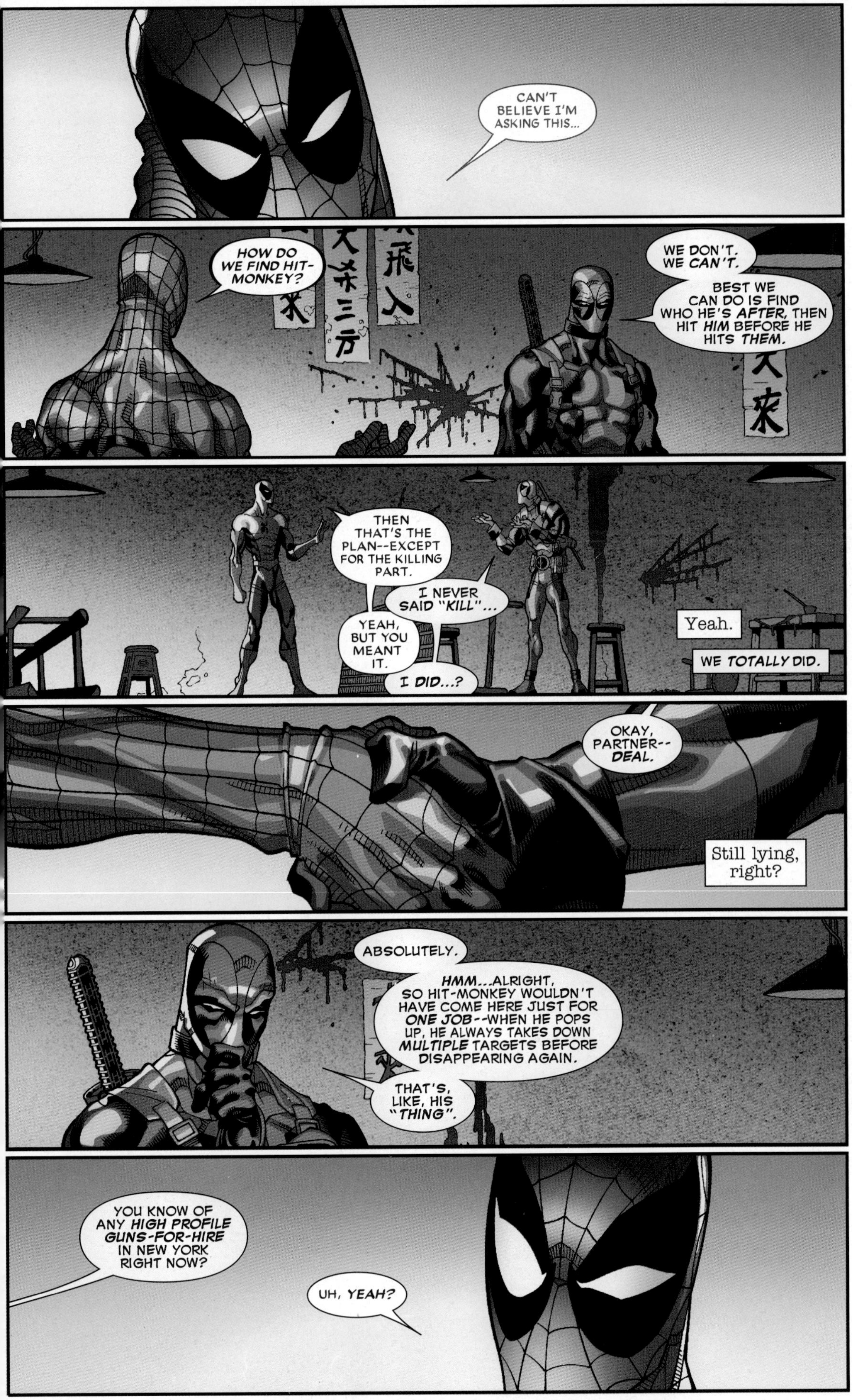
CAN'T BELIEVE I'M ASKING THIS...
HOW DO WE FIND HIT-MONKEY?
WE DON'T. WE CAN'T.
BEST WE CAN DO IS FIND WHO HE'S AFTER, THEN HIT HIM BEFORE HE HITS THEM.
THEN THAT'S THE PLAN--EXCEPT FOR THE KILLING PART.
I NEVER SAID "KILL"...
YEAH, BUT YOU MEANT IT.
I DID...?
Yeah.
WE TOTALLY DID.
OKAY, PARTNER--DEAL.
Still lying, right?
ABSOLUTELY.
HMM...ALRIGHT, SO HIT-MONKEY WOULDN'T HAVE COME HERE JUST FOR ONE JOB--WHEN HE POPS UP, HE ALWAYS TAKES DOWN MULTIPLE TARGETS BEFORE DISAPPEARING AGAIN.
THAT'S, LIKE, HIS "THING".
YOU KNOW OF ANY HIGH PROFILE GUNS-FOR-HIRE IN NEW YORK RIGHT NOW?
UH, YEAH?

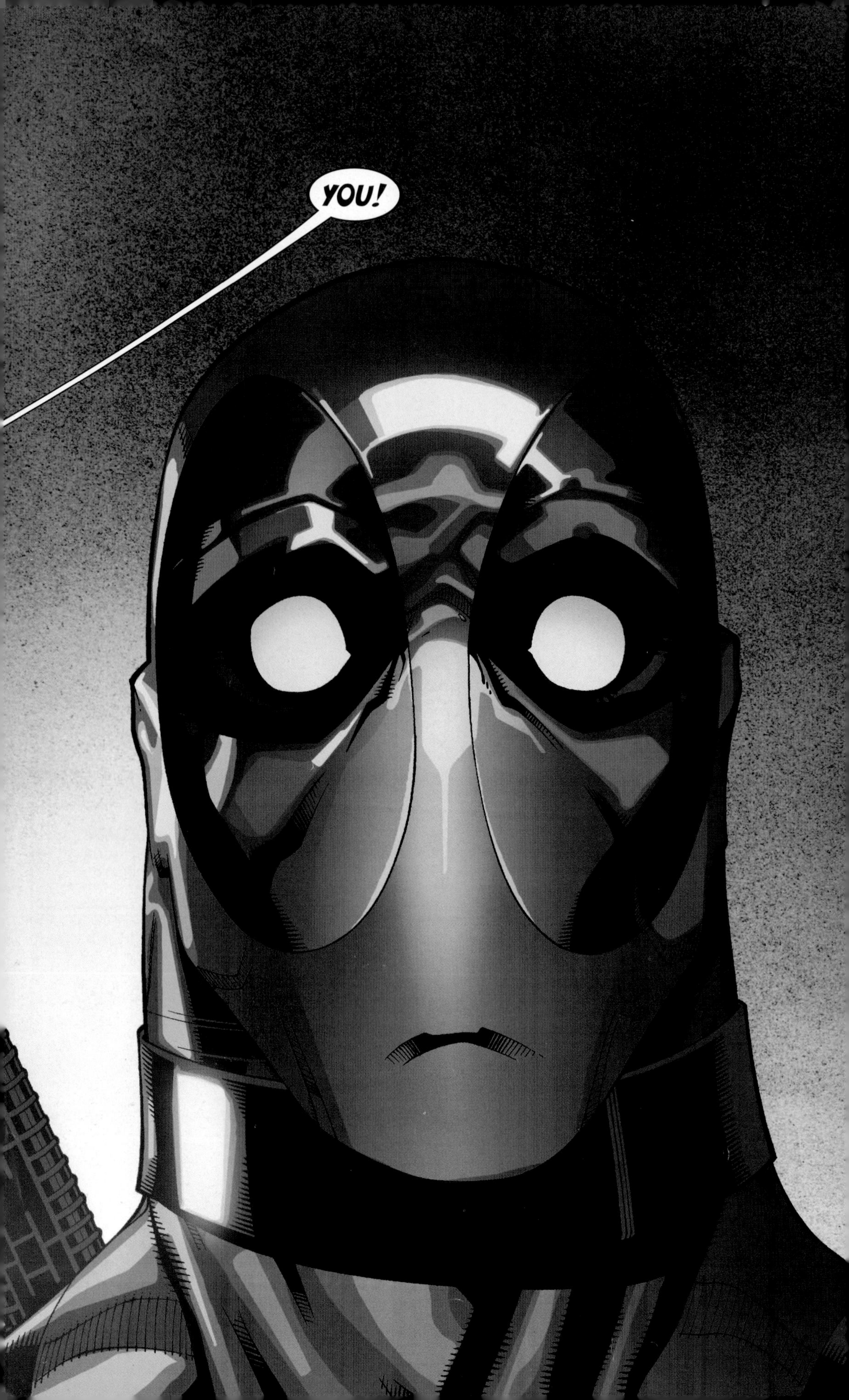
YOU!

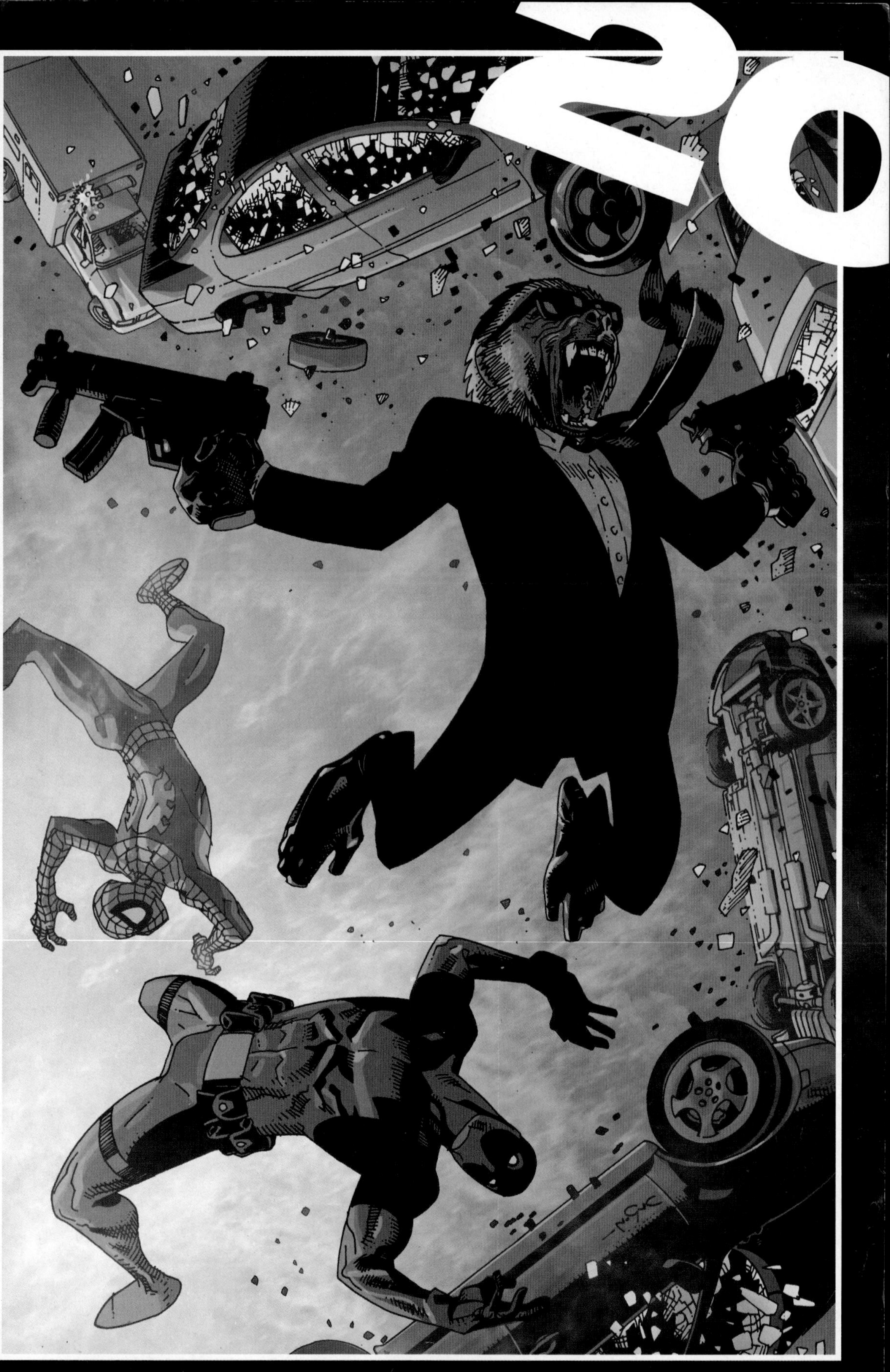
20

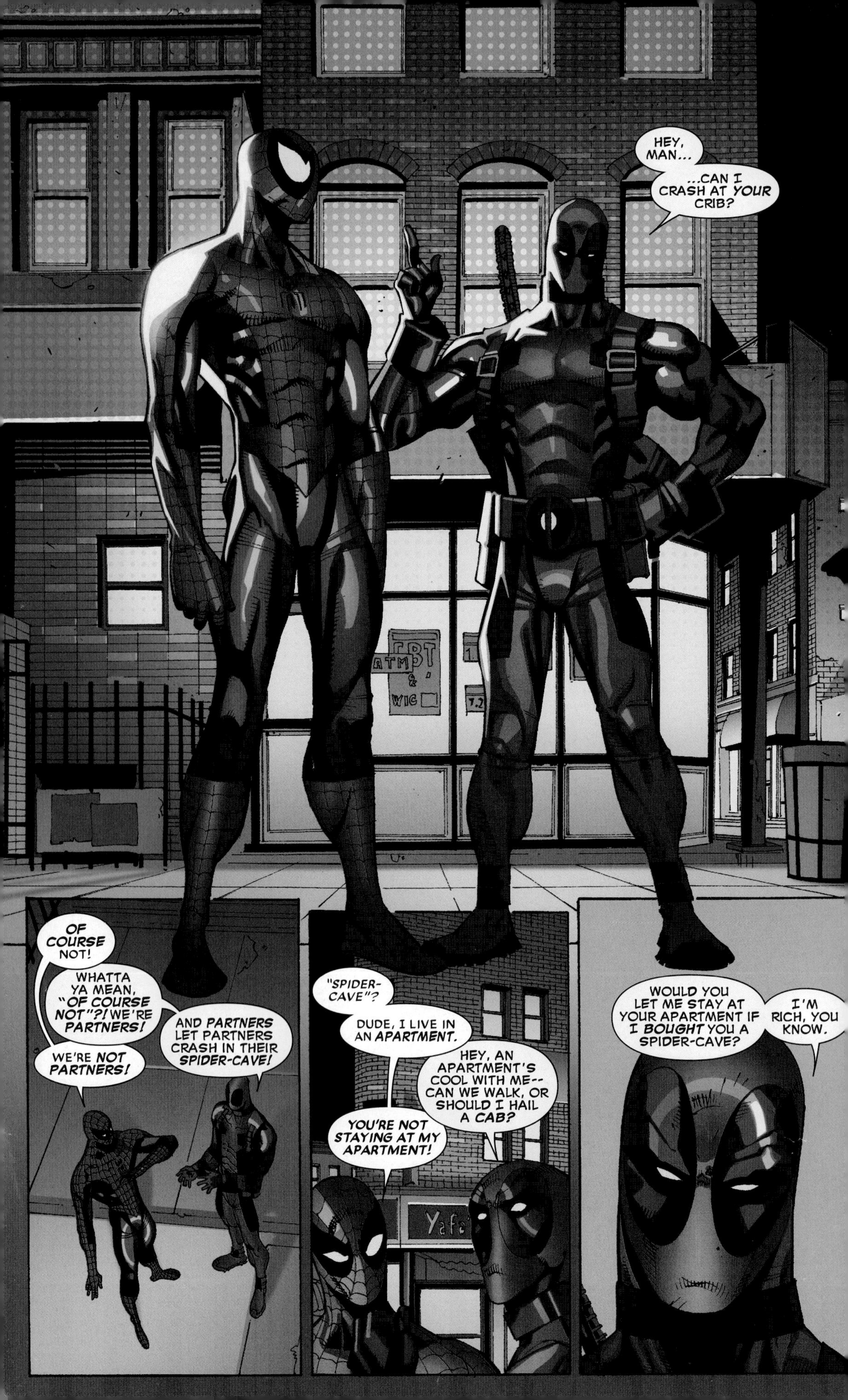
HEY, MAN...
...CAN I CRASH AT YOUR CRIB?
OF COURSE NOT!
WHATTA YA MEAN, "OF COURSE NOT"?! WE'RE PARTNERS!
WE'RE NOT PARTNERS!
AND PARTNERS LET PARTNERS CRASH IN THEIR SPIDER-CAVE!
"SPIDER-CAVE"?
DUDE, I LIVE IN AN APARTMENT.
HEY, AN APARTMENT'S COOL WITH ME-- CAN WE WALK, OR SHOULD I HAIL A CAB?
YOU'RE NOT STAYING AT MY APARTMENT!
WOULD YOU LET ME STAY AT YOUR APARTMENT IF I BOUGHT YOU A SPIDER-CAVE?
I'M RICH, YOU KNOW.

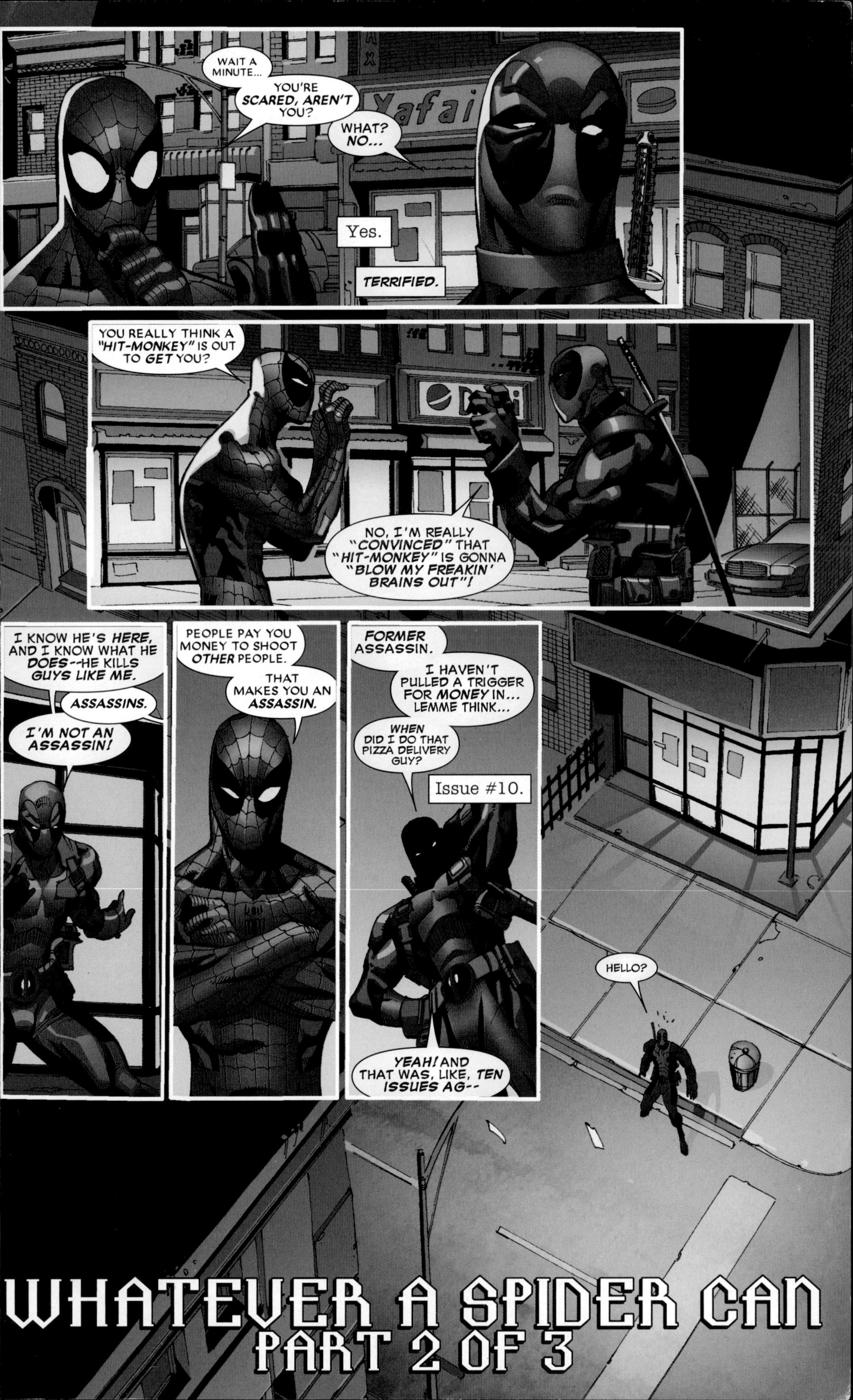
WAIT A MINUTE...
YOU'RE SCARED, AREN'T YOU?
WHAT? NO...
Yes.
TERRIFIED.
YOU REALLY THINK A "HIT-MONKEY" IS OUT TO GET YOU?
NO, I'M REALLY "CONVINCED" THAT "HIT-MONKEY" IS GONNA "BLOW MY FREAKIN' BRAINS OUT"!
I KNOW HE'S HERE, AND I KNOW WHAT HE DOES--HE KILLS GUYS LIKE ME.
ASSASSINS.
I'M NOT AN ASSASSIN!
PEOPLE PAY YOU MONEY TO SHOOT OTHER PEOPLE.
THAT MAKES YOU AN ASSASSIN.
FORMER ASSASSIN.
I HAVEN'T PULLED A TRIGGER FOR MONEY IN... LEMME THINK...
WHEN DID I DO THAT PIZZA DELIVERY GUY?
Issue #10.
YEAH! AND THAT WAS, LIKE, TEN ISSUES AG--
HELLO?
WHATEVER A SPIDER CAN
PART 2 OF 3

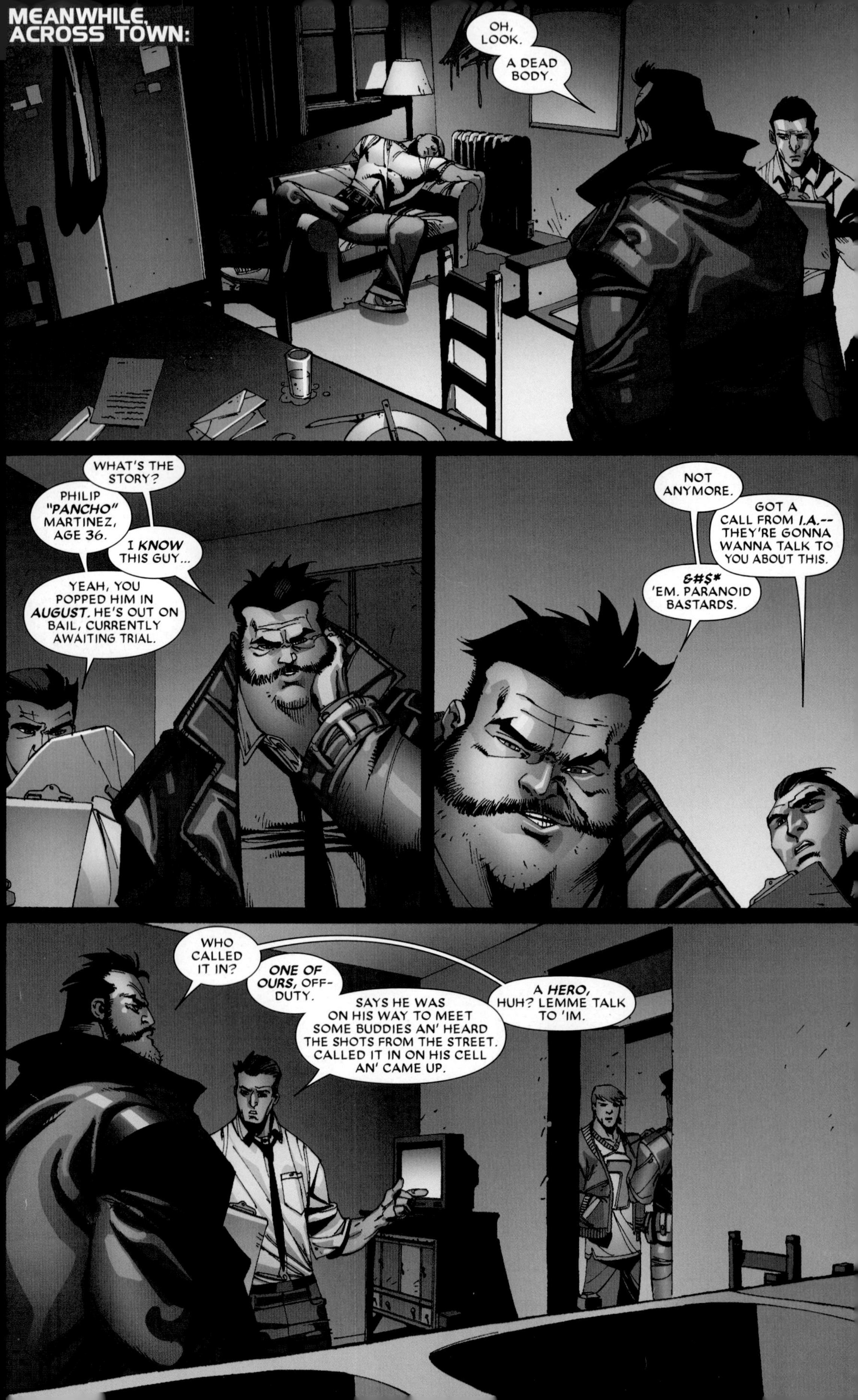
MEANWHILE, ACROSS TOWN:
OH, LOOK.
A DEAD BODY.
WHAT'S THE STORY?
PHILIP "PANCHO" MARTINEZ, AGE 36.
I KNOW THIS GUY...
YEAH, YOU POPPED HIM IN AUGUST. HE'S OUT ON BAIL, CURRENTLY AWAITING TRIAL.
NOT ANYMORE.
GOT A CALL FROM I.A.-- THEY'RE GONNA WANNA TALK TO YOU ABOUT THIS.
&#$* 'EM. PARANOID BASTARDS.
WHO CALLED IT IN?
ONE OF OURS, OFF-DUTY.
SAYS HE WAS ON HIS WAY TO MEET SOME BUDDIES AN' HEARD THE SHOTS FROM THE STREET. CALLED IT IN ON HIS CELL AN' CAME UP.
A HERO, HUH? LEMME TALK TO 'IM.

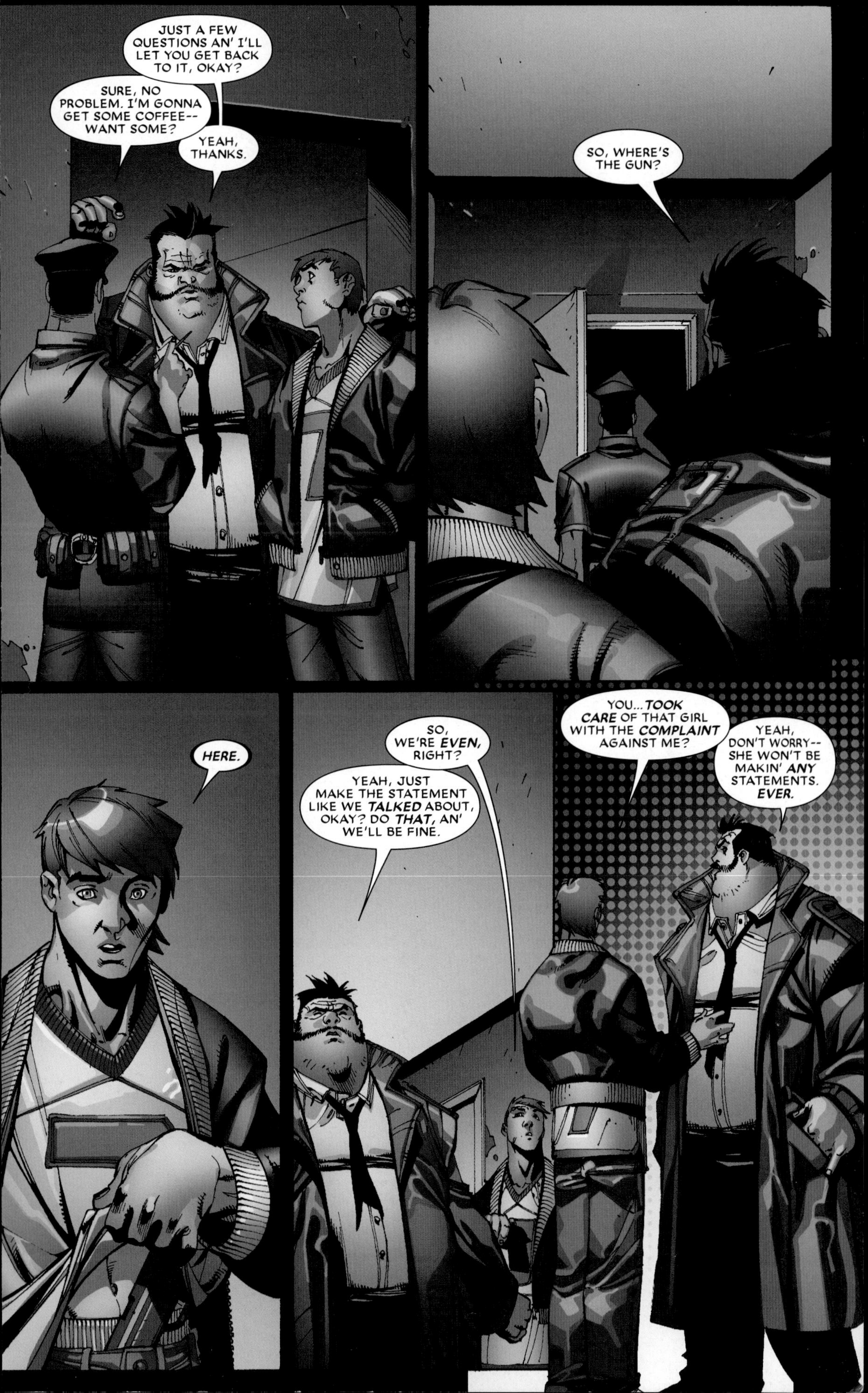
JUST A FEW QUESTIONS AN' I'LL LET YOU GET BACK TO IT, OKAY?
SURE, NO PROBLEM. I'M GONNA GET SOME COFFEE-- WANT SOME?
YEAH, THANKS.
SO, WHERE'S THE GUN?
HERE.
SO, WE'RE EVEN, RIGHT?
YEAH, JUST MAKE THE STATEMENT LIKE WE TALKED ABOUT, OKAY? DO THAT, AN' WE'LL BE FINE.
YOU...TOOK CARE OF THAT GIRL WITH THE COMPLAINT AGAINST ME?
YEAH, DON'T WORRY-- SHE WON'T BE MAKIN' ANY STATEMENTS. EVER.

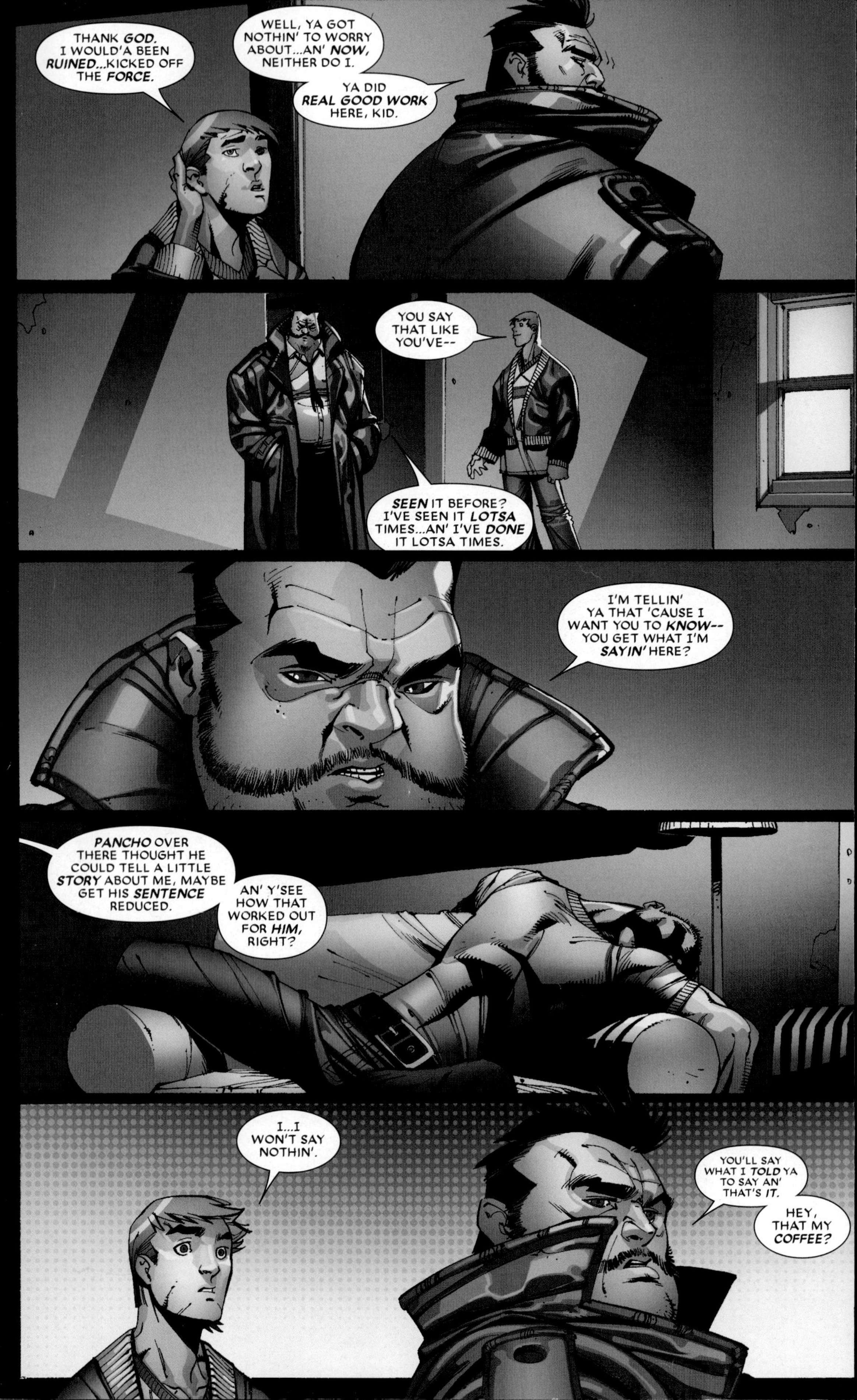

THANK GOD. I WOULD'A BEEN RUINED...KICKED OFF THE FORCE.
WELL, YA GOT NOTHIN' TO WORRY ABOUT...AN' NOW, NEITHER DO I.
YA DID REAL GOOD WORK HERE, KID.
YOU SAY THAT LIKE YOU'VE--
SEEN IT BEFORE? I'VE SEEN IT LOTSA TIMES...AN' I'VE DONE IT LOTSA TIMES.
I'M TELLIN' YA THAT 'CAUSE I WANT YOU TO KNOW-- YOU GET WHAT I'M SAYIN' HERE?
PANCHO OVER THERE THOUGHT HE COULD TELL A LITTLE STORY ABOUT ME, MAYBE GET HIS SENTENCE REDUCED.
AN' Y'SEE HOW THAT WORKED OUT FOR HIM, RIGHT?
I...I WON'T SAY NOTHIN'.
YOU'LL SAY WHAT I TOLD YA TO SAY AN' THAT'S IT.
HEY, THAT MY COFFEE?

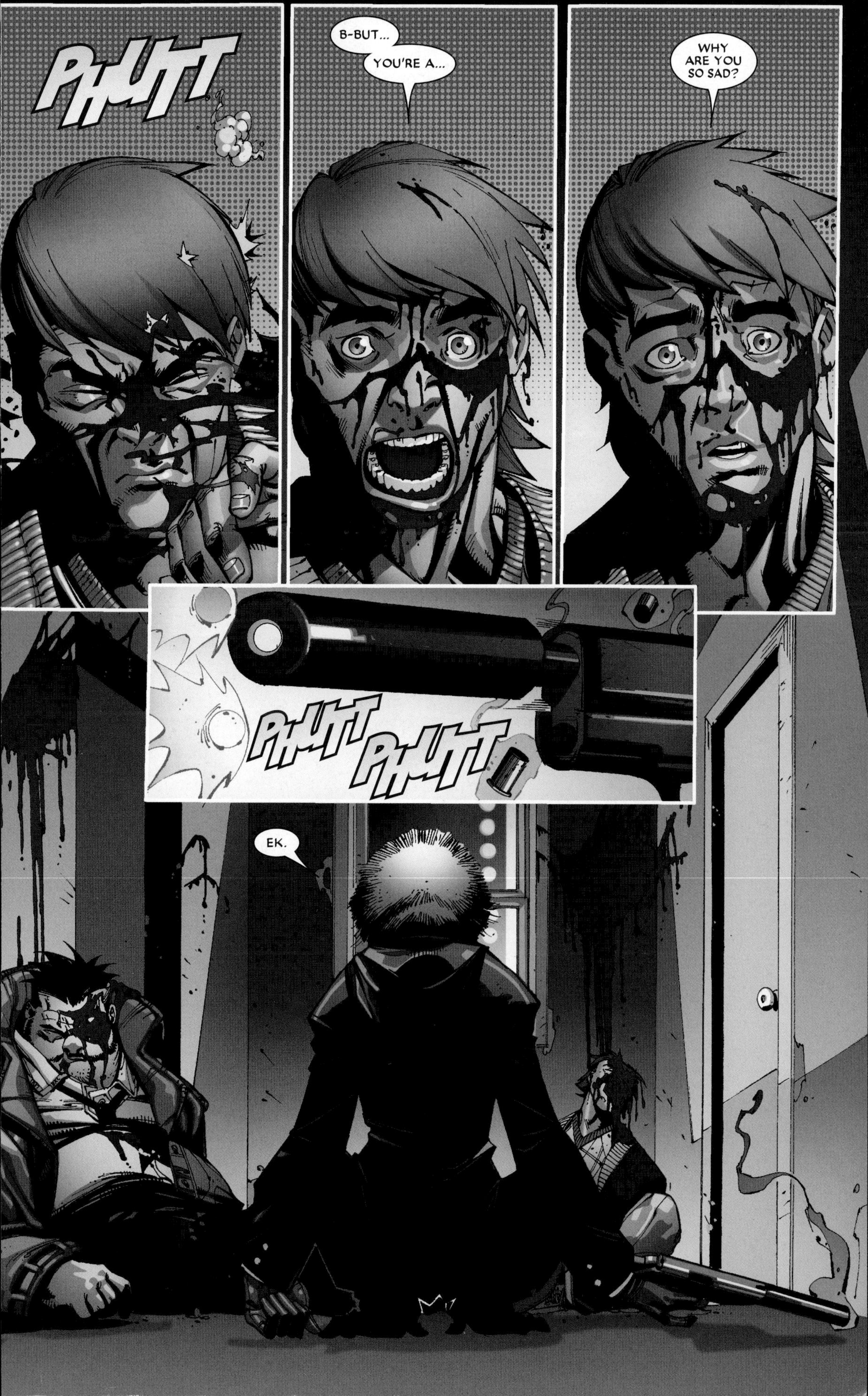
PHUTT
B-BUT...
YOU'RE A...
WHY ARE YOU SO SAD?
PHUTT PHUTT
EK.

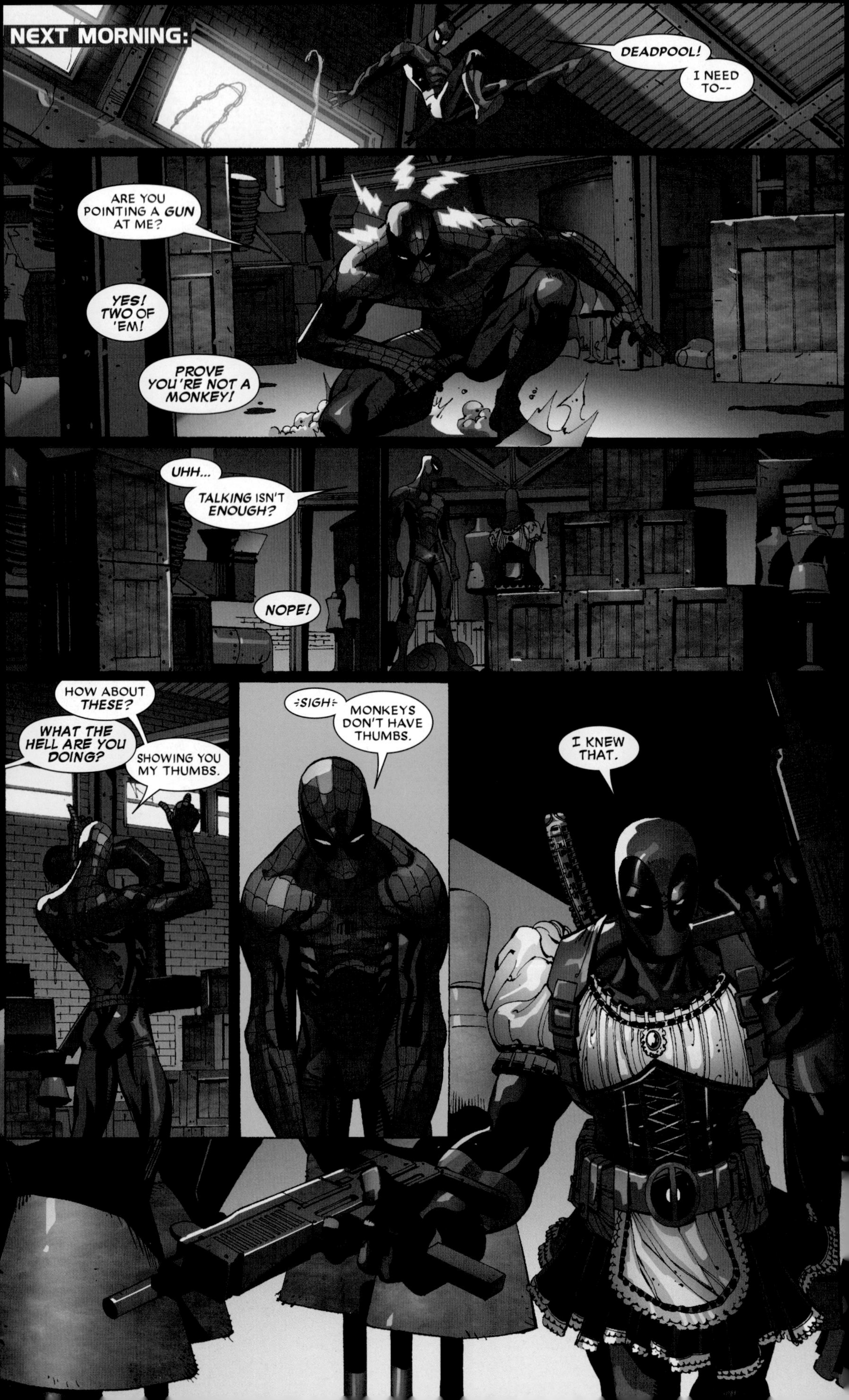
NEXT MORNING:
DEADPOOL!
I NEED TO--
ARE YOU POINTING A GUN AT ME?
YES! TWO OF 'EM!
PROVE YOU'RE NOT A MONKEY!
UHH...
TALKING ISN'T ENOUGH?
NOPE!
HOW ABOUT THESE?
WHAT THE HELL ARE YOU DOING?
SHOWING YOU MY THUMBS.
SIGH
MONKEYS DON'T HAVE THUMBS.
I KNEW THAT.

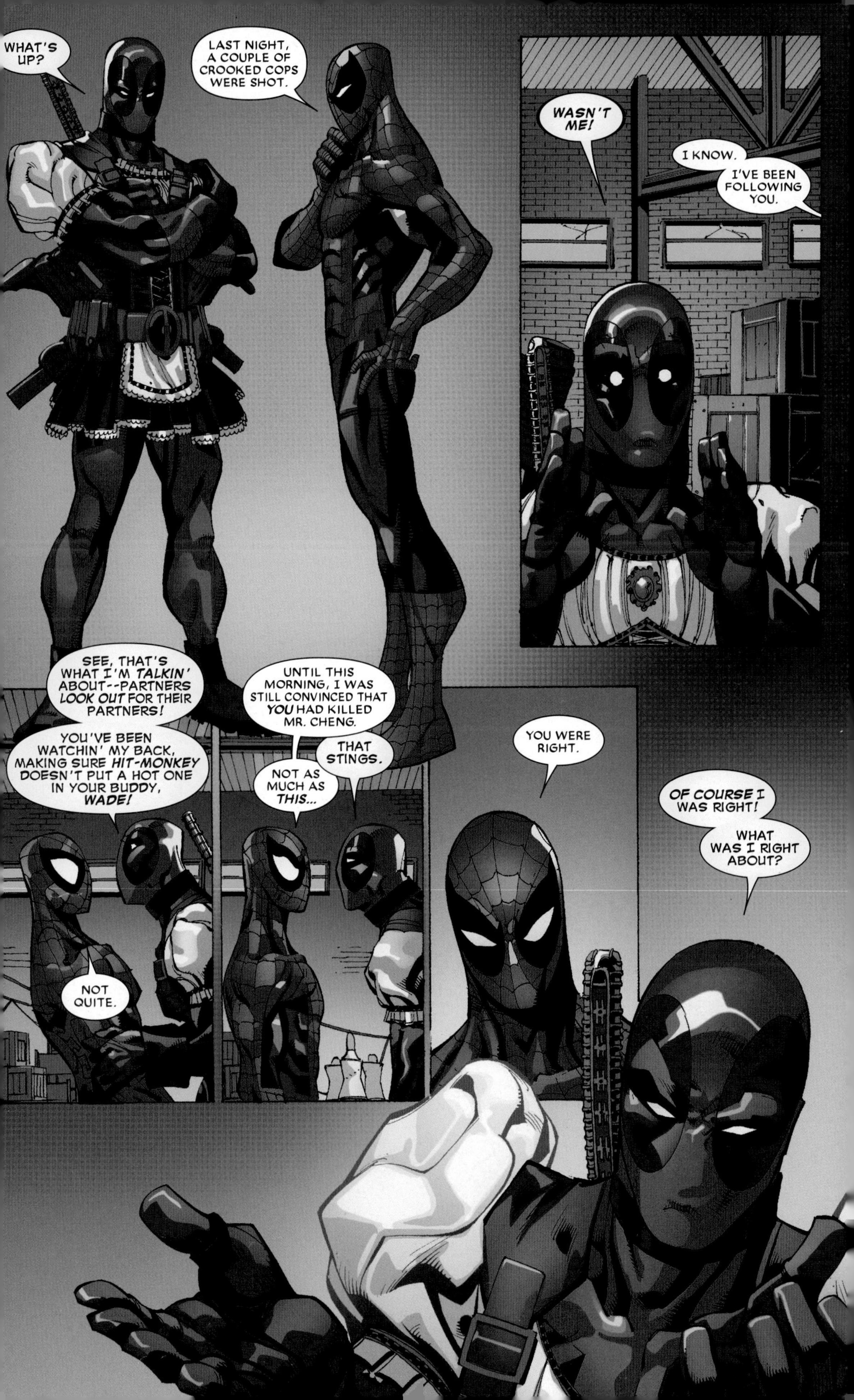
WHAT'S UP?
LAST NIGHT, A COUPLE OF CROOKED COPS WERE SHOT.
WASN'T ME!
I KNOW.
I'VE BEEN FOLLOWING YOU.
SEE, THAT'S WHAT I'M TALKIN' ABOUT--PARTNERS LOOK OUT FOR THEIR PARTNERS!
YOU'VE BEEN WATCHIN' MY BACK, MAKING SURE HIT-MONKEY DOESN'T PUT A HOT ONE IN YOUR BUDDY, WADE!
NOT QUITE.
UNTIL THIS MORNING, I WAS STILL CONVINCED THAT YOU HAD KILLED MR. CHENG.
THAT STINGS.
NOT AS MUCH AS THIS...
YOU WERE RIGHT.
OF COURSE I WAS RIGHT!
WHAT WAS I RIGHT ABOUT?

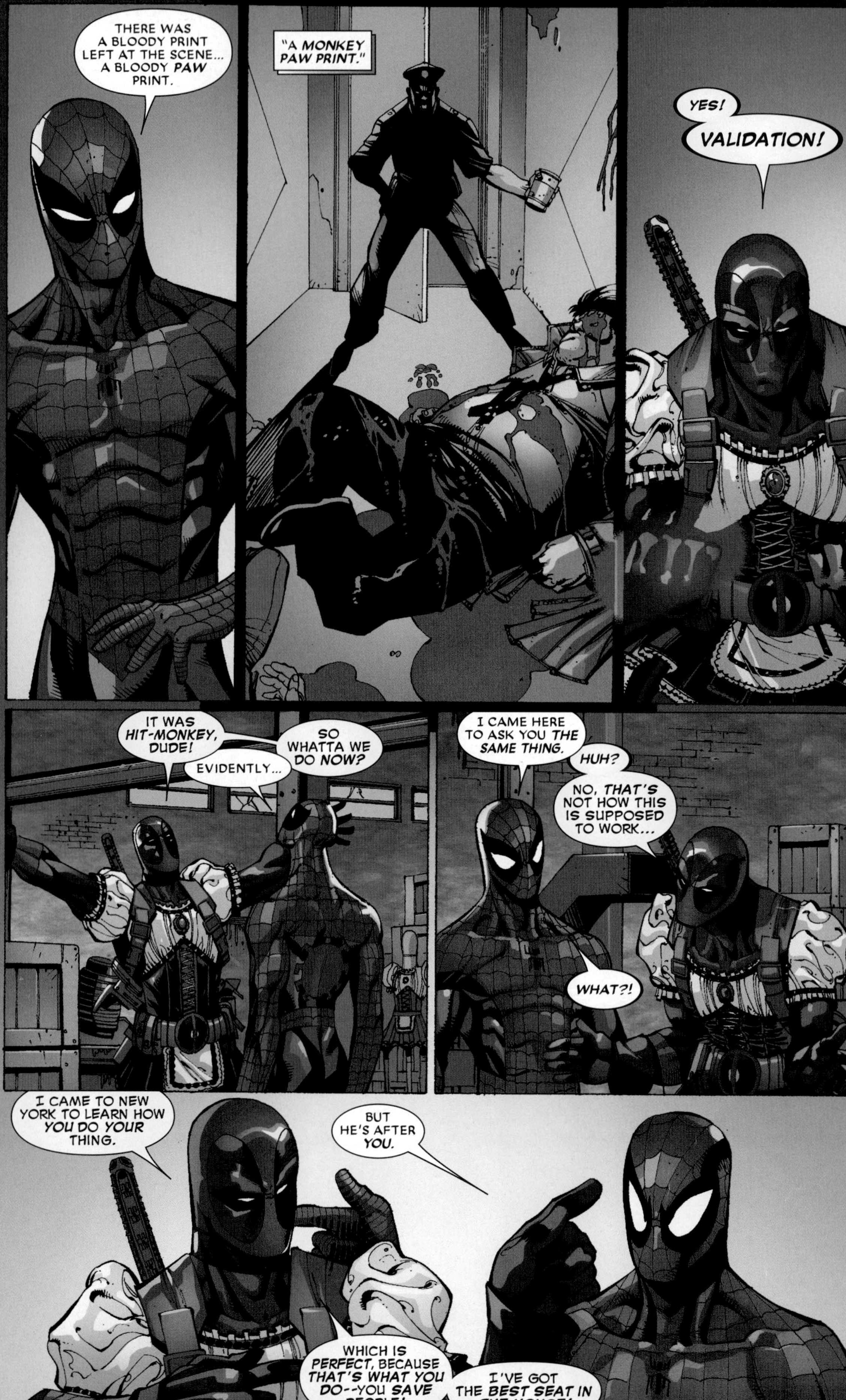

THERE WAS A BLOODY PRINT LEFT AT THE SCENE... A BLOODY *PAW* PRINT.
"A *MONKEY PAW PRINT.*"
YES!
VALIDATION!
IT WAS *HIT-MONKEY*, DUDE!
SO WHATTA WE DO *NOW?*
EVIDENTLY...
I CAME HERE TO ASK YOU *THE SAME THING.*
HUH?
NO, *THAT'S* NOT HOW THIS IS SUPPOSED TO WORK...
WHAT?!
I CAME TO NEW YORK TO LEARN HOW *YOU DO YOUR* THING.
BUT HE'S AFTER *YOU.*
WHICH IS *PERFECT*, BECAUSE *THAT'S WHAT YOU DO*--YOU *SAVE* PEOPLE!
I'VE GOT THE *BEST SEAT IN THE HOUSE!*

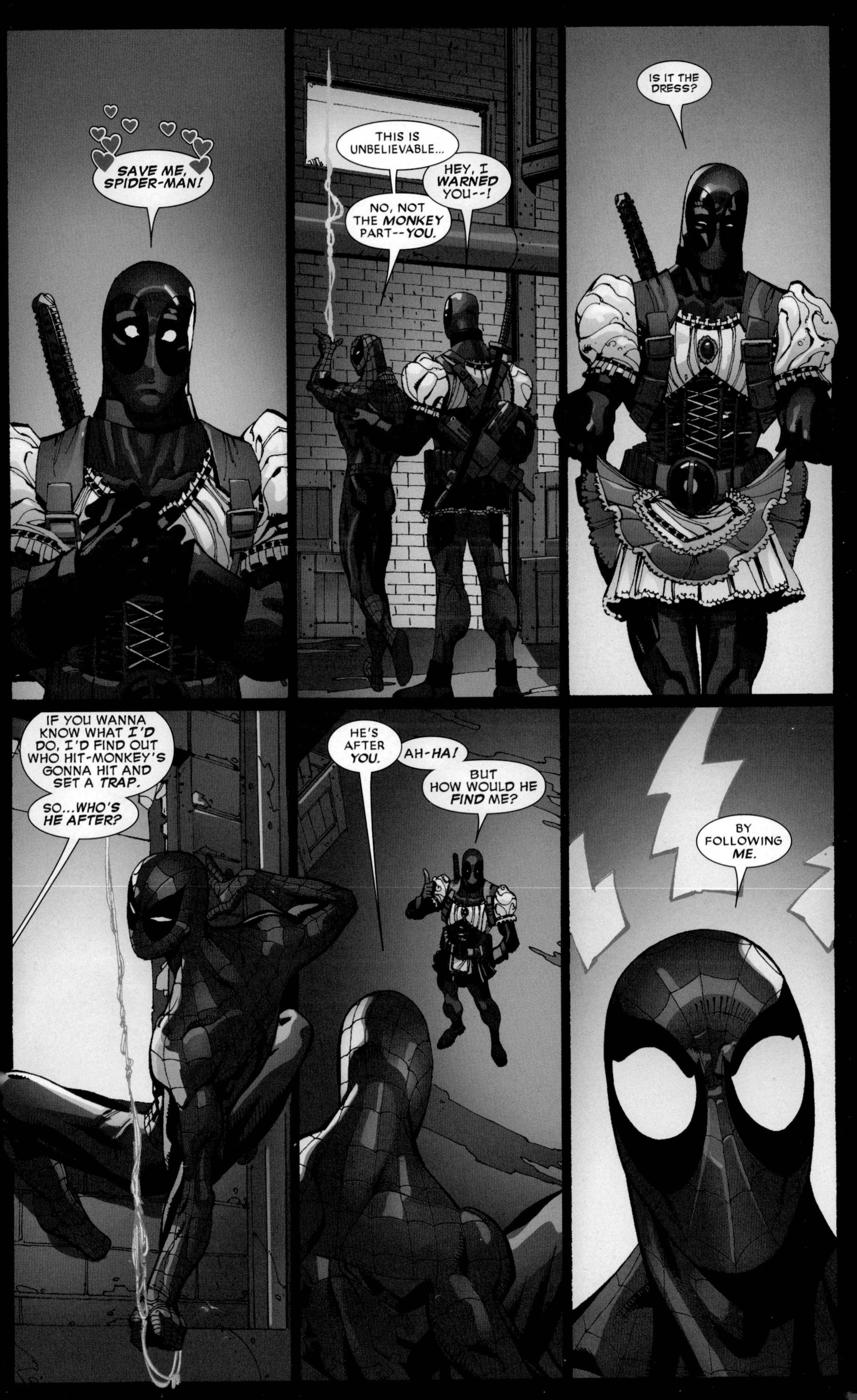
SAVE ME, SPIDER-MAN!
THIS IS UNBELIEVABLE...
NO, NOT THE MONKEY PART--YOU.
HEY, I WARNED YOU--!
IS IT THE DRESS?
IF YOU WANNA KNOW WHAT I'D DO, I'D FIND OUT WHO HIT-MONKEY'S GONNA HIT AND SET A TRAP.
SO...WHO'S HE AFTER?
HE'S AFTER YOU.
AH-HA!
BUT HOW WOULD HE FIND ME?
BY FOLLOWING ME.

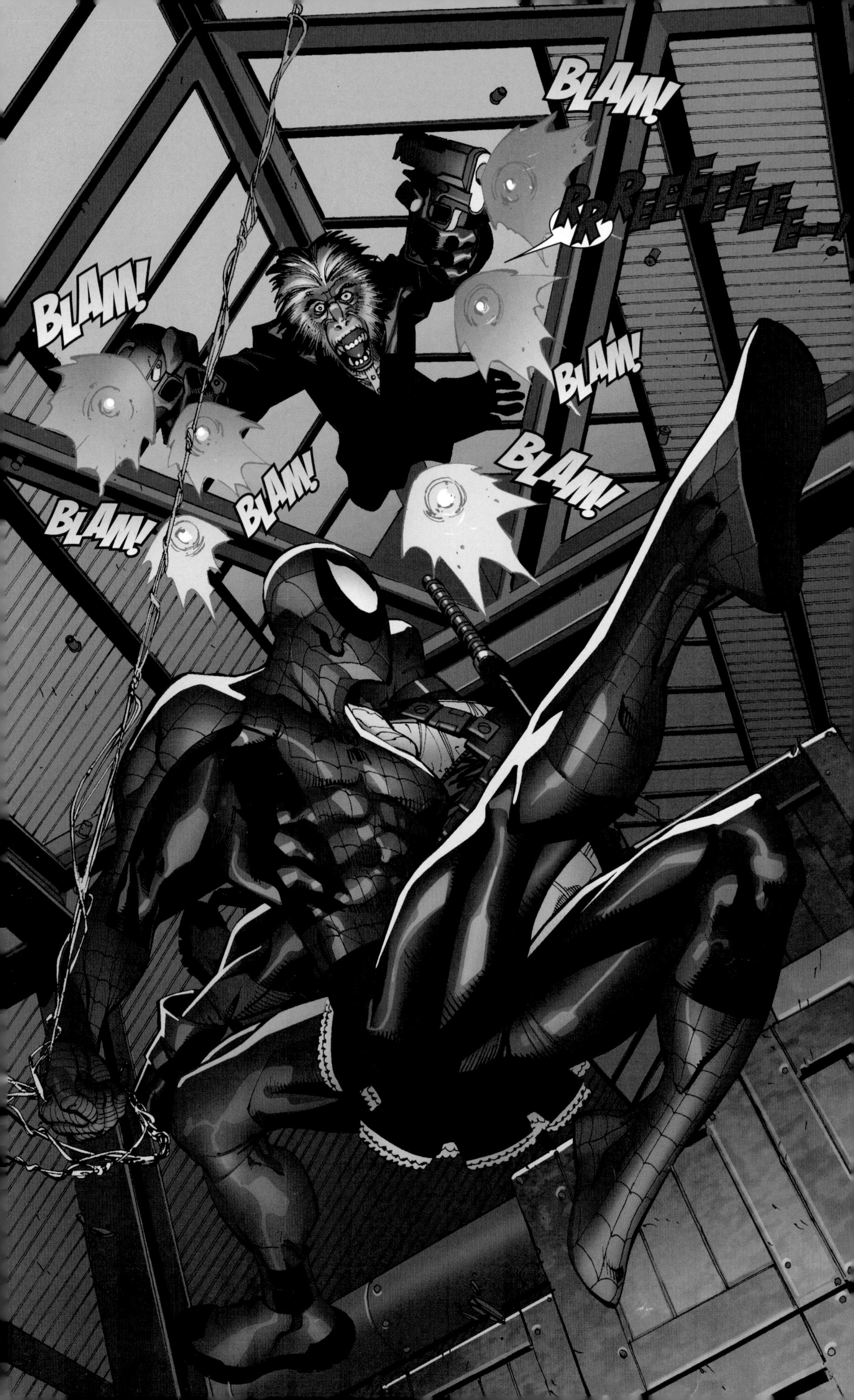
BLAM!
RRREEEEEEEEE--!
BLAM!
BLAM!
BLAM!
BLAM!
BLAM!

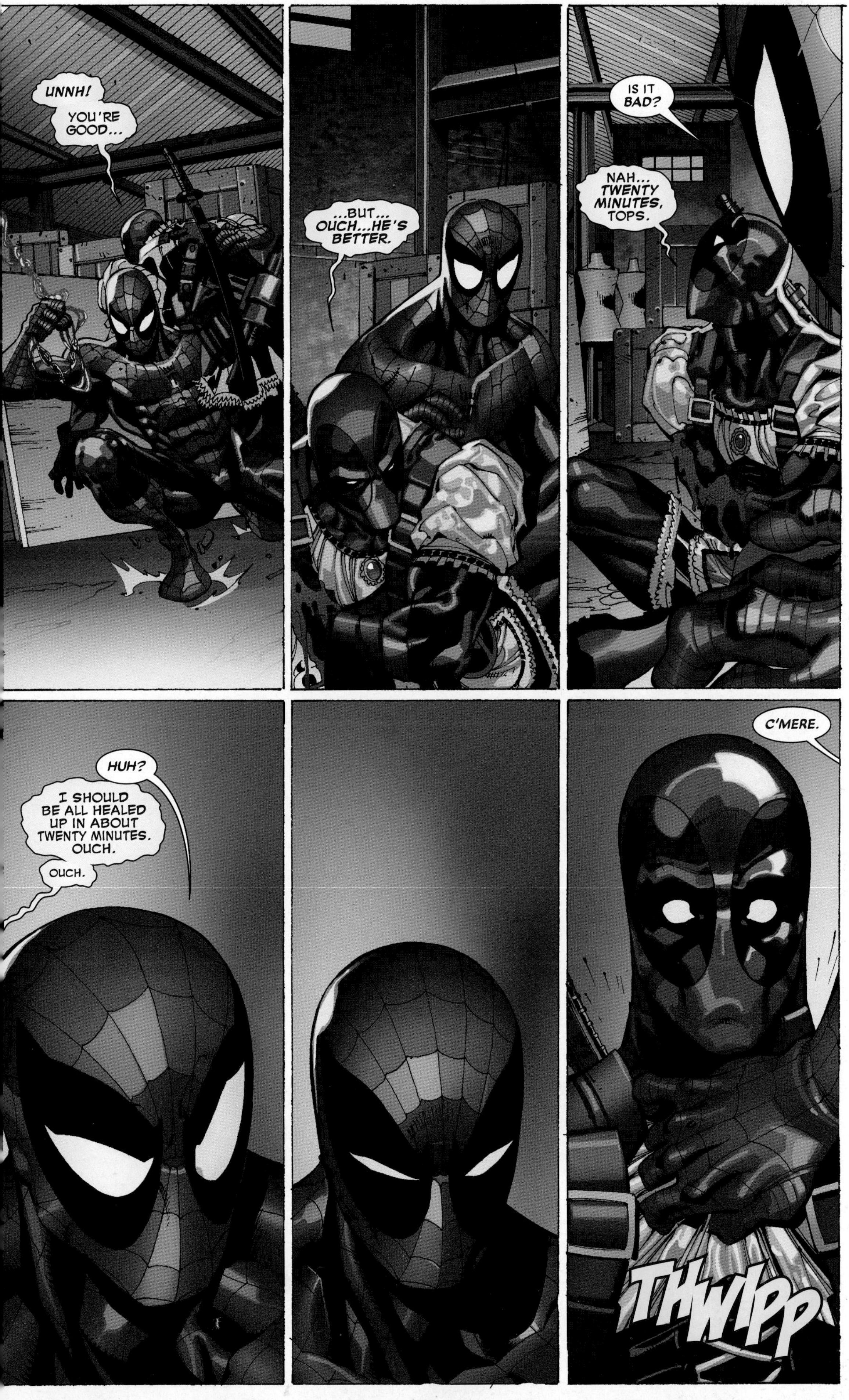
UNNH!
YOU'RE GOOD...
...BUT... OUCH...HE'S BETTER.
IS IT BAD?
NAH... TWENTY MINUTES, TOPS.
HUH?
I SHOULD BE ALL HEALED UP IN ABOUT TWENTY MINUTES. OUCH.
OUCH.
C'MERE.
THWIPP

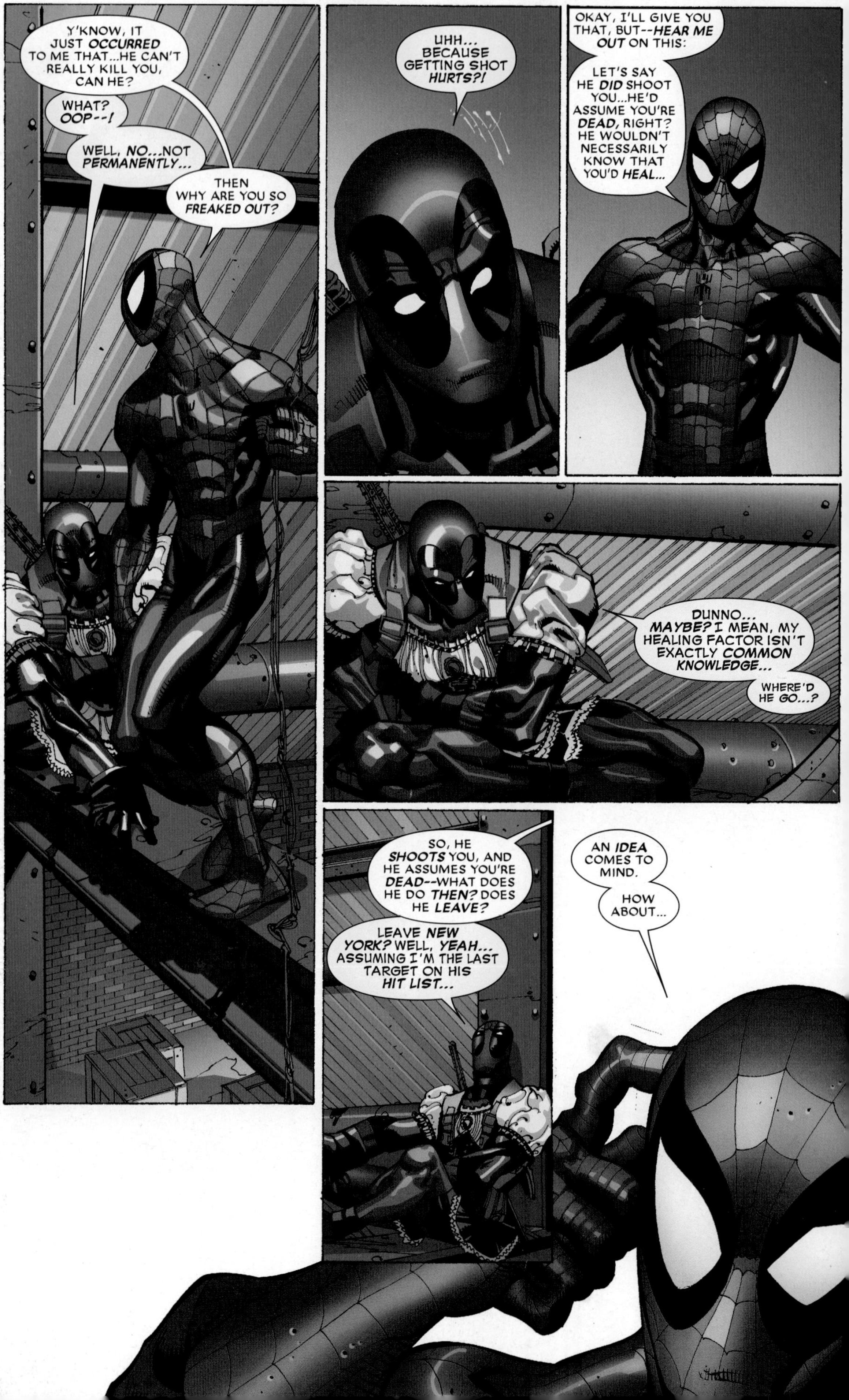

Y'KNOW, IT JUST OCCURRED TO ME THAT...HE CAN'T REALLY KILL YOU, CAN HE?
WHAT? OOP--!
WELL, NO...NOT PERMANENTLY...
THEN WHY ARE YOU SO FREAKED OUT?
UHH... BECAUSE GETTING SHOT HURTS?!
OKAY, I'LL GIVE YOU THAT, BUT--HEAR ME OUT ON THIS:
LET'S SAY HE DID SHOOT YOU...HE'D ASSUME YOU'RE DEAD, RIGHT? HE WOULDN'T NECESSARILY KNOW THAT YOU'D HEAL...
DUNNO... MAYBE? I MEAN, MY HEALING FACTOR ISN'T EXACTLY COMMON KNOWLEDGE...
WHERE'D HE GO...?
SO, HE SHOOTS YOU, AND HE ASSUMES YOU'RE DEAD--WHAT DOES HE DO THEN? DOES HE LEAVE?
LEAVE NEW YORK? WELL, YEAH... ASSUMING I'M THE LAST TARGET ON HIS HIT LIST...
AN IDEA COMES TO MIND.
HOW ABOUT...

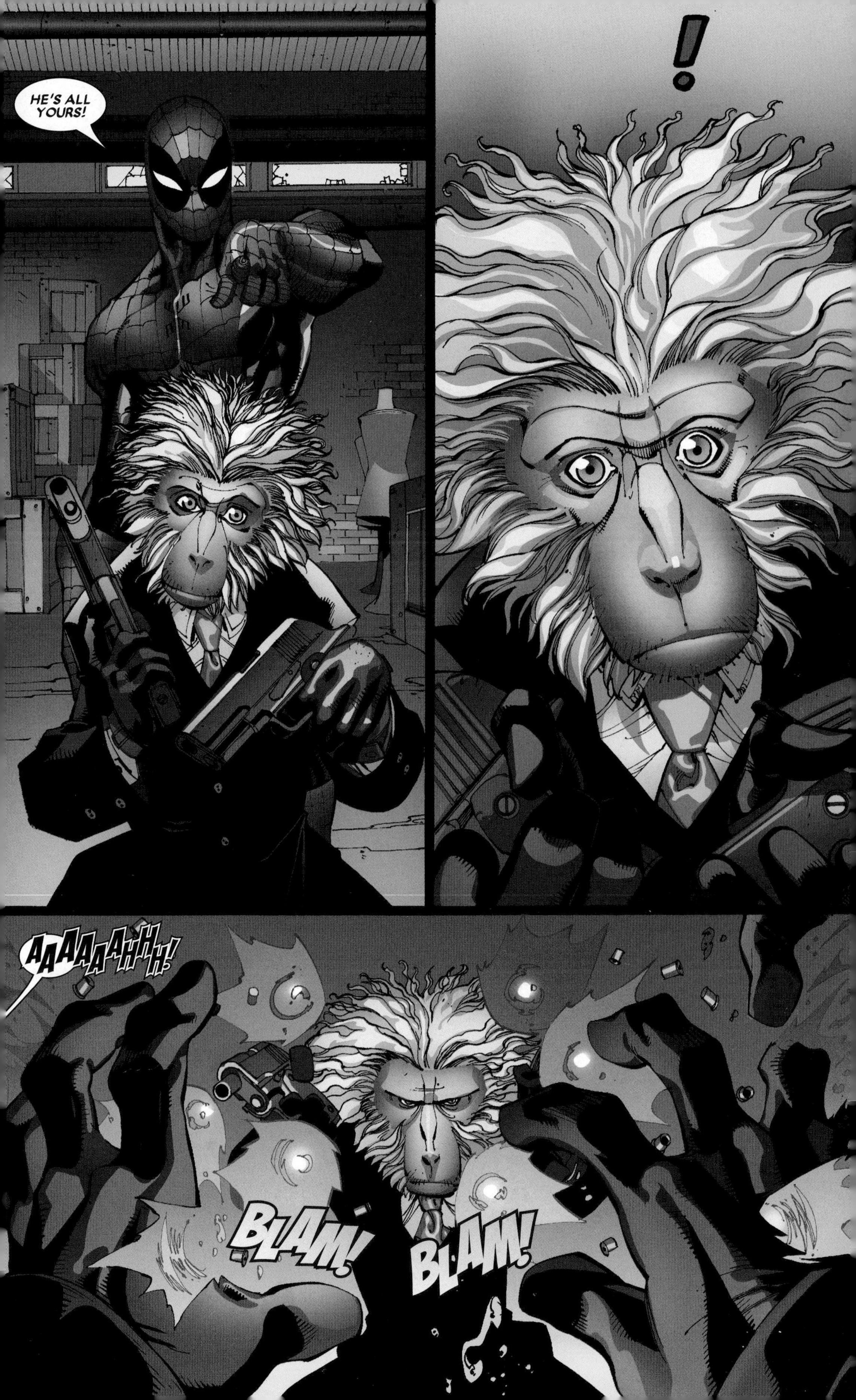
HE'S ALL YOURS!
!
AAAAAAHHHH!
BLAM!
BLAM!

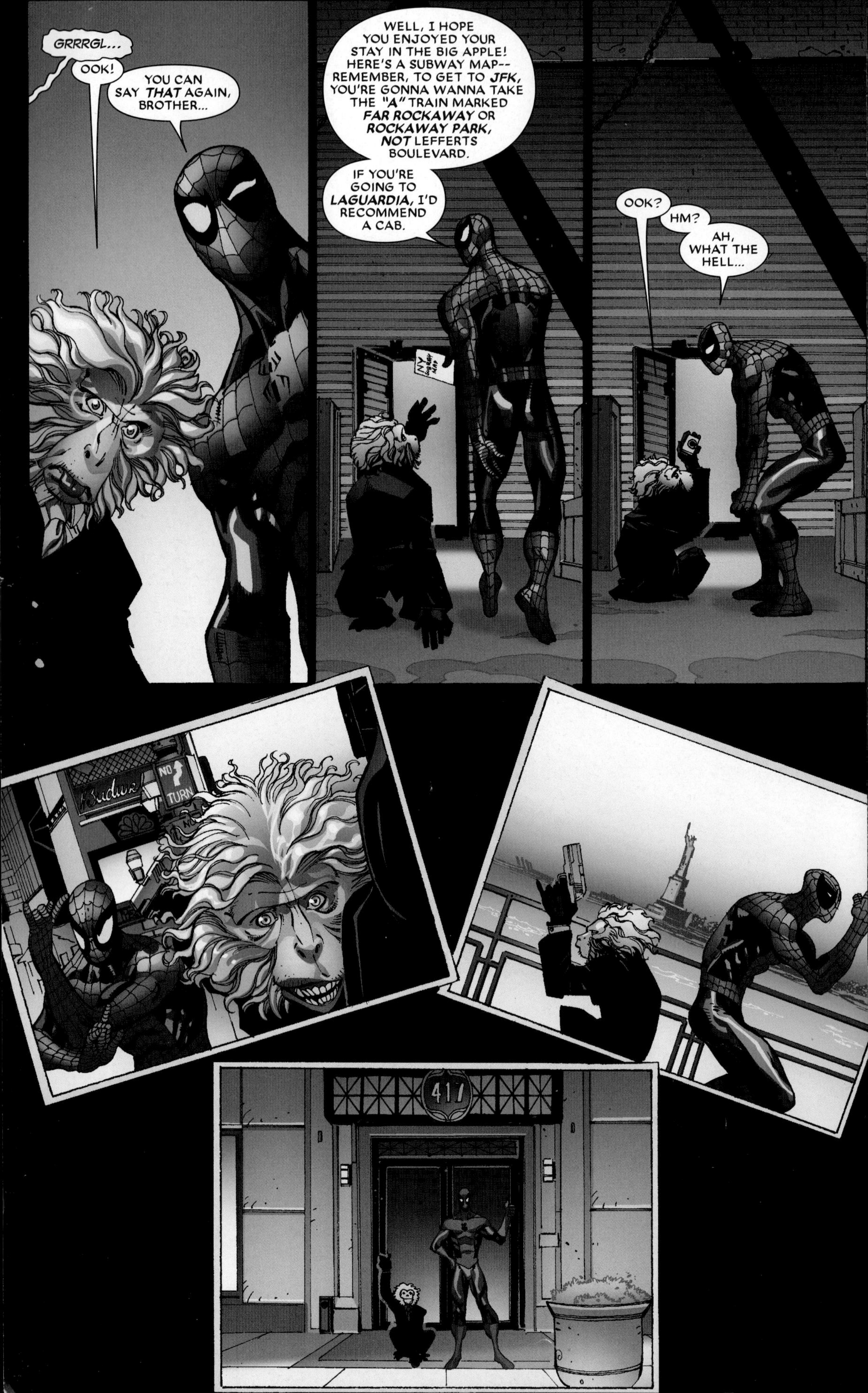
GRRRGL...
OOK!
YOU CAN SAY *THAT* AGAIN, BROTHER...
WELL, I HOPE YOU ENJOYED YOUR STAY IN THE BIG APPLE! HERE'S A SUBWAY MAP-- REMEMBER, TO GET TO *JFK*, YOU'RE GONNA WANNA TAKE THE *"A"* TRAIN MARKED *FAR ROCKAWAY* OR *ROCKAWAY PARK*, *NOT* LEFFERTS BOULEVARD.
IF YOU'RE GOING TO *LAGUARDIA*, I'D RECOMMEND A CAB.
OOK?
HM?
AH, WHAT THE HELL...
NO TURN
417

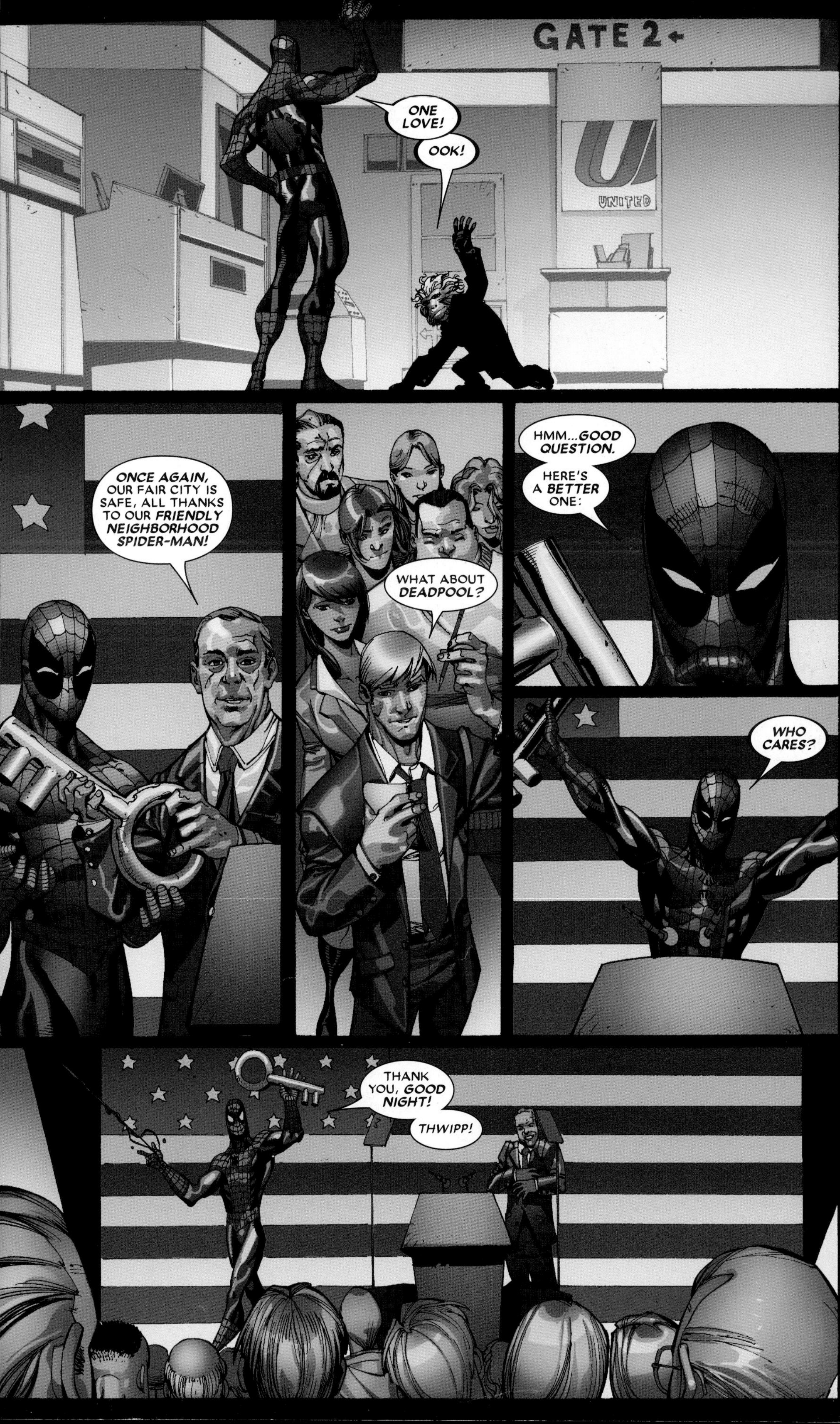
GATE 2
UNITED
ONE LOVE!
OOK!
ONCE AGAIN, OUR FAIR CITY IS SAFE, ALL THANKS TO OUR FRIENDLY NEIGHBORHOOD SPIDER-MAN!
WHAT ABOUT DEADPOOL?
HMM...GOOD QUESTION.
HERE'S A BETTER ONE:
WHO CARES?
THANK YOU, GOOD NIGHT!
THWIPP!

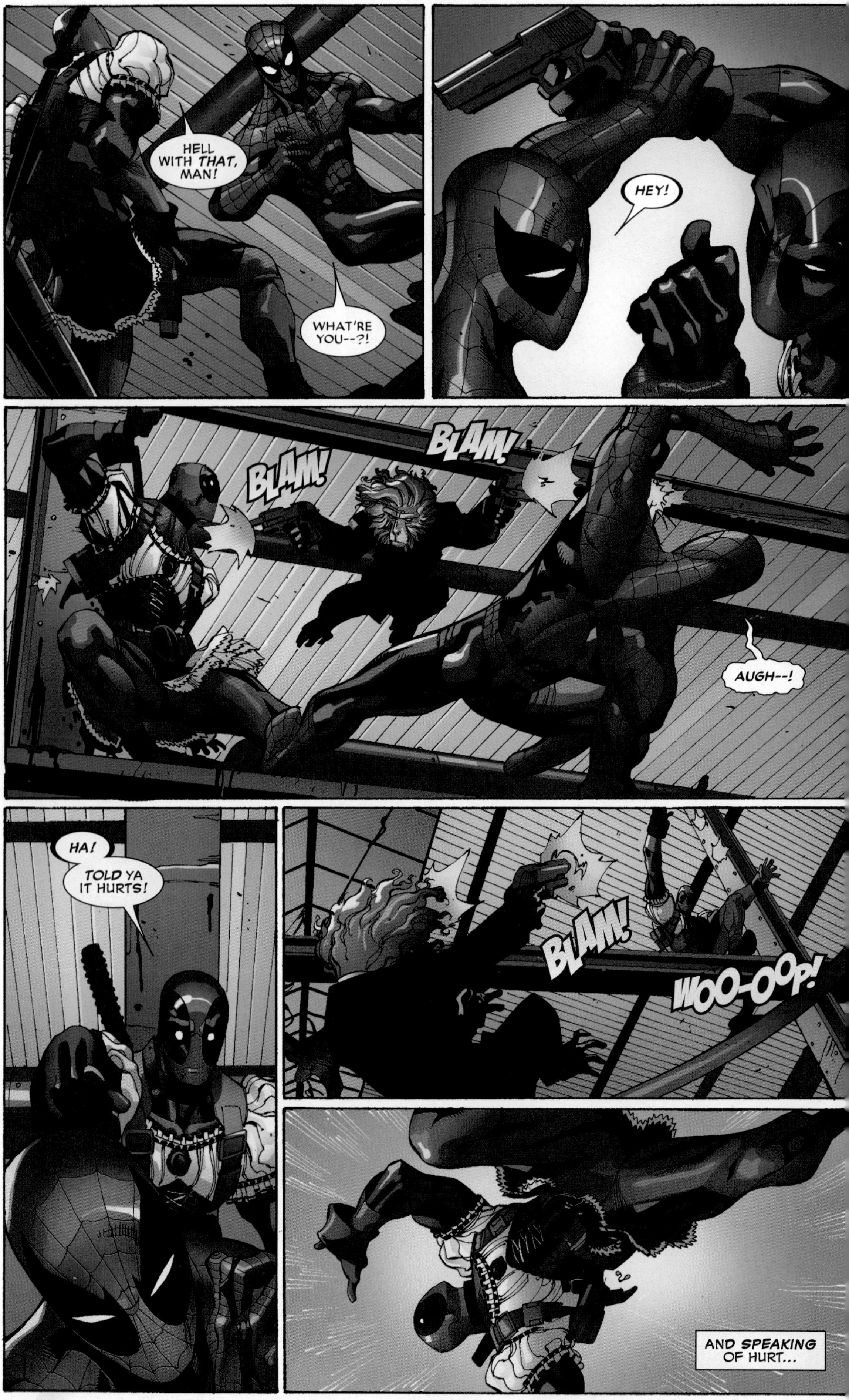
HELL WITH THAT, MAN!
WHAT'RE YOU--?!
HEY!
BLAM!
BLAM!
AUGH--!
HA!
TOLD YA IT HURTS!
BLAM!
WOO-OOP!
AND SPEAKING OF HURT...

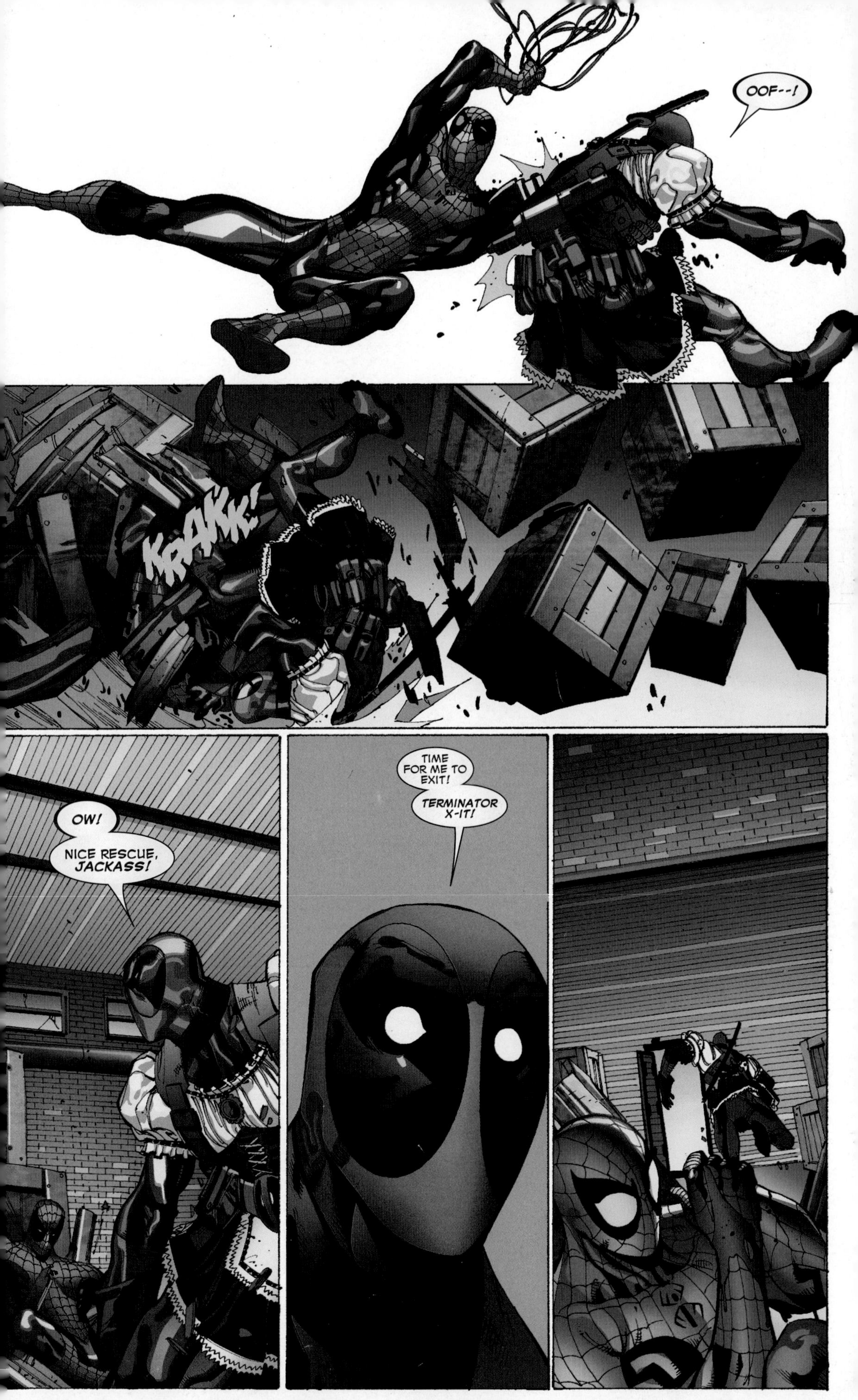
OOF--!
KRAKK!
OW!
NICE RESCUE, JACKASS!
TIME FOR ME TO EXIT!
TERMINATOR X-IT!

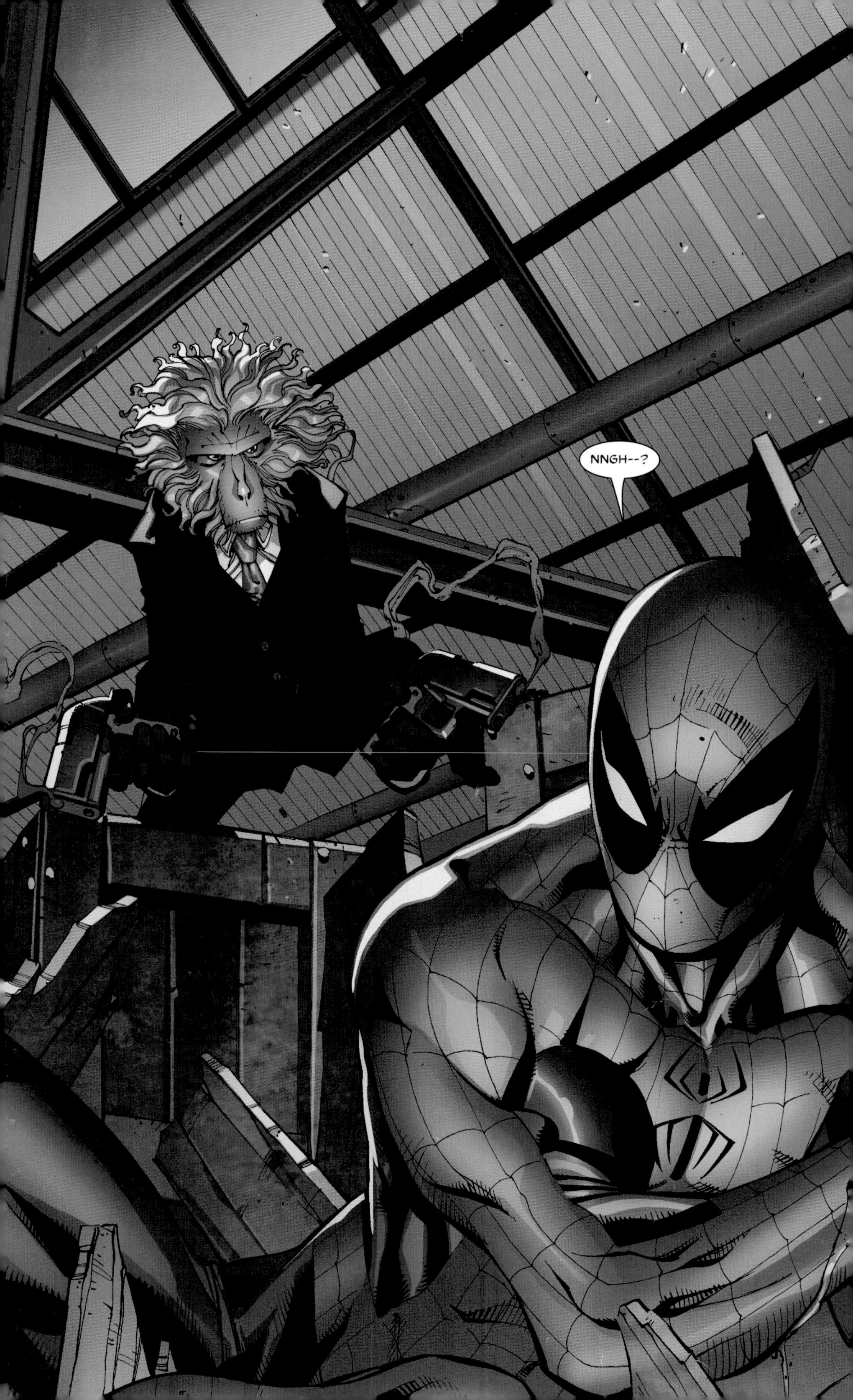
NNGH--?

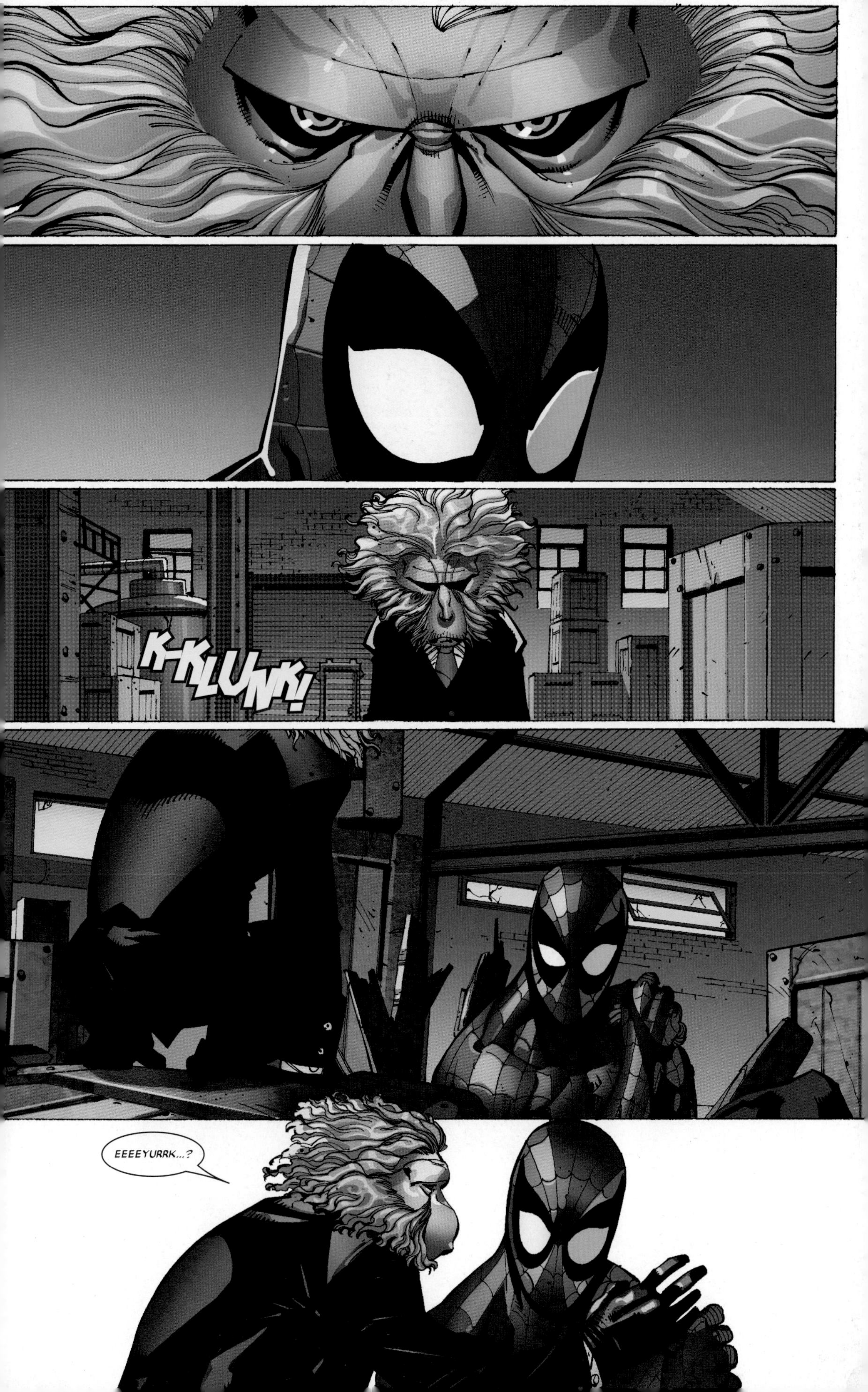
K-KLUNK!
EEEEYURRK...?

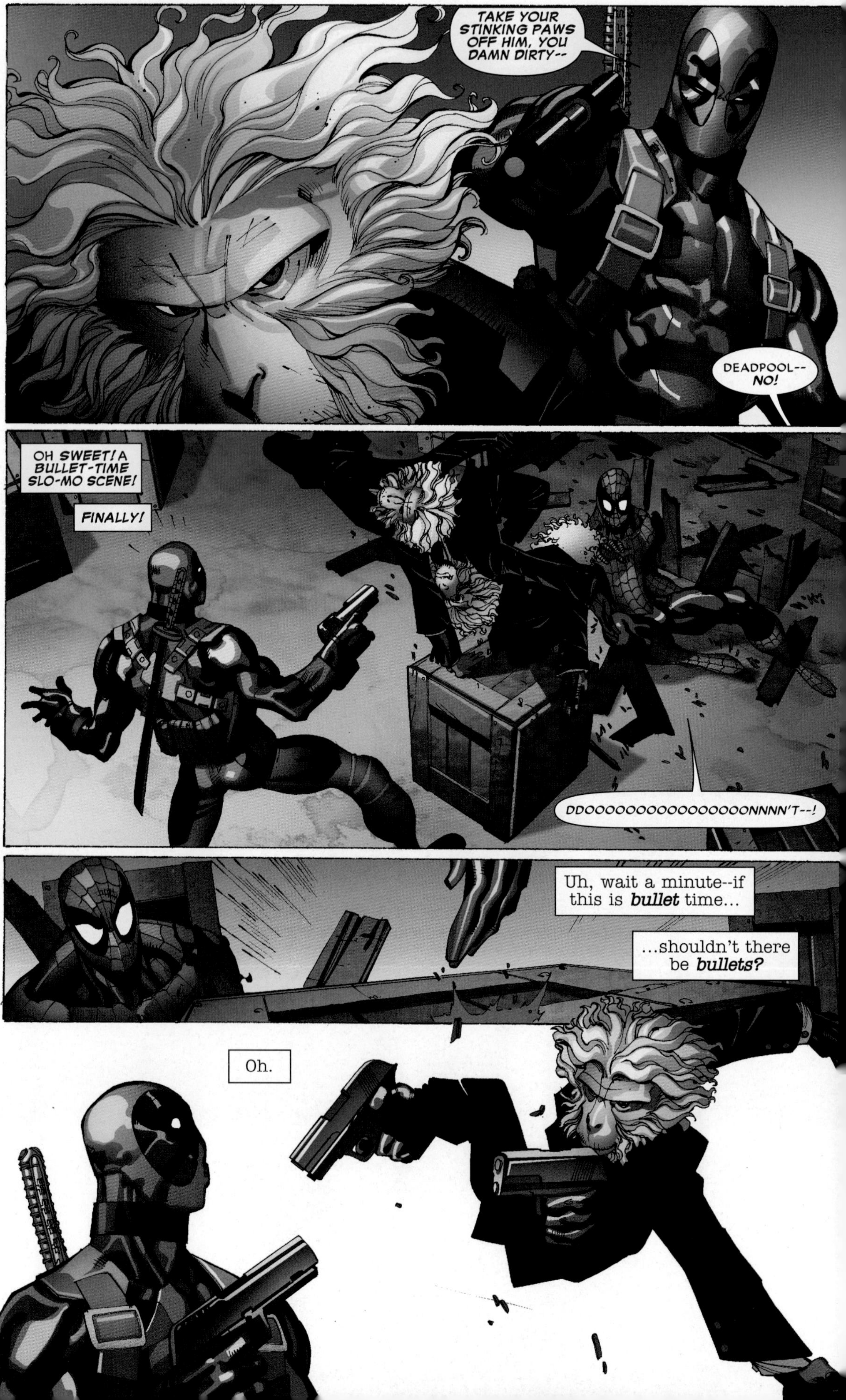
TAKE YOUR STINKING PAWS OFF HIM, YOU DAMN DIRTY--
DEADPOOL-- NO!
OH SWEET! A BULLET-TIME SLO-MO SCENE!
FINALLY!
DDOOOOOOOOOOOOOOOOONNNN'T--!
Uh, wait a minute--if this is bullet time...
...shouldn't there be bullets?
Oh.

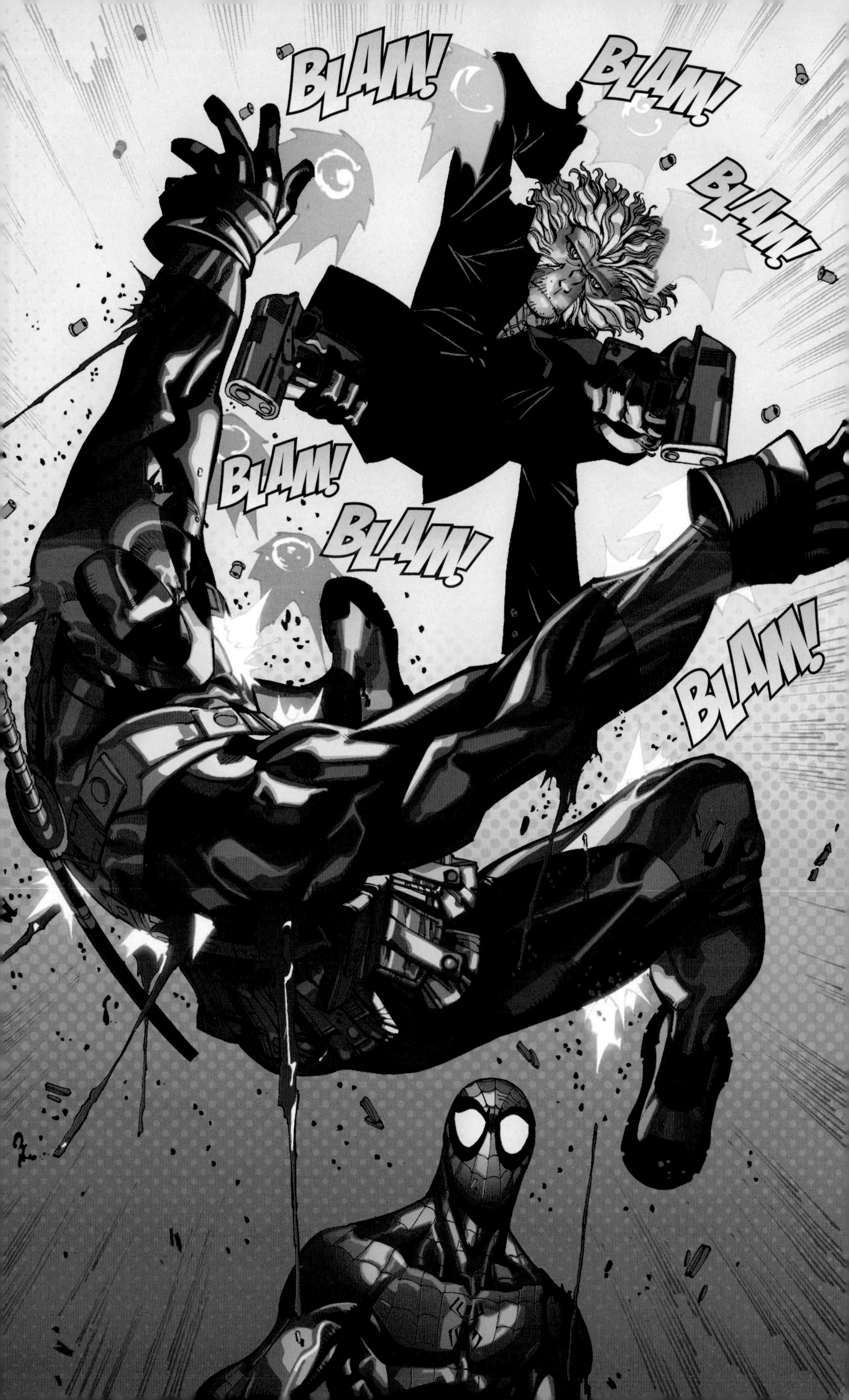
BLAM!
BLAM!
BLAM!
BLAM!
BLAM!
BLAM!

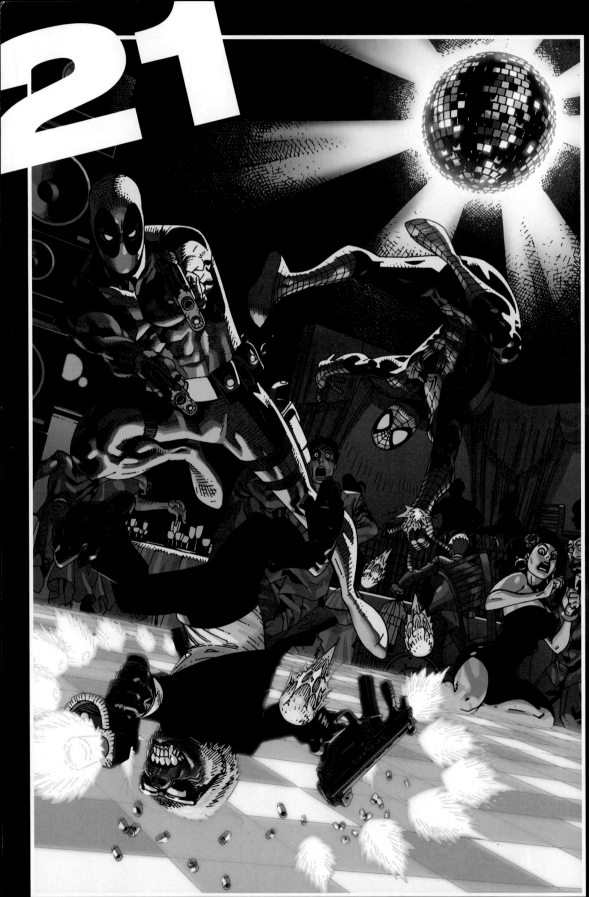

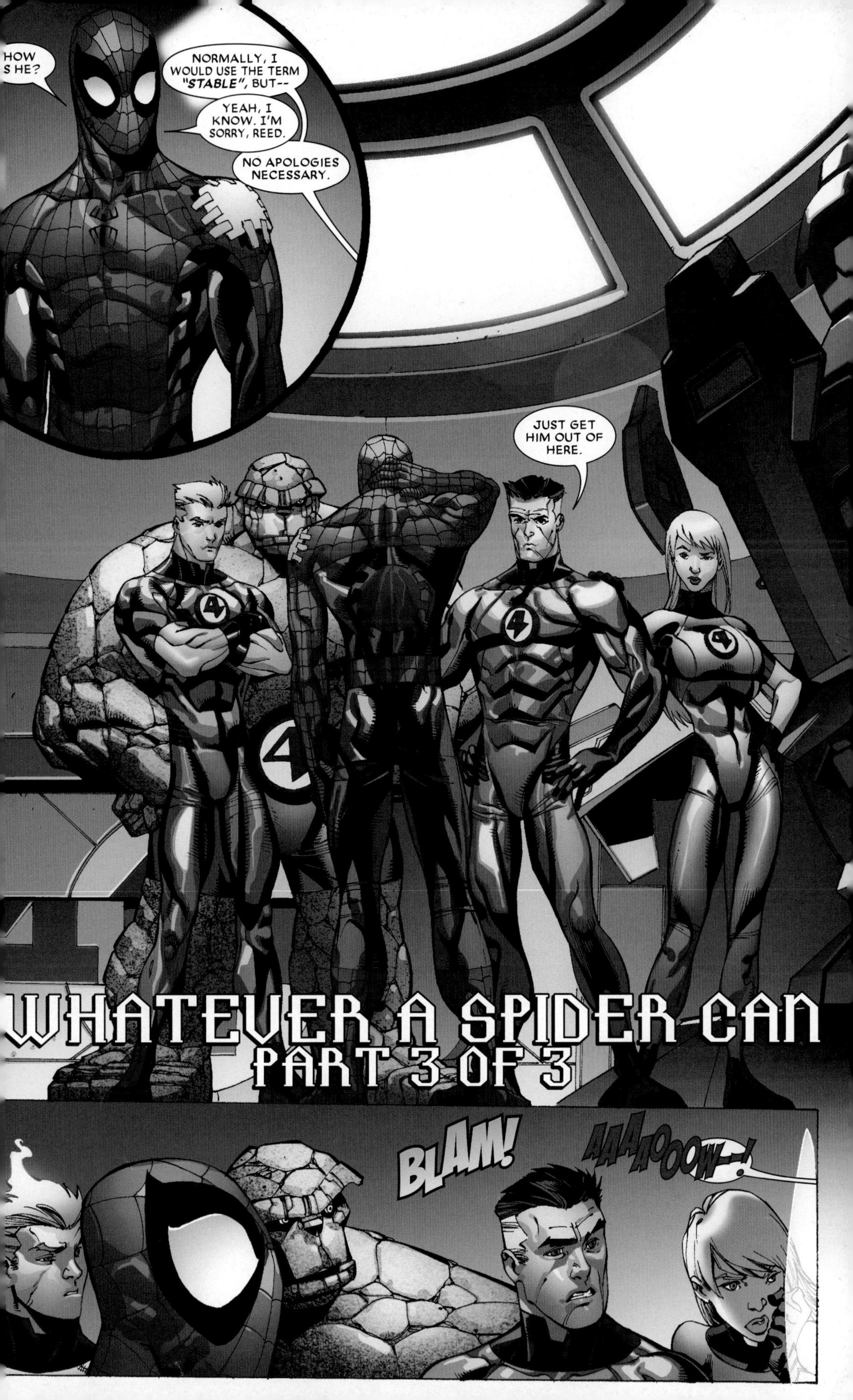
HOW S HE?
NORMALLY, I WOULD USE THE TERM "STABLE", BUT--
YEAH, I KNOW. I'M SORRY, REED.
NO APOLOGIES NECESSARY.
JUST GET HIM OUT OF HERE.
WHATEVER A SPIDER CAN
PART 3 OF 3
BLAM!
AAAAOOOW--!

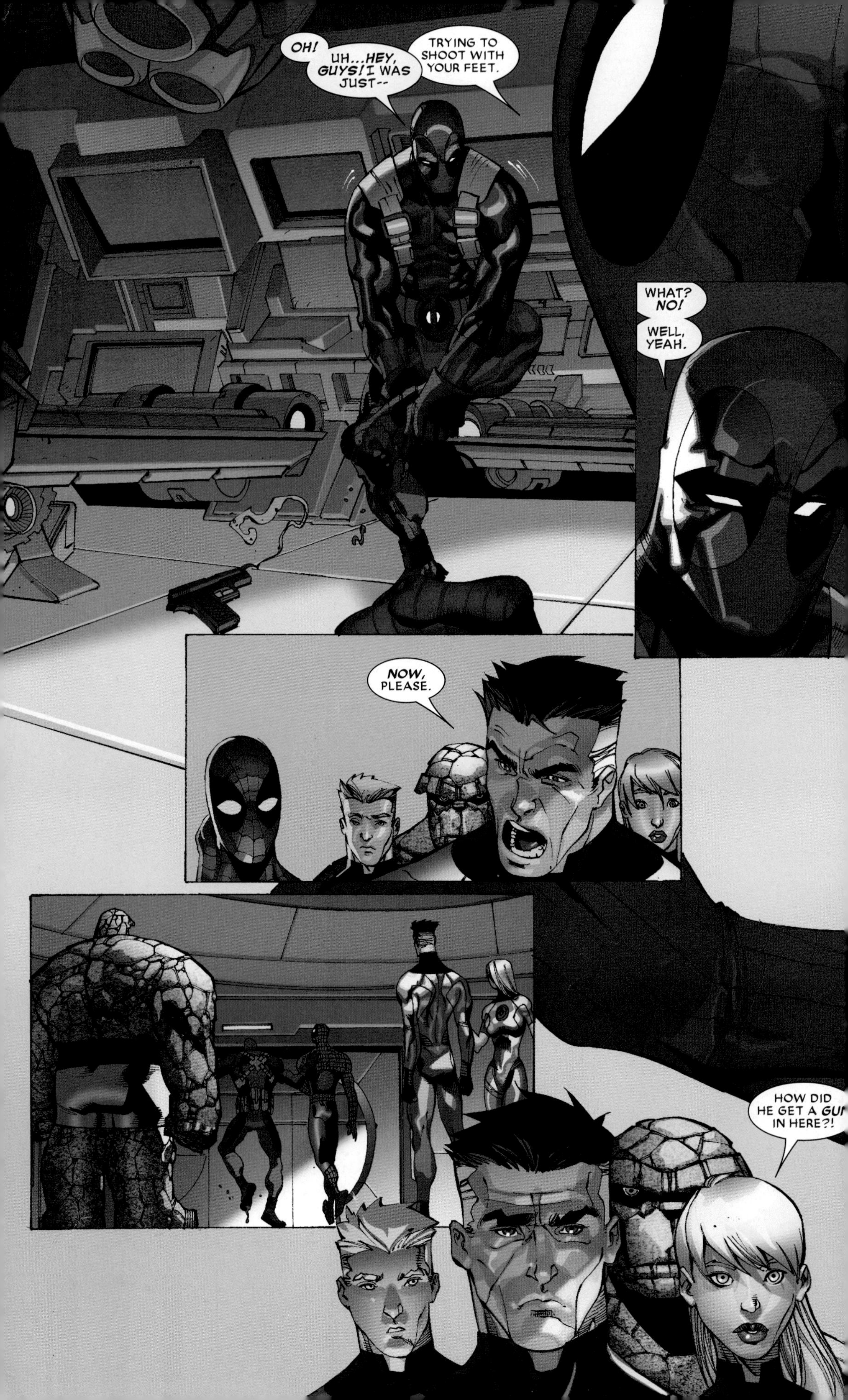
OH!
UH...HEY, GUYS! I WAS JUST--
TRYING TO SHOOT WITH YOUR FEET.
WHAT? NO!
WELL, YEAH.
NOW, PLEASE.
HOW DID HE GET A GU
IN HERE?!

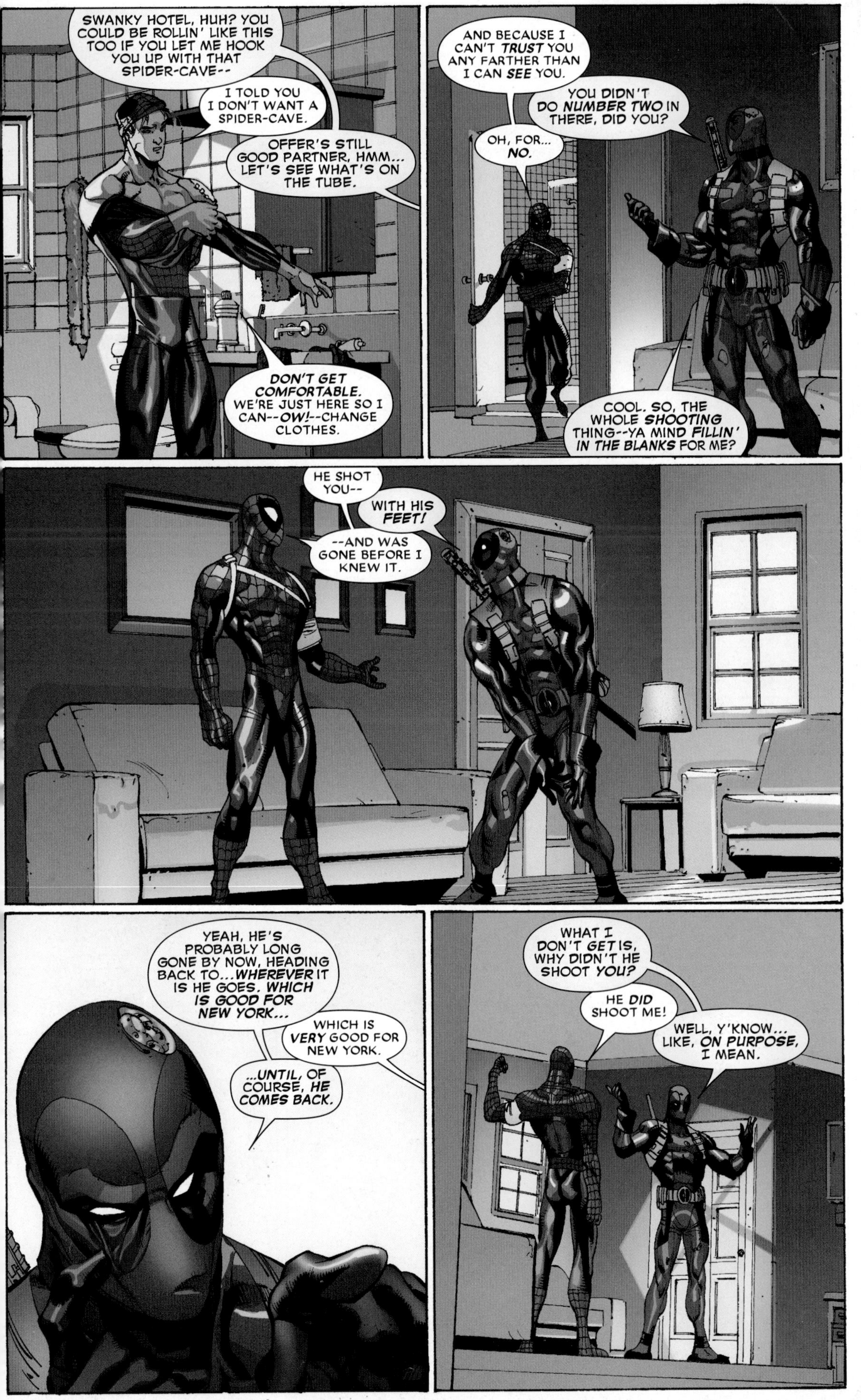
SWANKY HOTEL, HUH? YOU COULD BE ROLLIN' LIKE THIS TOO IF YOU LET ME HOOK YOU UP WITH THAT SPIDER-CAVE--
I TOLD YOU I DON'T WANT A SPIDER-CAVE.
OFFER'S STILL GOOD PARTNER, HMM... LET'S SEE WHAT'S ON THE TUBE.
DON'T GET COMFORTABLE. WE'RE JUST HERE SO I CAN--OW!--CHANGE CLOTHES.
AND BECAUSE I CAN'T TRUST YOU ANY FARTHER THAN I CAN SEE YOU.
YOU DIDN'T DO NUMBER TWO IN THERE, DID YOU?
OH, FOR... NO.
COOL. SO, THE WHOLE SHOOTING THING--YA MIND FILLIN' IN THE BLANKS FOR ME?
HE SHOT YOU--
WITH HIS FEET!
--AND WAS GONE BEFORE I KNEW IT.
YEAH, HE'S PROBABLY LONG GONE BY NOW, HEADING BACK TO...WHEREVER IT IS HE GOES. WHICH IS GOOD FOR NEW YORK...
WHICH IS VERY GOOD FOR NEW YORK.
...UNTIL, OF COURSE, HE COMES BACK.
WHAT I DON'T GET IS, WHY DIDN'T HE SHOOT YOU?
HE DID SHOOT ME!
WELL, Y'KNOW... LIKE, ON PURPOSE, I MEAN.

YOU'RE RIGHT ABOUT THAT, IT *WAS* AN *ACCIDENT*...AND FROM WHAT I COULD TELL HE SEEMED REALLY... *SAD* ABOUT SHOOTING ME.

REALLY? *THAT'S WEIRD*...

NO, ACTUALLY, IT'S *NOT*. UNLIKE *YOU*, *MOST* PEOPLE WOULD REGRET--

UNLIKE *ME*, MOST PEOPLE WOULD BE DEAD RIGHT NOW, BECAUSE *THAT'S WHAT HAPPENS WHEN HIT-MONKEY SHOOTS YOU*.

LET THAT SINK IN WHILE I HANDLE A LITTLE BIT O' BUSINESS.

WHOO-BOY...

UHH, SINCE WE'RE *PARTNERS* AN' ALL, I THINK I SHOULD *WARN* YOU ABOUT WHAT'S ABOUT TO HAPPEN...

OPEN THE WINDOW!

I WAS GONNA DO THAT ANYWAY, BUT--

WHATEVER YOU'RE DOING IN THERE, I DO *NOT* WANT TO HEAR ABOUT IT.

OKAY... *UNNH!*

DON'T SAY I DIDN'T TRY TO WARN YA...

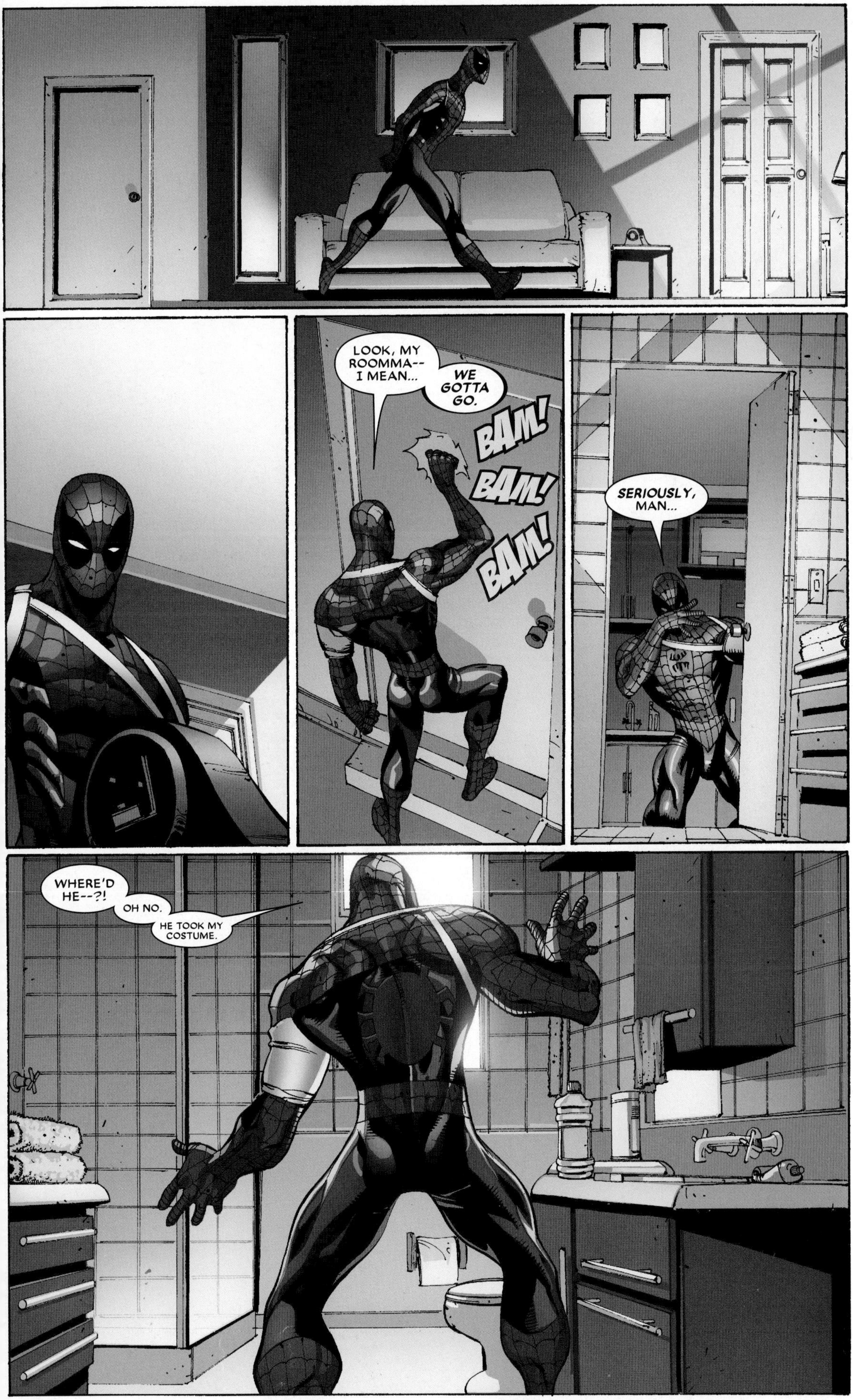

LOOK, MY ROOMMA-- I MEAN...
WE GOTTA GO.
BAM!
BAM!
BAM!
SERIOUSLY, MAN...
WHERE'D HE--?!
OH NO.
HE TOOK MY COSTUME.

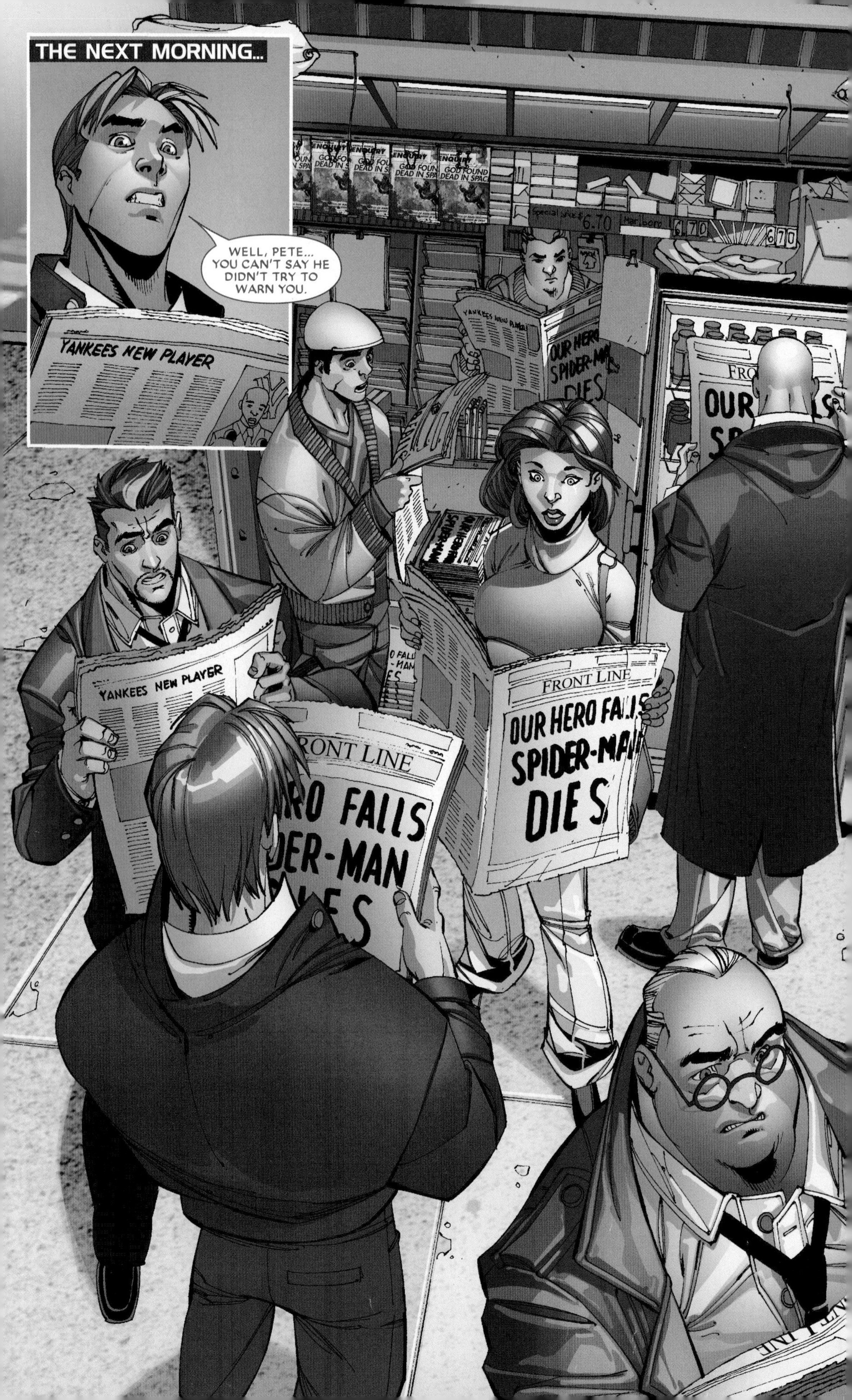
THE NEXT MORNING...
WELL, PETE... YOU CAN'T SAY HE DIDN'T TRY TO WARN YOU.
YANKEES NEW PLAYER
OUR HERO SPIDER-MAN DIES
FRONT LINE
GOD FOUND DEAD IN SPA

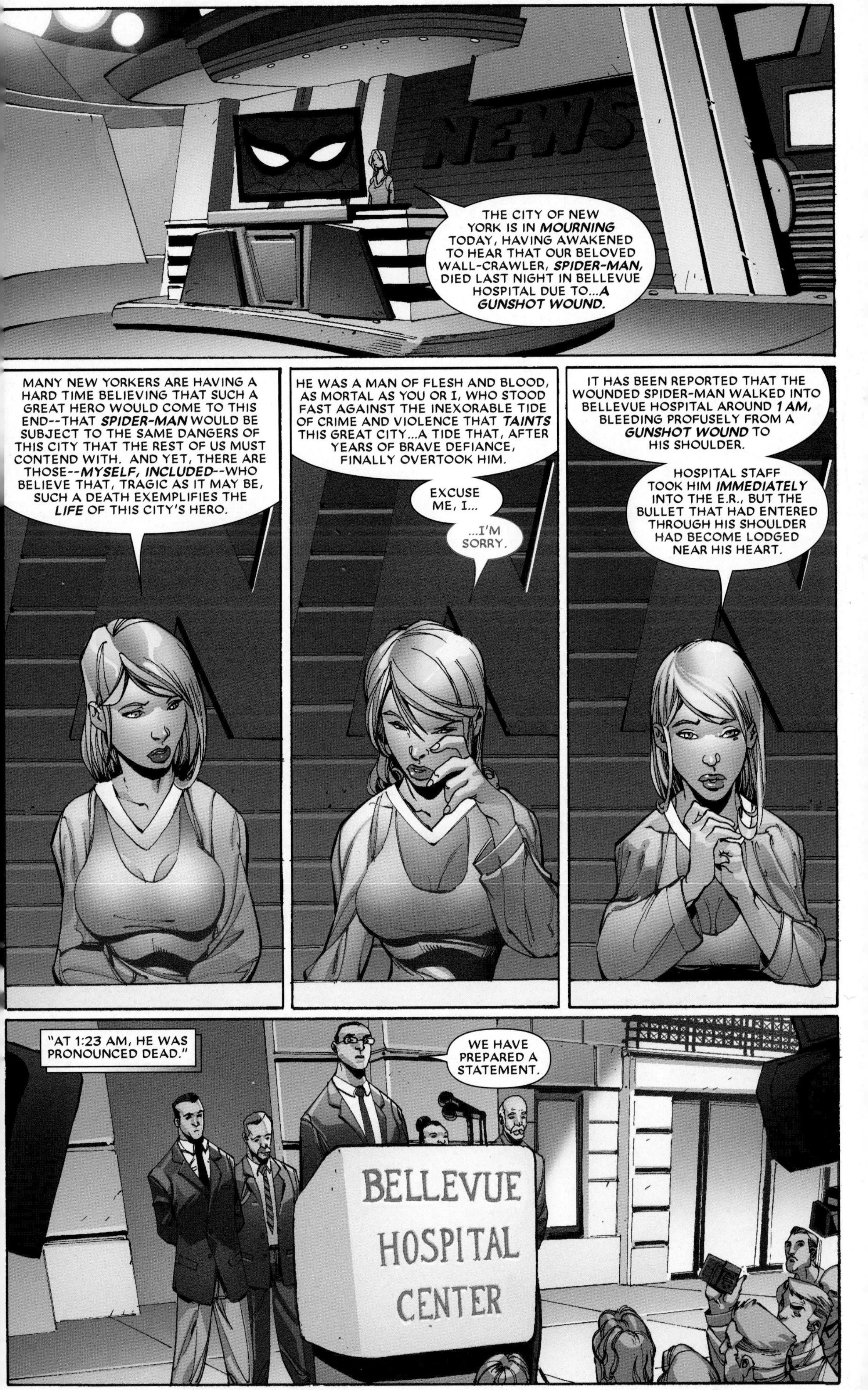
NEWS
THE CITY OF NEW YORK IS IN MOURNING TODAY, HAVING AWAKENED TO HEAR THAT OUR BELOVED WALL-CRAWLER, SPIDER-MAN, DIED LAST NIGHT IN BELLEVUE HOSPITAL DUE TO...A GUNSHOT WOUND.
MANY NEW YORKERS ARE HAVING A HARD TIME BELIEVING THAT SUCH A GREAT HERO WOULD COME TO THIS END--THAT SPIDER-MAN WOULD BE SUBJECT TO THE SAME DANGERS OF THIS CITY THAT THE REST OF US MUST CONTEND WITH. AND YET, THERE ARE THOSE--MYSELF, INCLUDED--WHO BELIEVE THAT, TRAGIC AS IT MAY BE, SUCH A DEATH EXEMPLIFIES THE LIFE OF THIS CITY'S HERO.
HE WAS A MAN OF FLESH AND BLOOD, AS MORTAL AS YOU OR I, WHO STOOD FAST AGAINST THE INEXORABLE TIDE OF CRIME AND VIOLENCE THAT TAINTS THIS GREAT CITY...A TIDE THAT, AFTER YEARS OF BRAVE DEFIANCE, FINALLY OVERTOOK HIM.
EXCUSE ME, I...
...I'M SORRY.
IT HAS BEEN REPORTED THAT THE WOUNDED SPIDER-MAN WALKED INTO BELLEVUE HOSPITAL AROUND 1 AM, BLEEDING PROFUSELY FROM A GUNSHOT WOUND TO HIS SHOULDER.
HOSPITAL STAFF TOOK HIM IMMEDIATELY INTO THE E.R., BUT THE BULLET THAT HAD ENTERED THROUGH HIS SHOULDER HAD BECOME LODGED NEAR HIS HEART.
"AT 1:23 AM, HE WAS PRONOUNCED DEAD."
WE HAVE PREPARED A STATEMENT.
BELLEVUE HOSPITAL CENTER

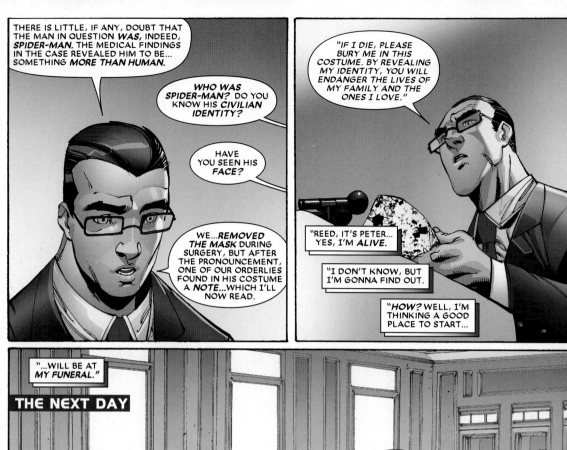

THERE IS LITTLE, IF ANY, DOUBT THAT THE MAN IN QUESTION *WAS*, INDEED, *SPIDER-MAN*. THE MEDICAL FINDINGS IN THE CASE REVEALED HIM TO BE... SOMETHING *MORE THAN HUMAN*.

WHO WAS SPIDER-MAN? DO YOU KNOW HIS *CIVILIAN IDENTITY?*

HAVE YOU SEEN HIS *FACE?*

WE...*REMOVED THE MASK* DURING SURGERY, BUT AFTER THE PRONOUNCEMENT, ONE OF OUR ORDERLIES FOUND IN HIS COSTUME A *NOTE*...WHICH I'LL NOW READ.

"IF I DIE, PLEASE BURY ME IN THIS COSTUME. BY REVEALING MY IDENTITY, YOU WILL ENDANGER THE LIVES OF MY FAMILY AND THE ONES I LOVE."

"REED, IT'S PETER... YES, I'M *ALIVE*."

"I DON'T KNOW, BUT I'M GONNA FIND OUT."

"*HOW?* WELL, I'M THINKING A GOOD PLACE TO START..."

"...WILL BE AT *MY FUNERAL*."

THE NEXT DAY

WOW.

GET LOTSA *CROWD SHOTS*. IF YOU CAN FIND A *KID CRYING*, I *GUARANTEE* YOU THE FRONT PAGE.

HRRNN--!

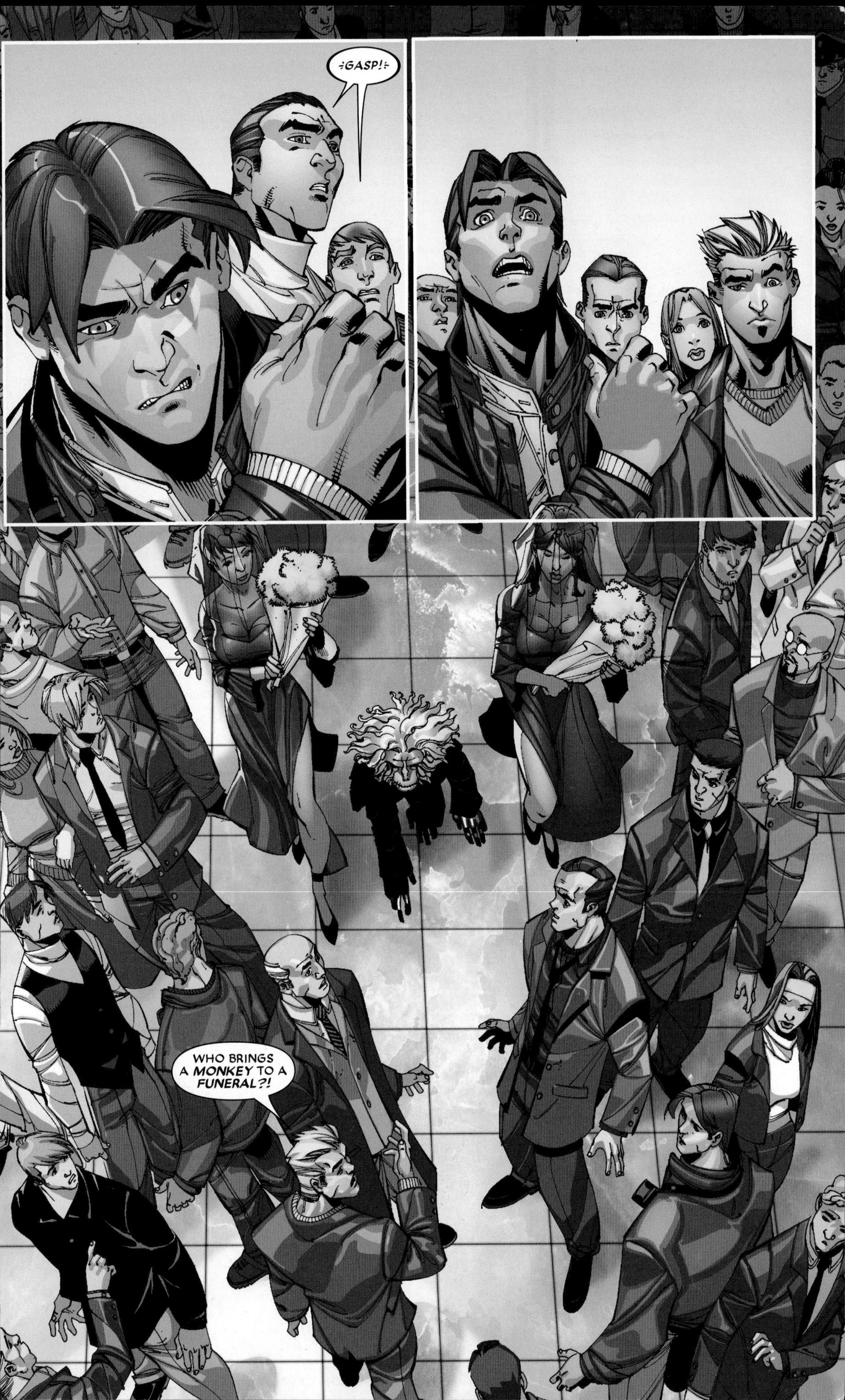

GASP!
WHO BRINGS A MONKEY TO A FUNERAL?!

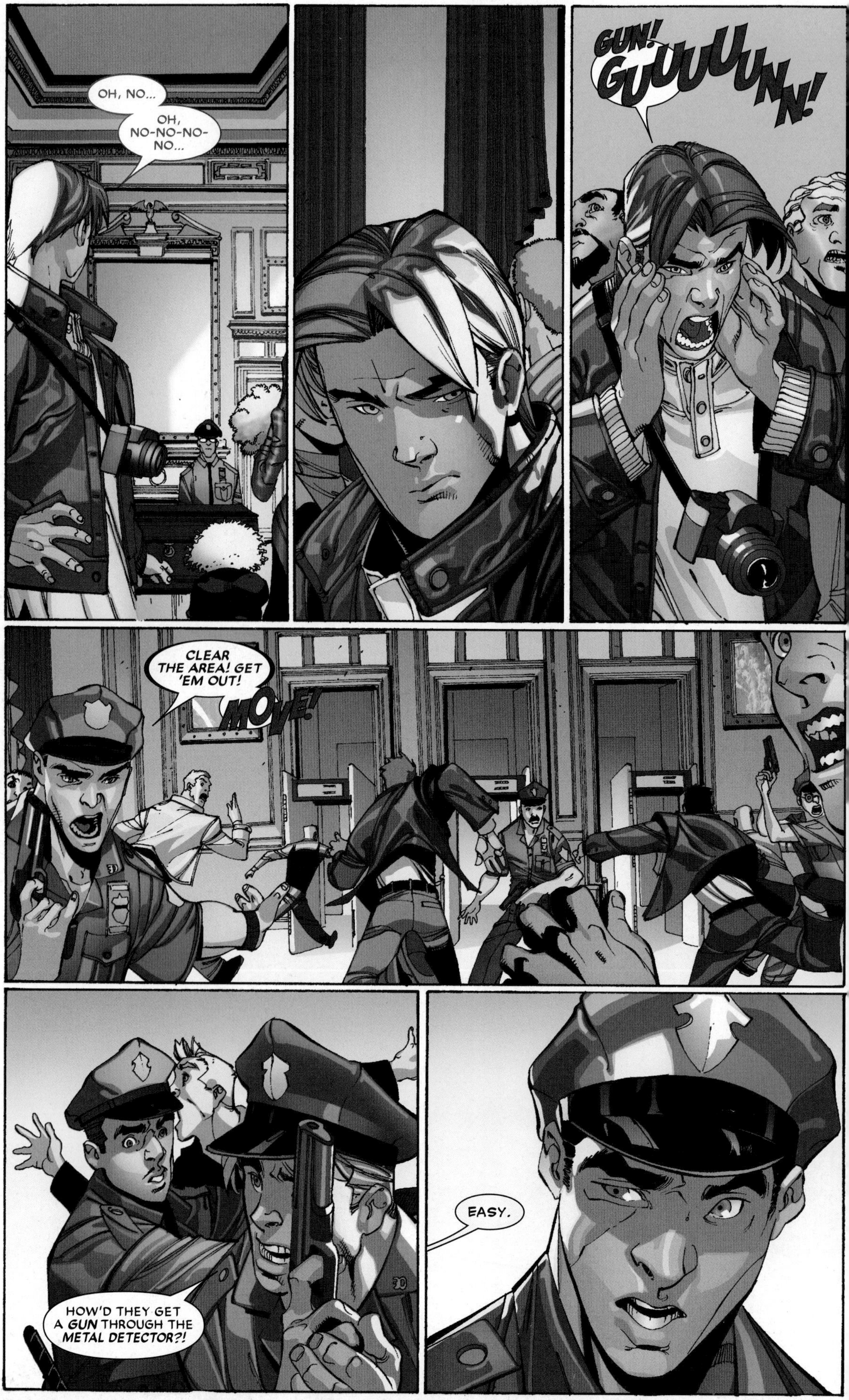
OH, NO...
OH, NO-NO-NO-NO...
GUN! GUUUUUNN!
CLEAR THE AREA! GET 'EM OUT!
MOVE!
HOW'D THEY GET A GUN THROUGH THE METAL DETECTOR?!
EASY.

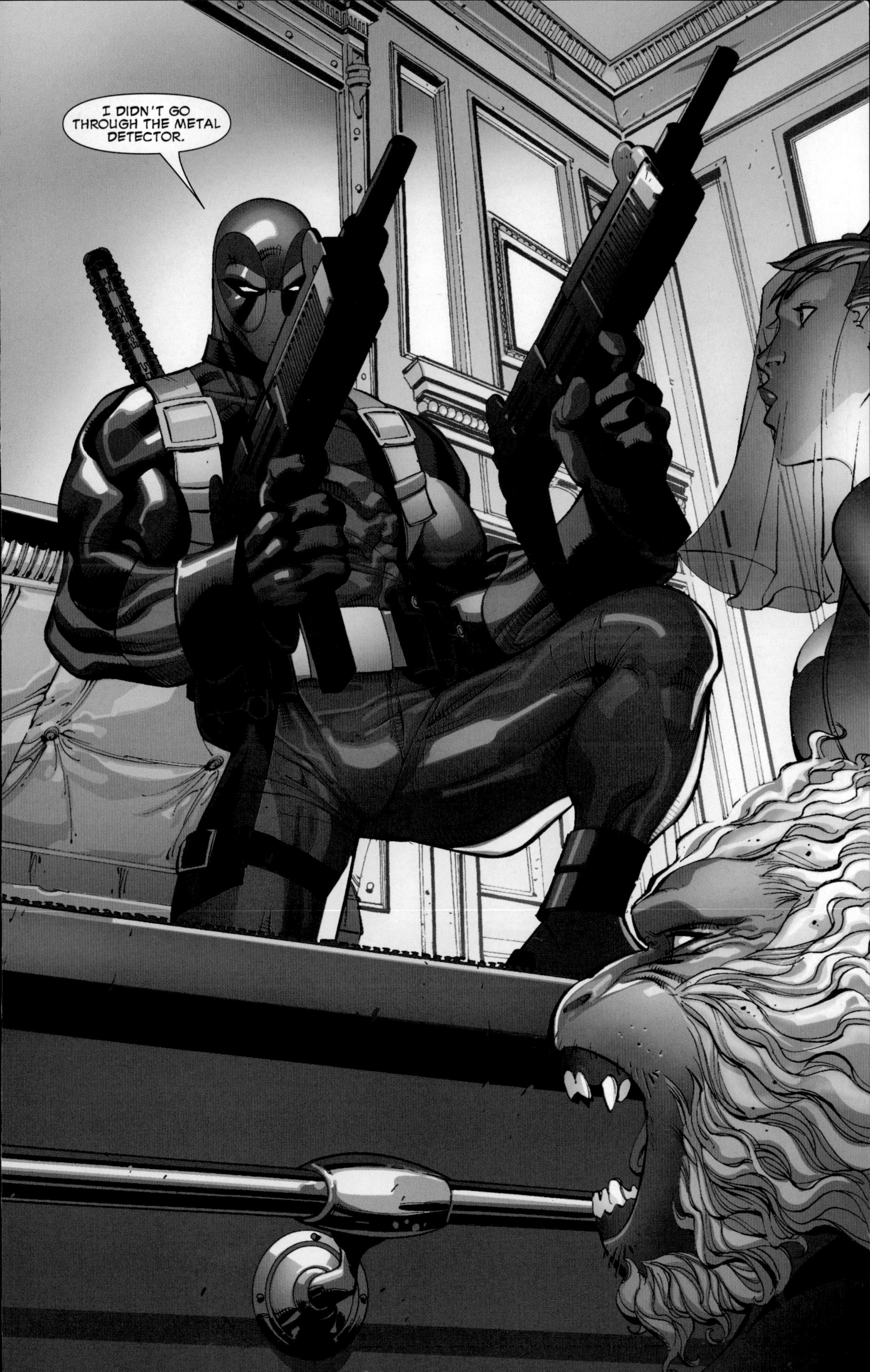
I DIDN'T GO THROUGH THE METAL DETECTOR.

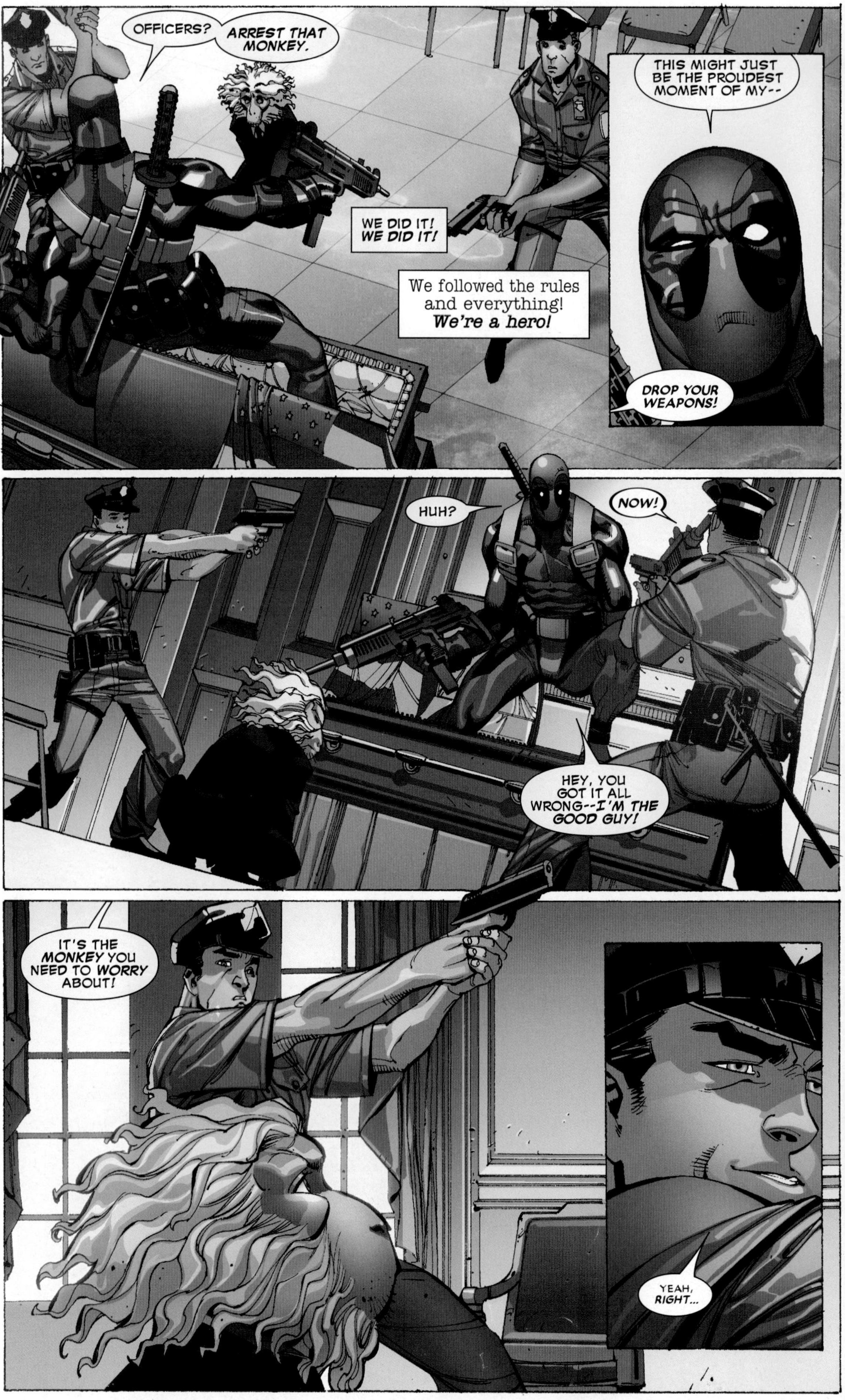
OFFICERS? ARREST THAT MONKEY.
WE DID IT! WE DID IT!
We followed the rules and everything! We're a hero!
THIS MIGHT JUST BE THE PROUDEST MOMENT OF MY--
DROP YOUR WEAPONS!
HUH?
NOW!
HEY, YOU GOT IT ALL WRONG--I'M THE GOOD GUY!
IT'S THE MONKEY YOU NEED TO WORRY ABOUT!
YEAH, RIGHT...

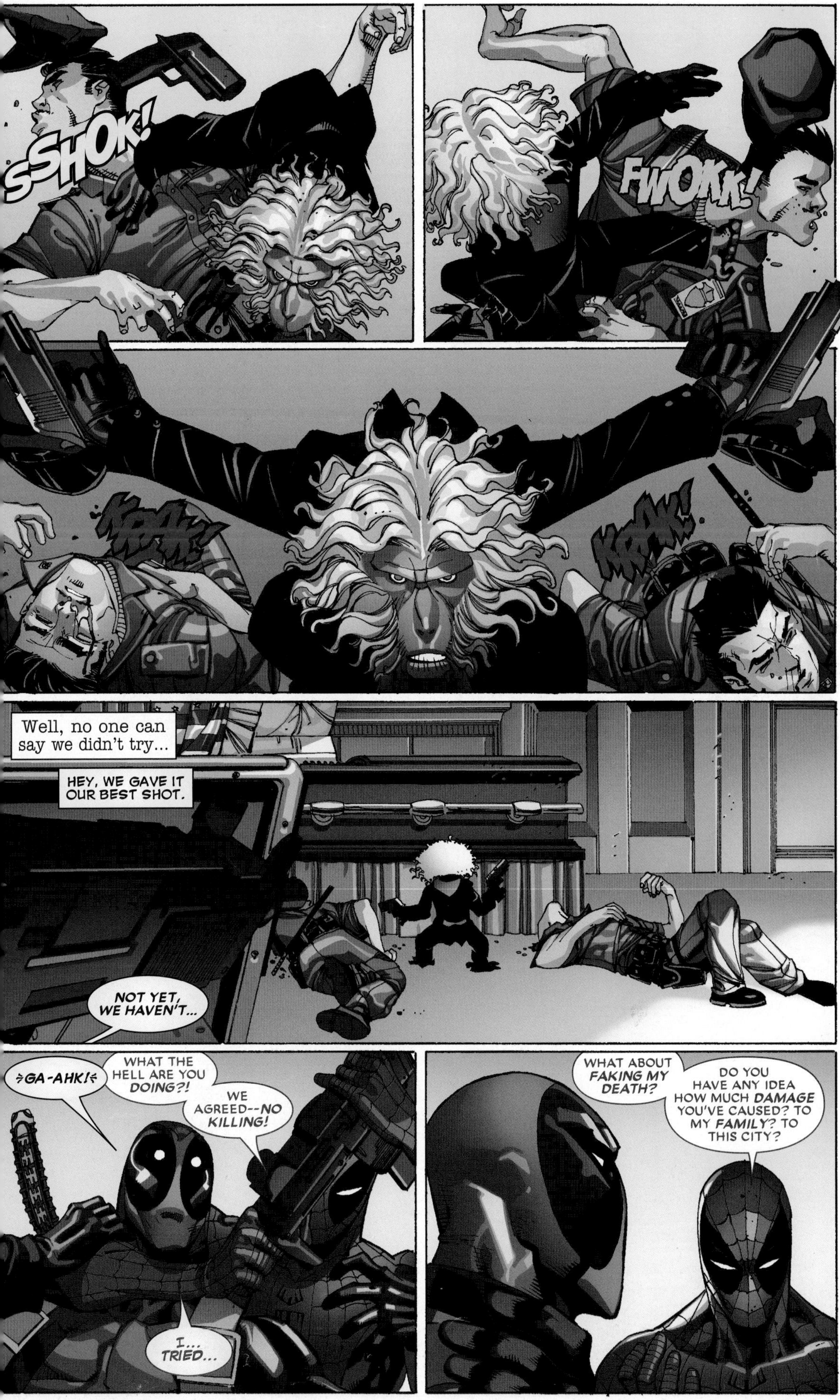
SSHOK!
FWOKK!
KRAK!
KRAK!
Well, no one can say we didn't try...
HEY, WE GAVE IT OUR BEST SHOT.
NOT YET, WE HAVEN'T...
⇒GA-AHK!⇐
WHAT THE HELL ARE YOU DOING?!
WE AGREED--NO KILLING!
I... TRIED...
WHAT ABOUT FAKING MY DEATH?
DO YOU HAVE ANY IDEA HOW MUCH DAMAGE YOU'VE CAUSED? TO MY FAMILY? TO THIS CITY?

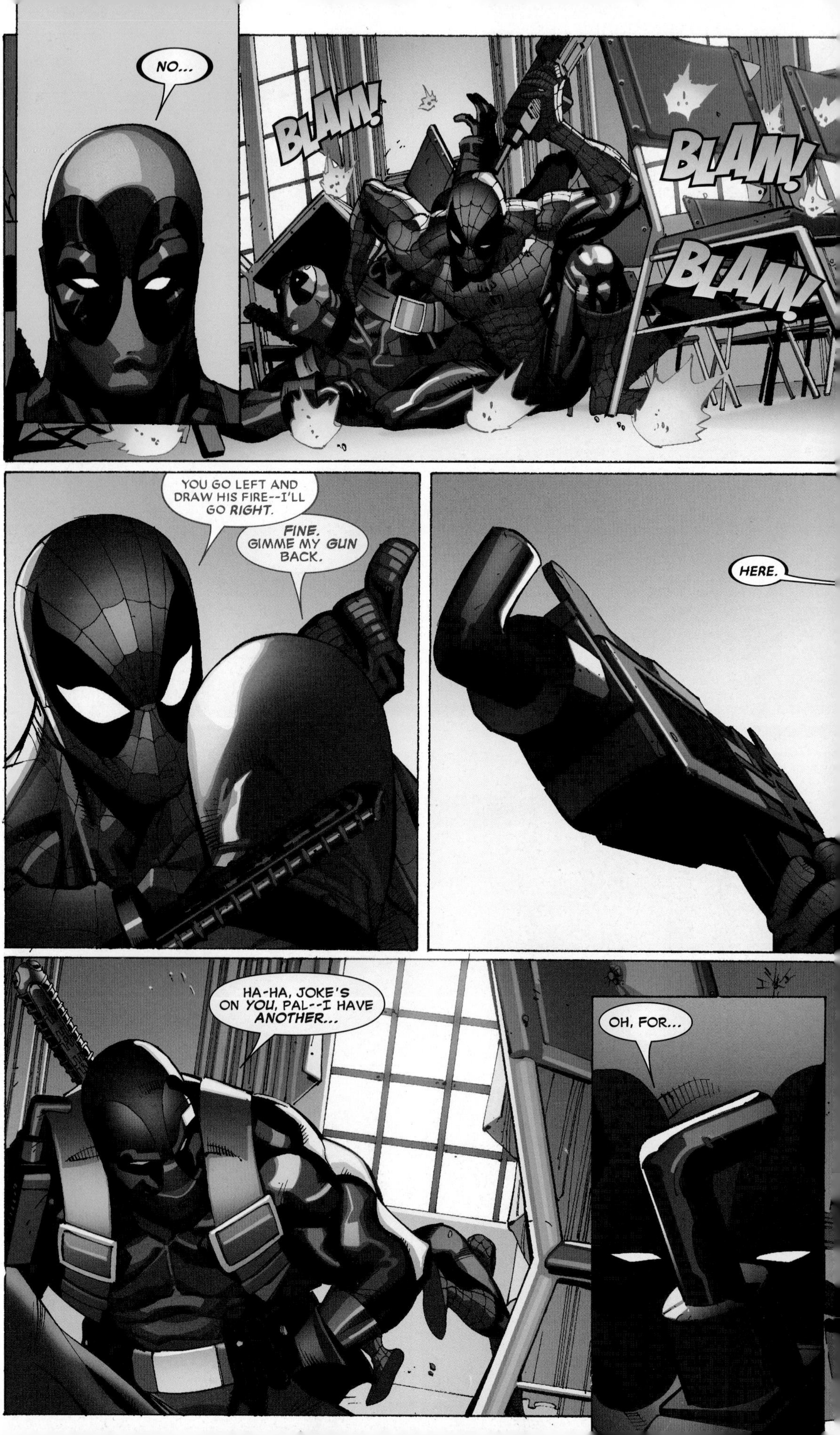
NO...
BLAM!
BLAM!
BLAM!
YOU GO LEFT AND DRAW HIS FIRE--I'LL GO RIGHT.
FINE. GIMME MY GUN BACK.
HERE.
HA-HA, JOKE'S ON YOU, PAL--I HAVE ANOTHER...
OH, FOR...

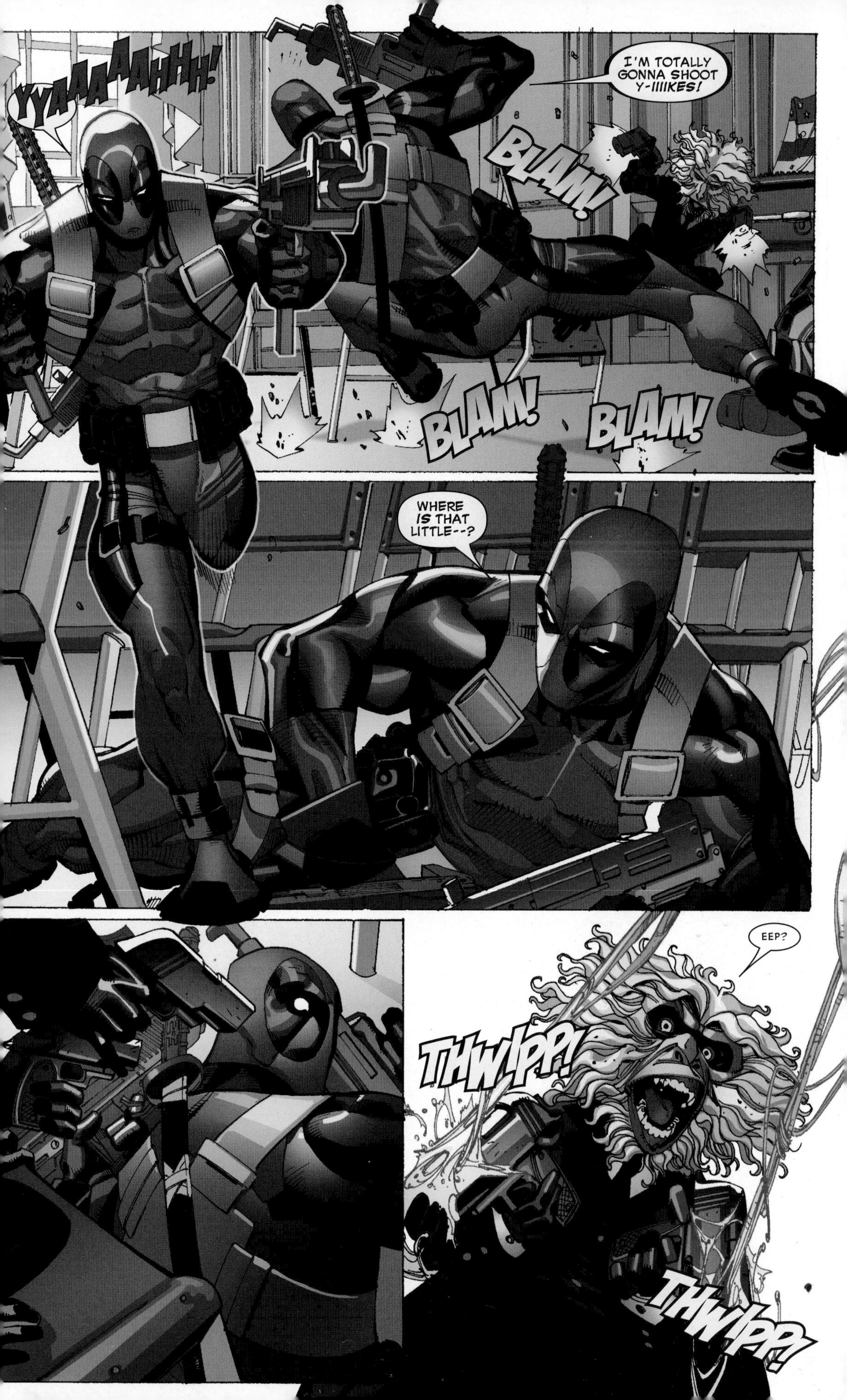
YYAAAAAHHH!
I'M TOTALLY GONNA SHOOT Y-IIIIKES!
BLAM!
BLAM!
BLAM!
WHERE IS THAT LITTLE--?
EEP?
THWIPP!
THWIPP!

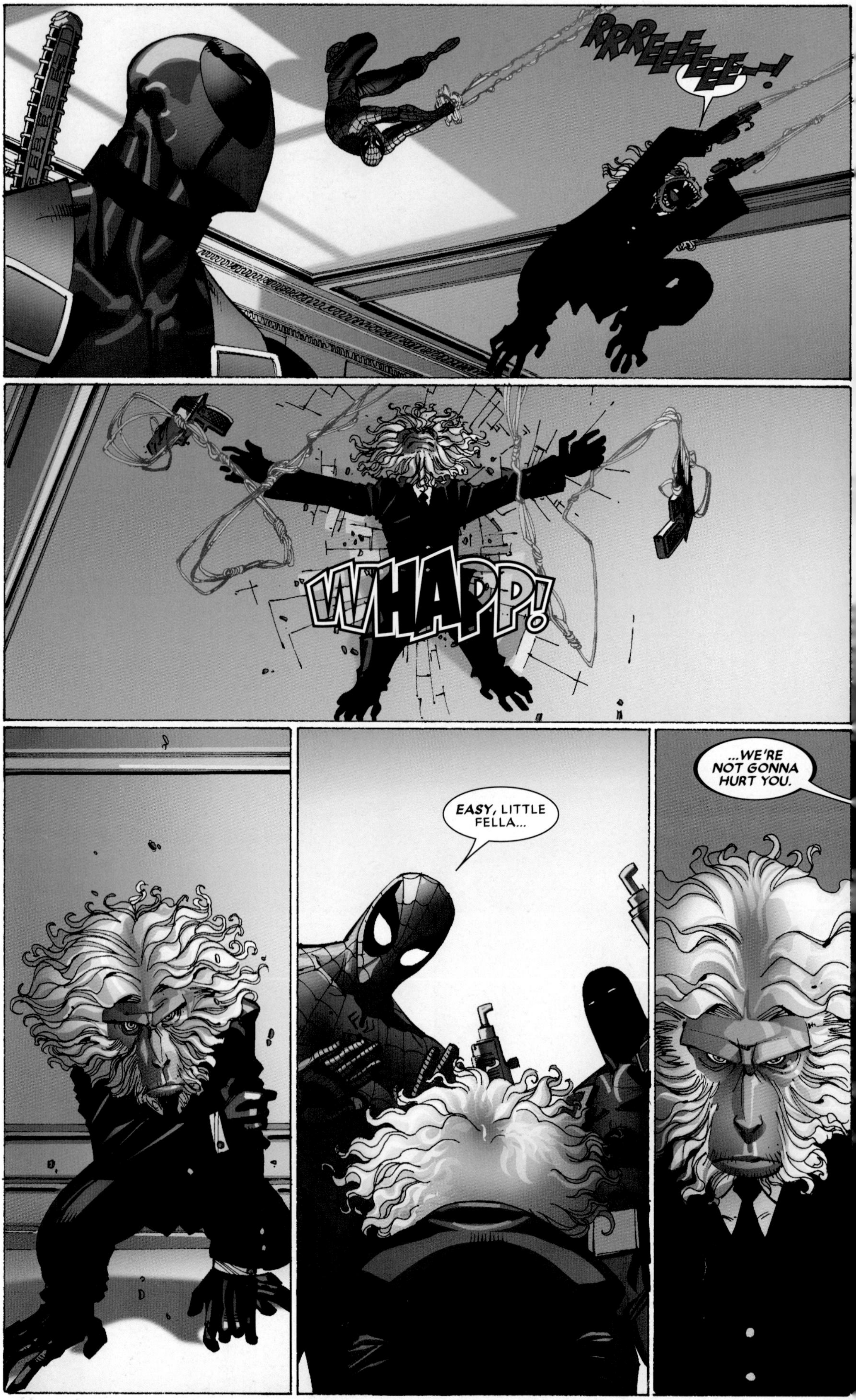
RRREEEEEEE--!
WHAPP!
EASY, LITTLE FELLA...
...WE'RE NOT GONNA HURT YOU.

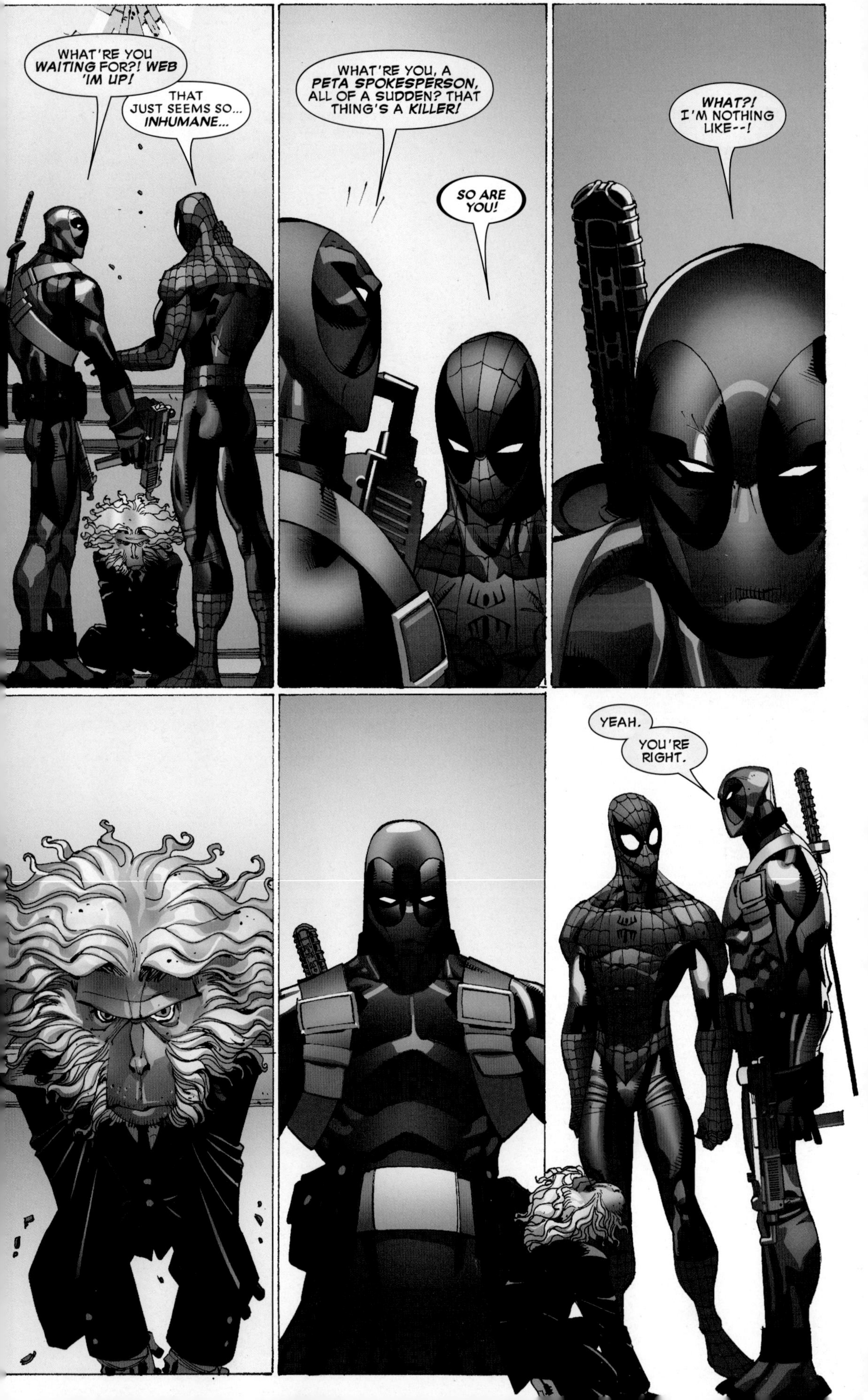

WHAT'RE YOU WAITING FOR?! WEB 'IM UP!
THAT JUST SEEMS SO... INHUMANE...
WHAT'RE YOU, A PETA SPOKESPERSON, ALL OF A SUDDEN? THAT THING'S A KILLER!
SO ARE YOU!
WHAT?! I'M NOTHING LIKE--!
YEAH.
YOU'RE RIGHT.

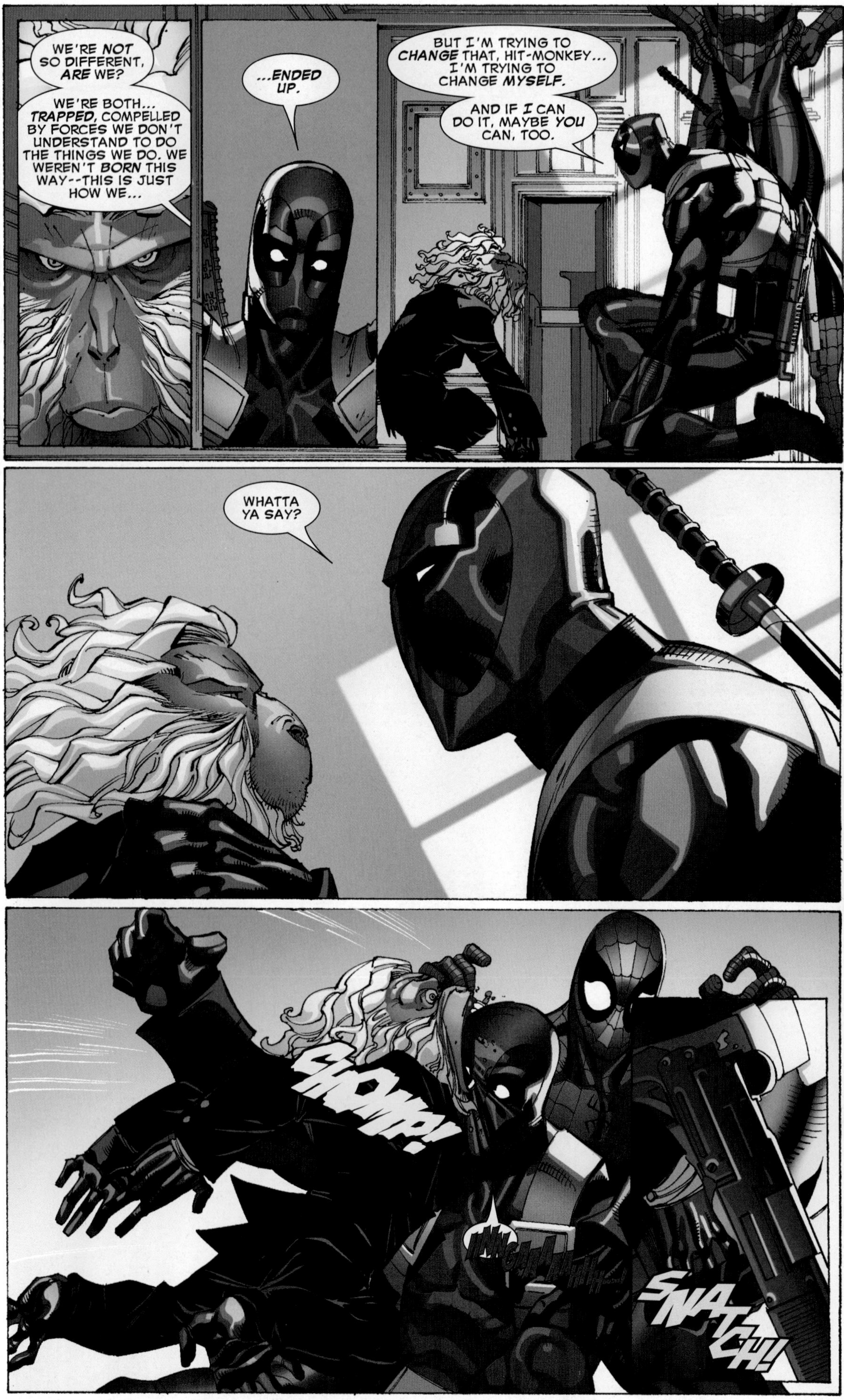
WE'RE NOT SO DIFFERENT, ARE WE?
WE'RE BOTH... TRAPPED, COMPELLED BY FORCES WE DON'T UNDERSTAND TO DO THE THINGS WE DO. WE WEREN'T BORN THIS WAY--THIS IS JUST HOW WE...
...ENDED UP.
BUT I'M TRYING TO CHANGE THAT, HIT-MONKEY... I'M TRYING TO CHANGE MYSELF.
AND IF I CAN DO IT, MAYBE YOU CAN, TOO.
WHATTA YA SAY?
CHOMP!
SNATCH!

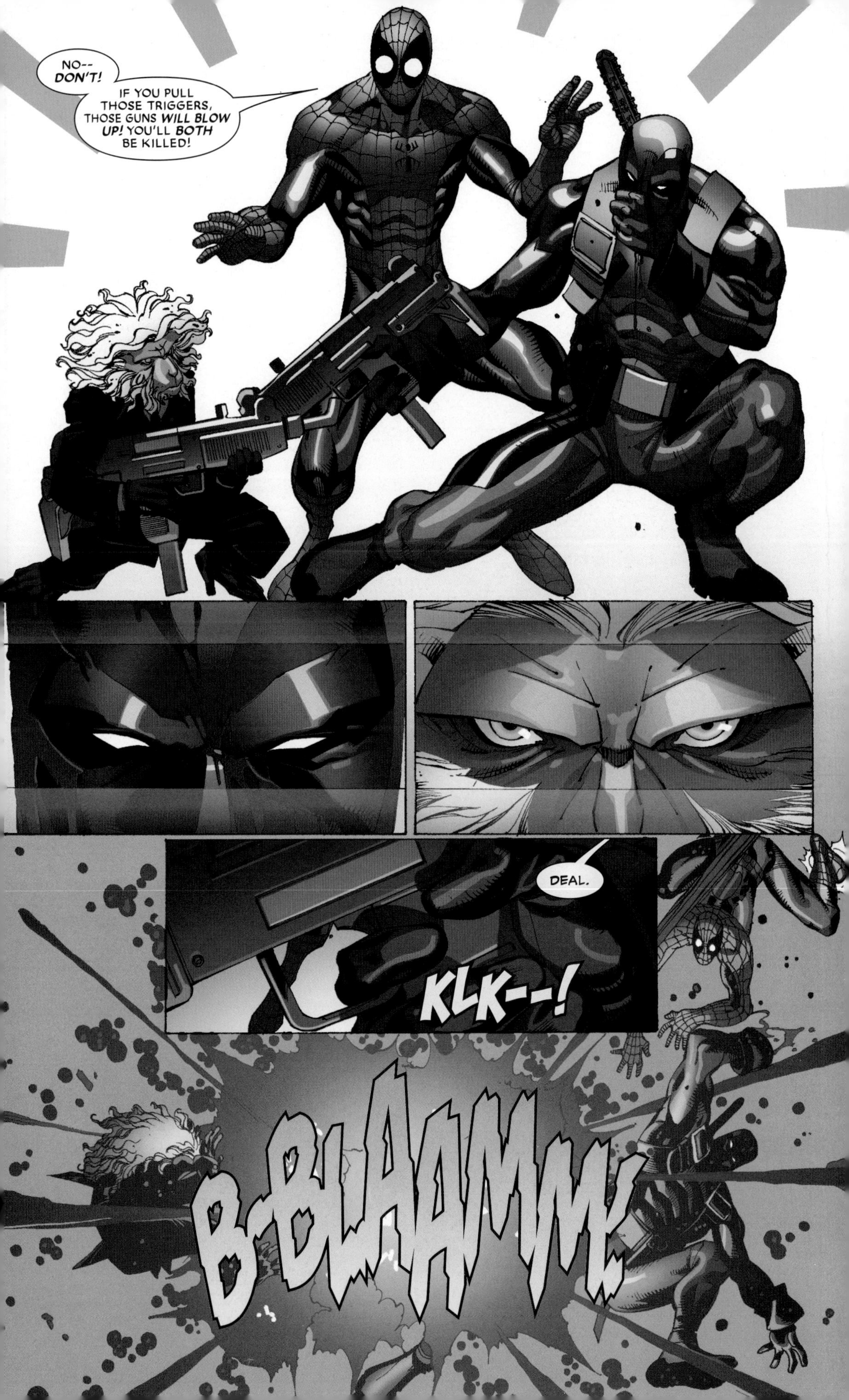
NO--
DON'T!
IF YOU PULL THOSE TRIGGERS, THOSE GUNS WILL BLOW UP! YOU'LL BOTH BE KILLED!
DEAL.
KLK--!
B-BLAMM!

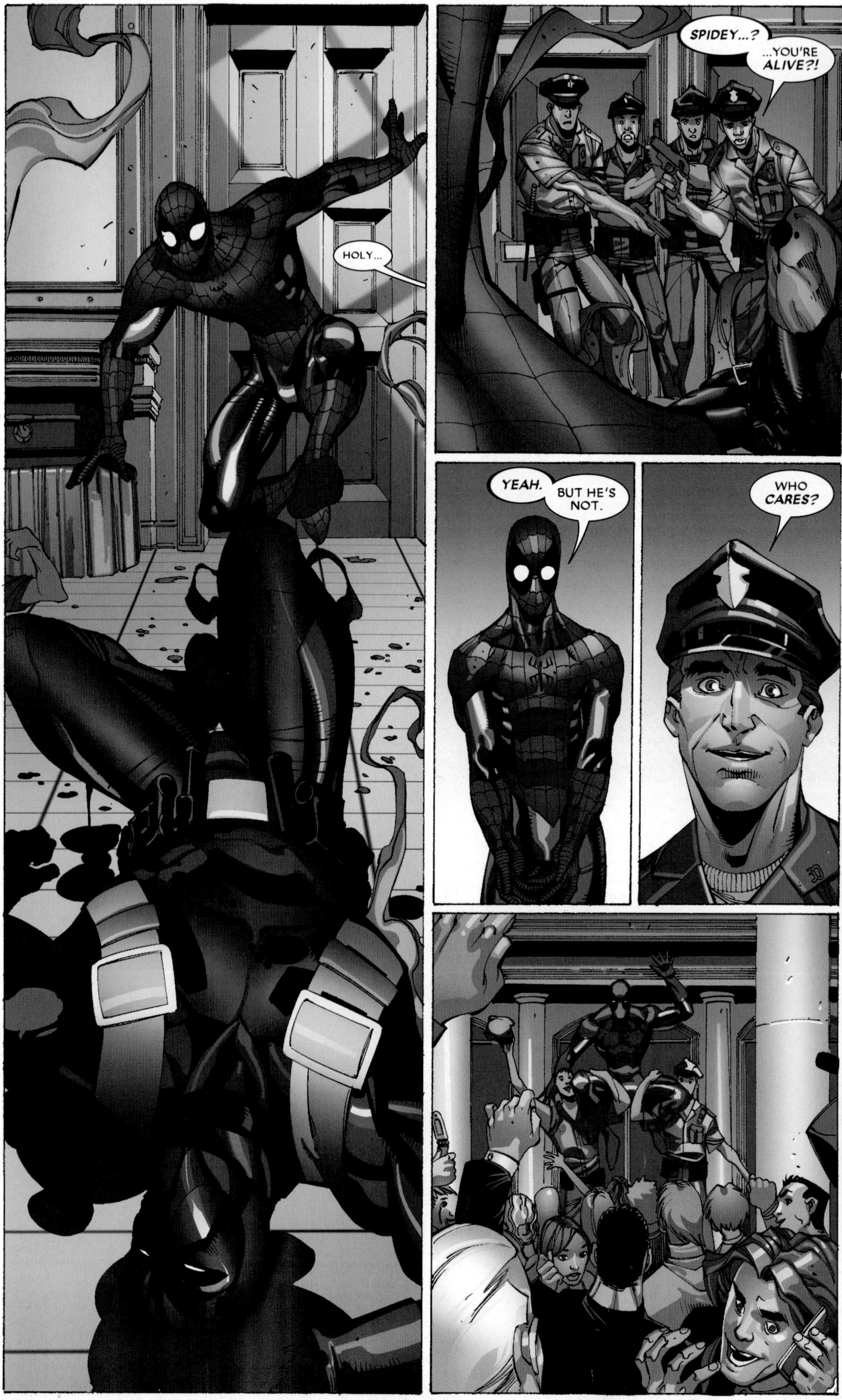
HOLY...
SPIDEY...?
...YOU'RE ALIVE?!
YEAH.
BUT HE'S NOT.
WHO CARES?

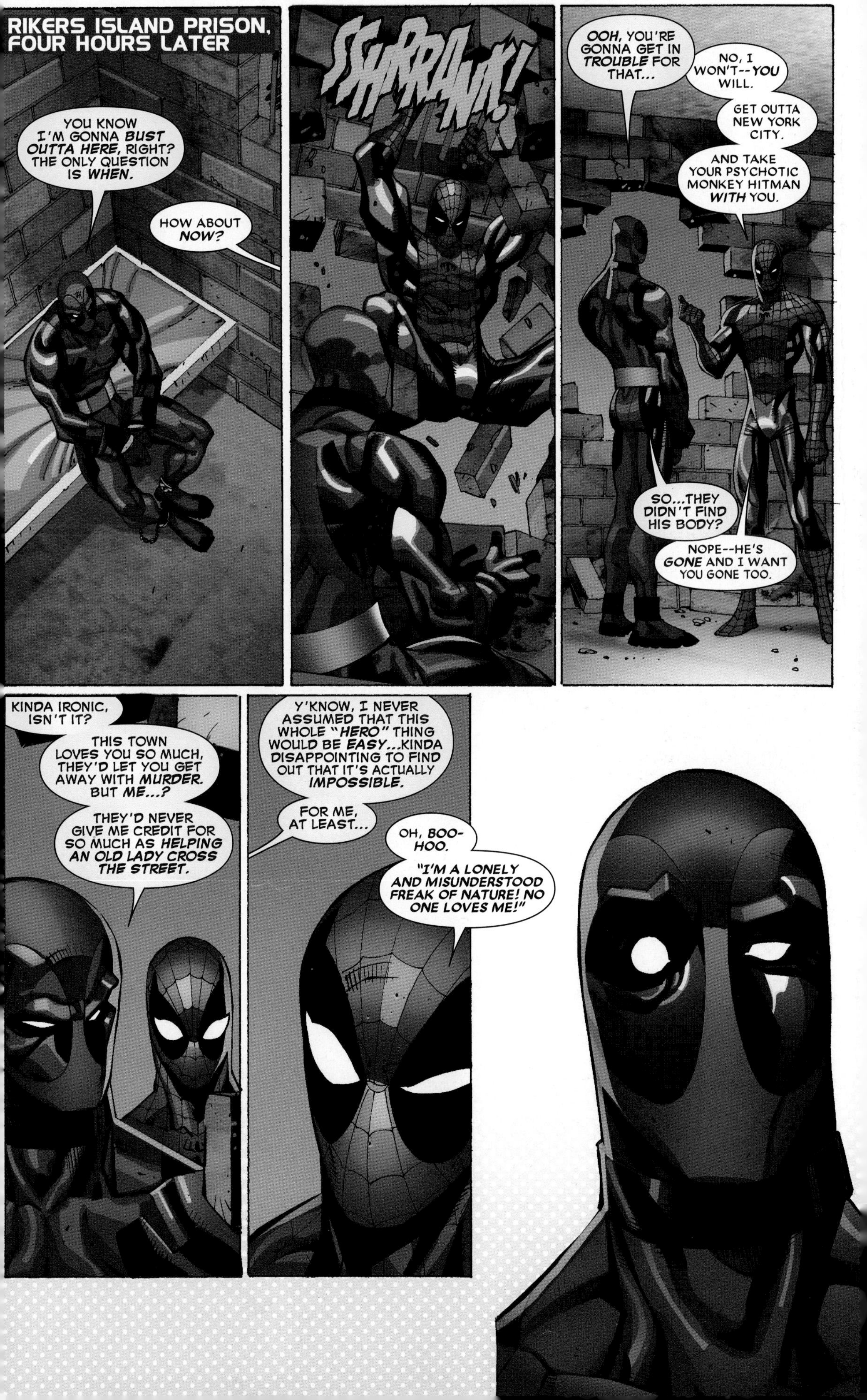
RIKERS ISLAND PRISON, FOUR HOURS LATER
YOU KNOW I'M GONNA BUST OUTTA HERE, RIGHT? THE ONLY QUESTION IS WHEN.
HOW ABOUT NOW?
SHRRANK!
OOH, YOU'RE GONNA GET IN TROUBLE FOR THAT...
NO, I WON'T--YOU WILL.
GET OUTTA NEW YORK CITY.
AND TAKE YOUR PSYCHOTIC MONKEY HITMAN WITH YOU.
SO...THEY DIDN'T FIND HIS BODY?
NOPE--HE'S GONE AND I WANT YOU GONE TOO.
KINDA IRONIC, ISN'T IT?
THIS TOWN LOVES YOU SO MUCH, THEY'D LET YOU GET AWAY WITH MURDER. BUT ME...?
THEY'D NEVER GIVE ME CREDIT FOR SO MUCH AS HELPING AN OLD LADY CROSS THE STREET.
Y'KNOW, I NEVER ASSUMED THAT THIS WHOLE "HERO" THING WOULD BE EASY...KINDA DISAPPOINTING TO FIND OUT THAT IT'S ACTUALLY IMPOSSIBLE.
FOR ME, AT LEAST...
OH, BOO-HOO.
"I'M A LONELY AND MISUNDERSTOOD FREAK OF NATURE! NO ONE LOVES ME!"

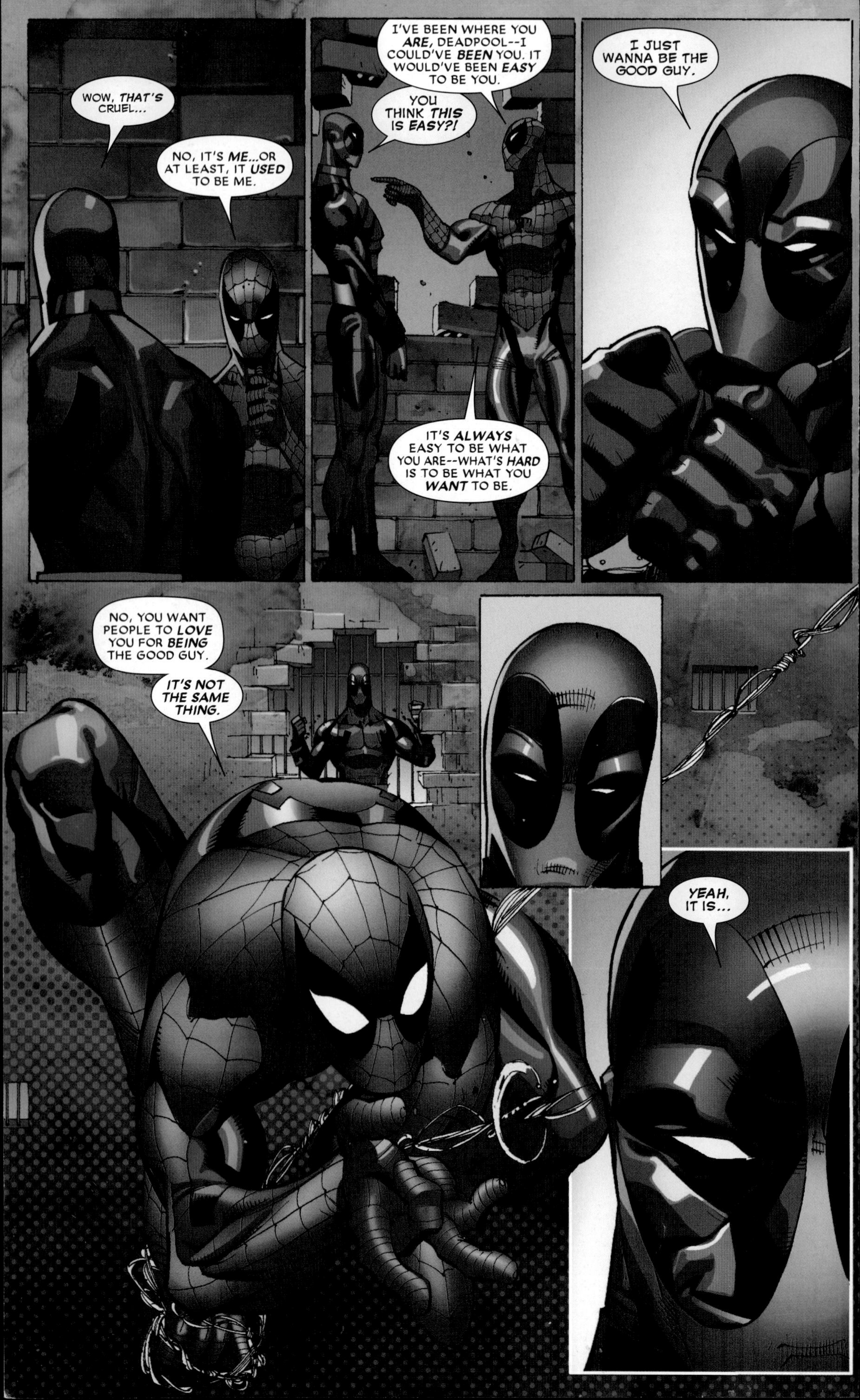
WOW, THAT'S CRUEL...
NO, IT'S ME...OR AT LEAST, IT USED TO BE ME.
I'VE BEEN WHERE YOU ARE, DEADPOOL--I COULD'VE BEEN YOU. IT WOULD'VE BEEN EASY TO BE YOU.
YOU THINK THIS IS EASY?!
IT'S ALWAYS EASY TO BE WHAT YOU ARE--WHAT'S HARD IS TO BE WHAT YOU WANT TO BE.
I JUST WANNA BE THE GOOD GUY.
NO, YOU WANT PEOPLE TO LOVE YOU FOR BEING THE GOOD GUY.
IT'S NOT THE SAME THING.
YEAH, IT IS...

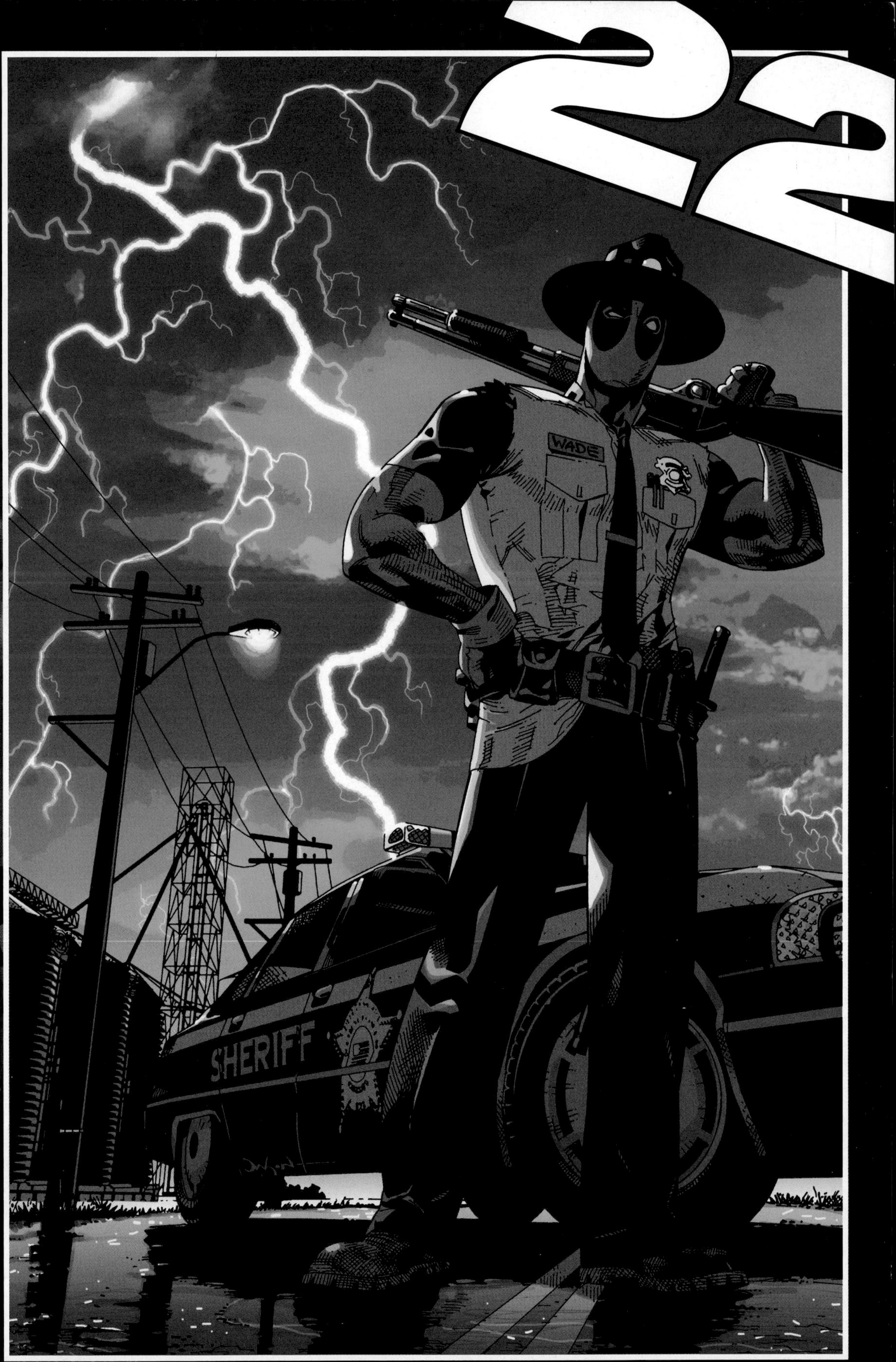
22
WADE
SHERIFF

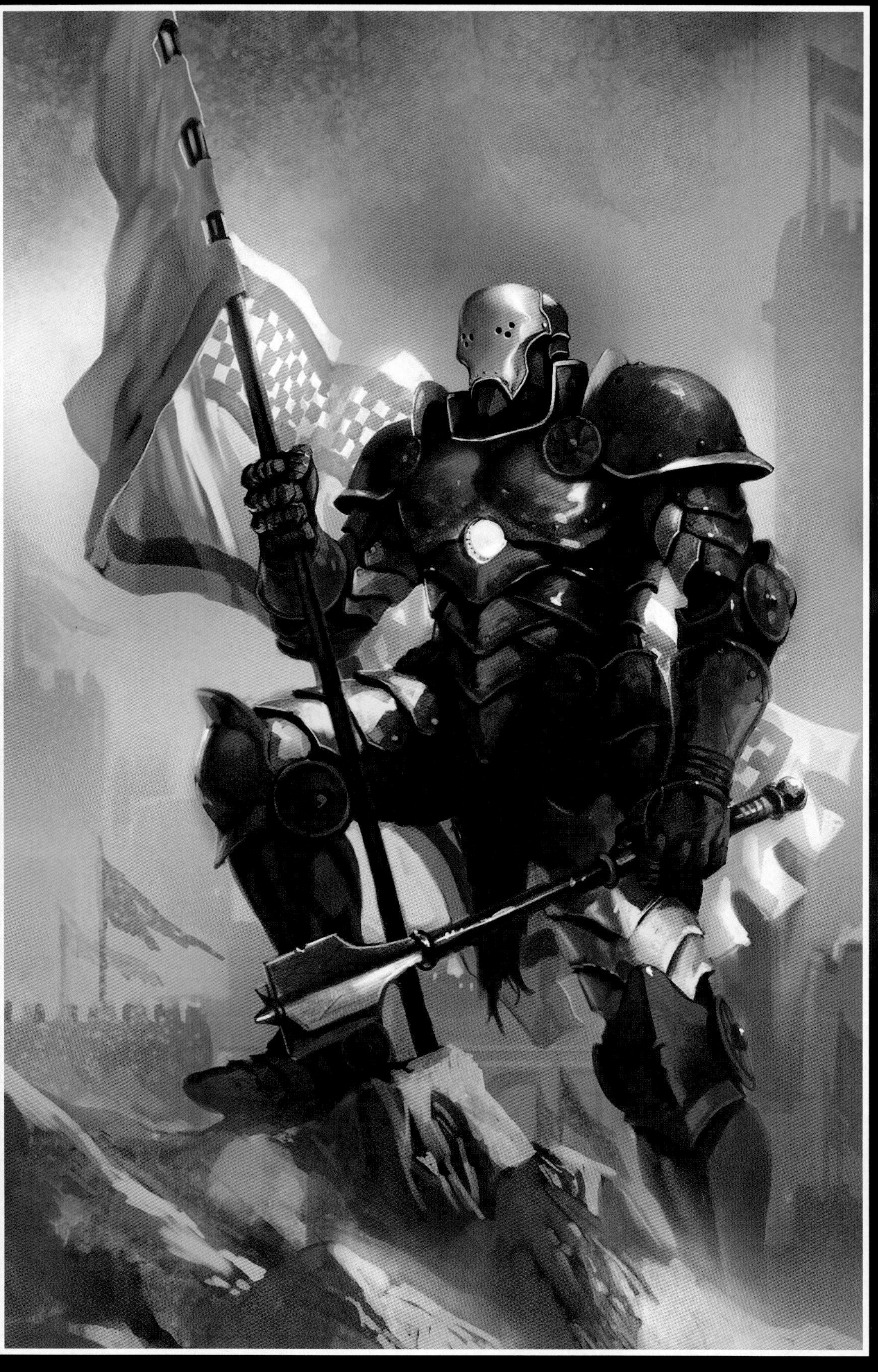

DEADPOOL #22 IRON MAN BY DESIGN VARIANT
by Marko Djurdjevic

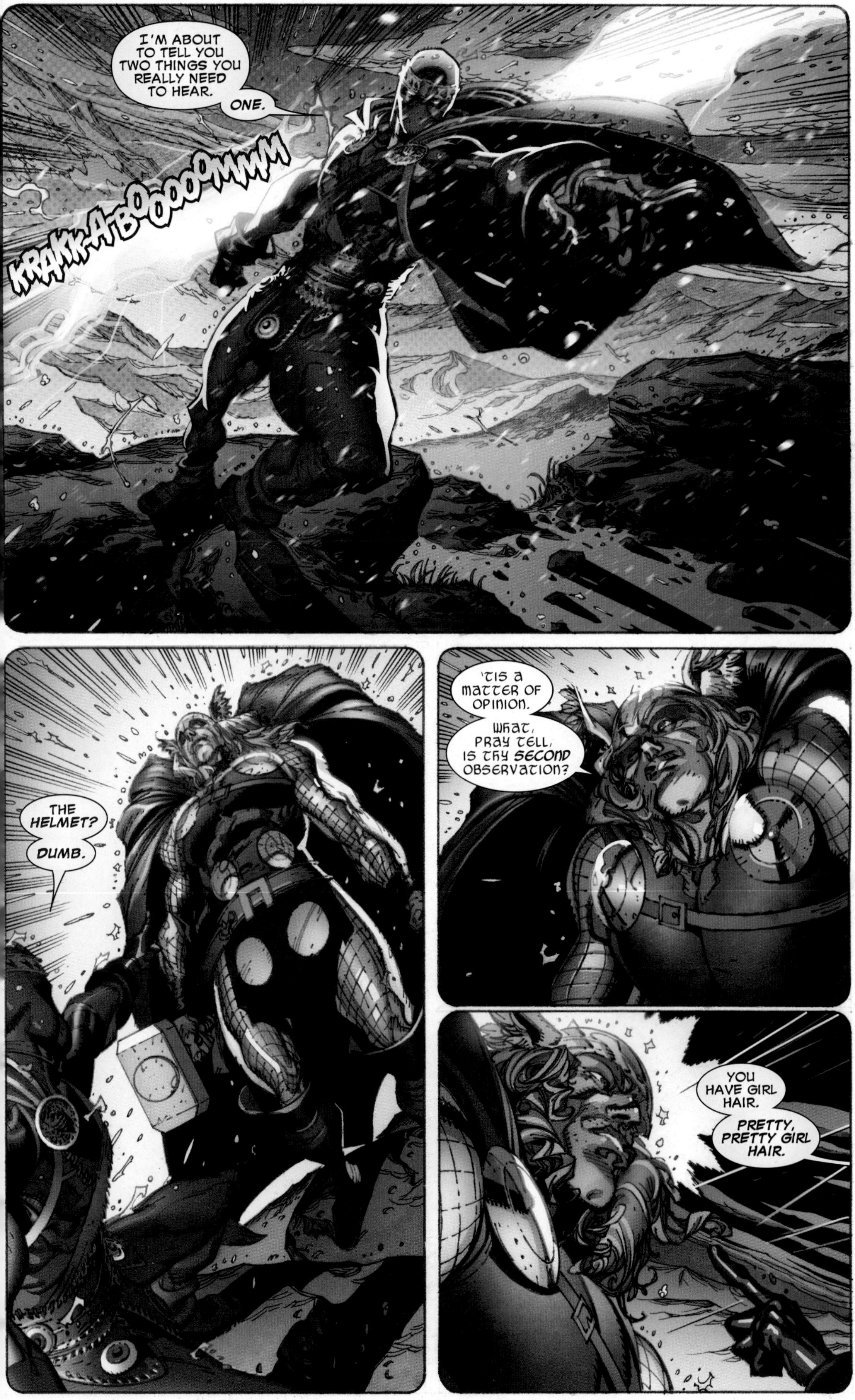
I'M ABOUT TO TELL YOU TWO THINGS YOU REALLY NEED TO HEAR.
ONE.
KRAKK-A-BOOOOOMMM
THE HELMET?
DUMB.
'TIS A MATTER OF OPINION.
WHAT, PRAY TELL, IS THY SECOND OBSERVATION?
YOU HAVE GIRL HAIR.
PRETTY, PRETTY GIRL HAIR.

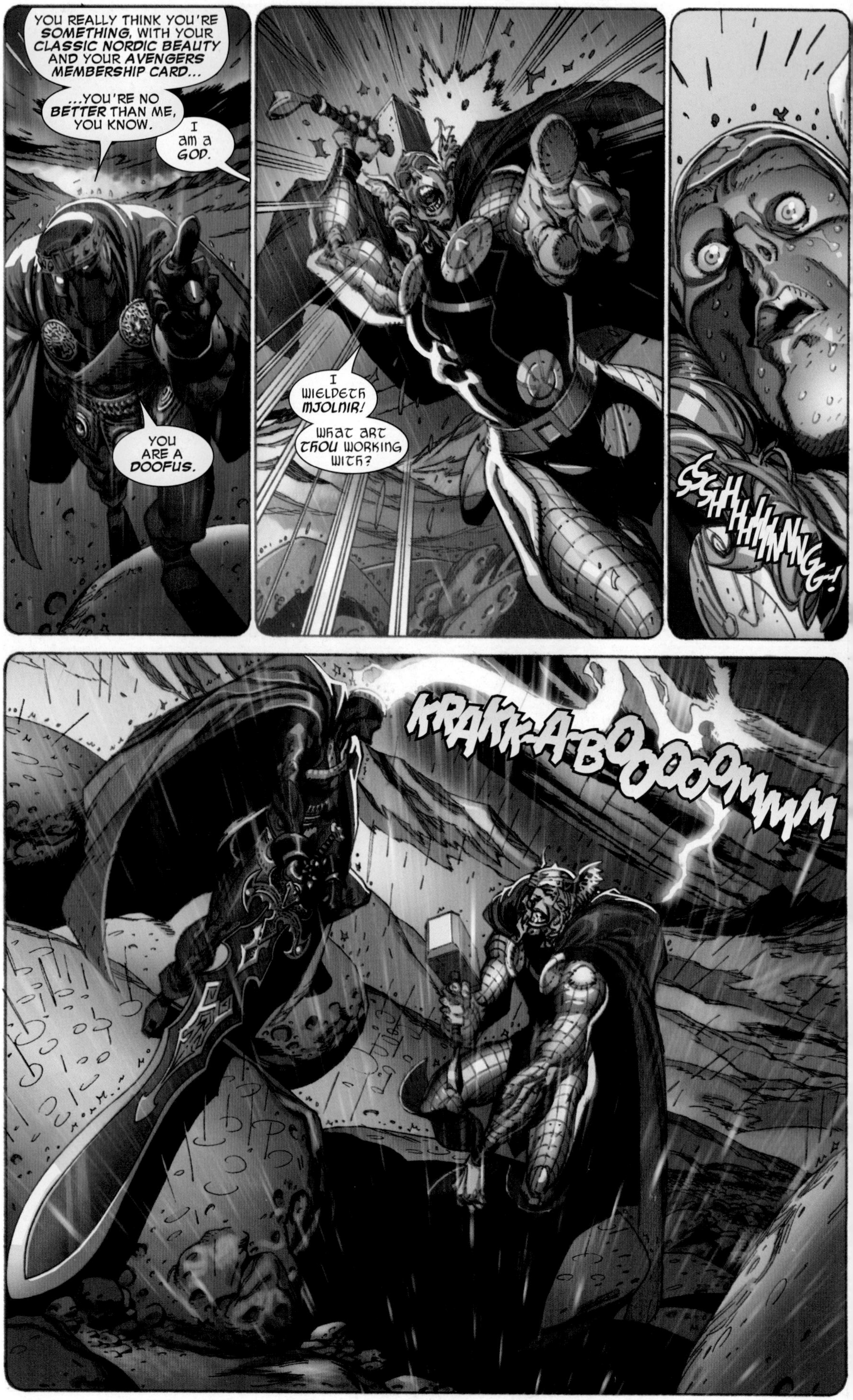
YOU REALLY THINK YOU'RE SOMETHING, WITH YOUR CLASSIC NORDIC BEAUTY AND YOUR AVENGERS MEMBERSHIP CARD...
...YOU'RE NO BETTER THAN ME, YOU KNOW.
I am a GOD.
YOU ARE A DOOFUS.
I WIELDETH MJOLNIR!
WHAT ART THOU WORKING WITH?
SSSHHHHMMNNGG!
KRAKK-A-BOOOOOOMMMM

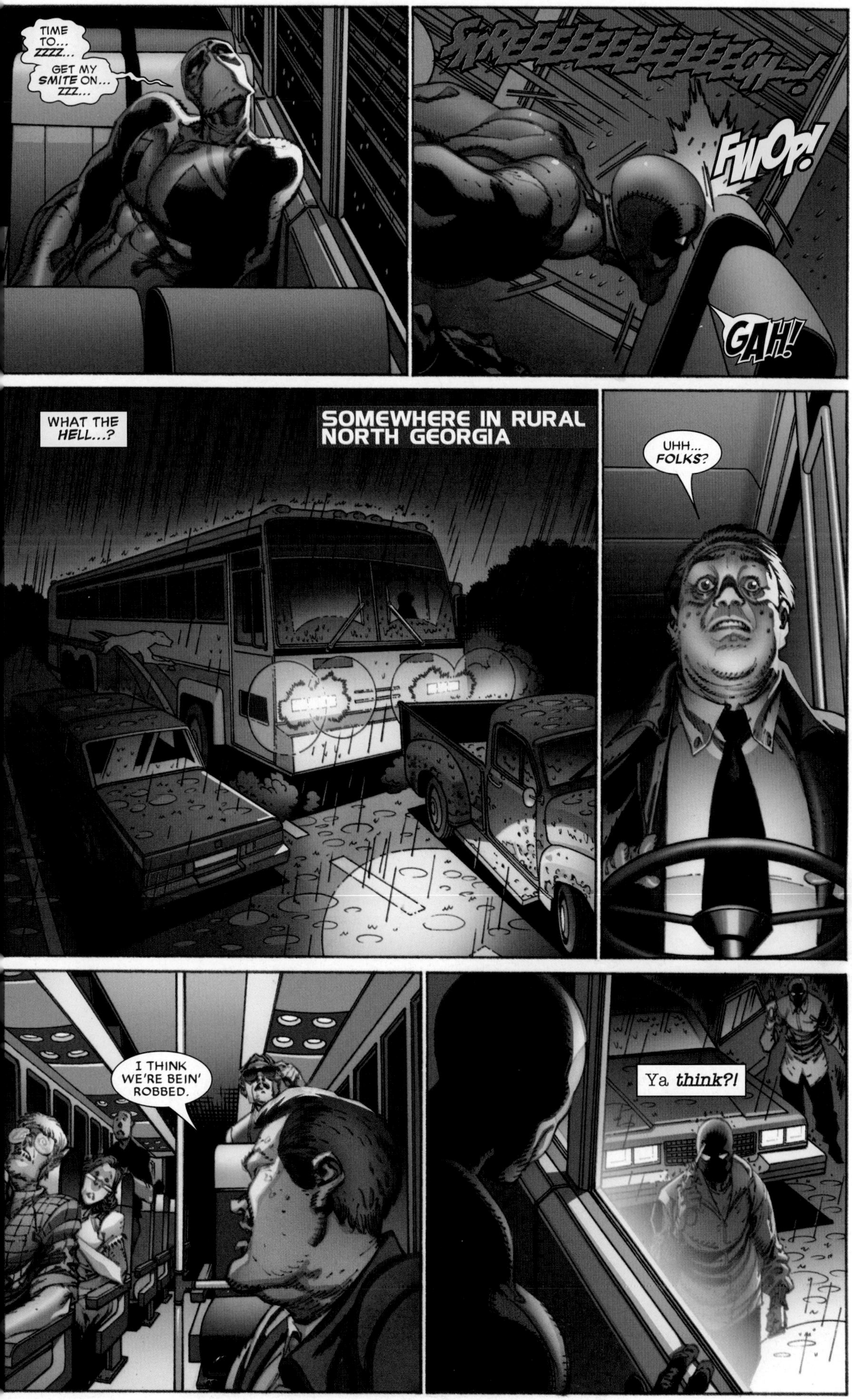
TIME TO... ZZZZ... GET MY SMITE ON... ZZZ...
SKREEEEEEEEEEEEECH--!
FWOP!
GAH!
WHAT THE HELL...?
SOMEWHERE IN RURAL NORTH GEORGIA
UHH... FOLKS?
I THINK WE'RE BEIN' ROBBED.
Ya think?!

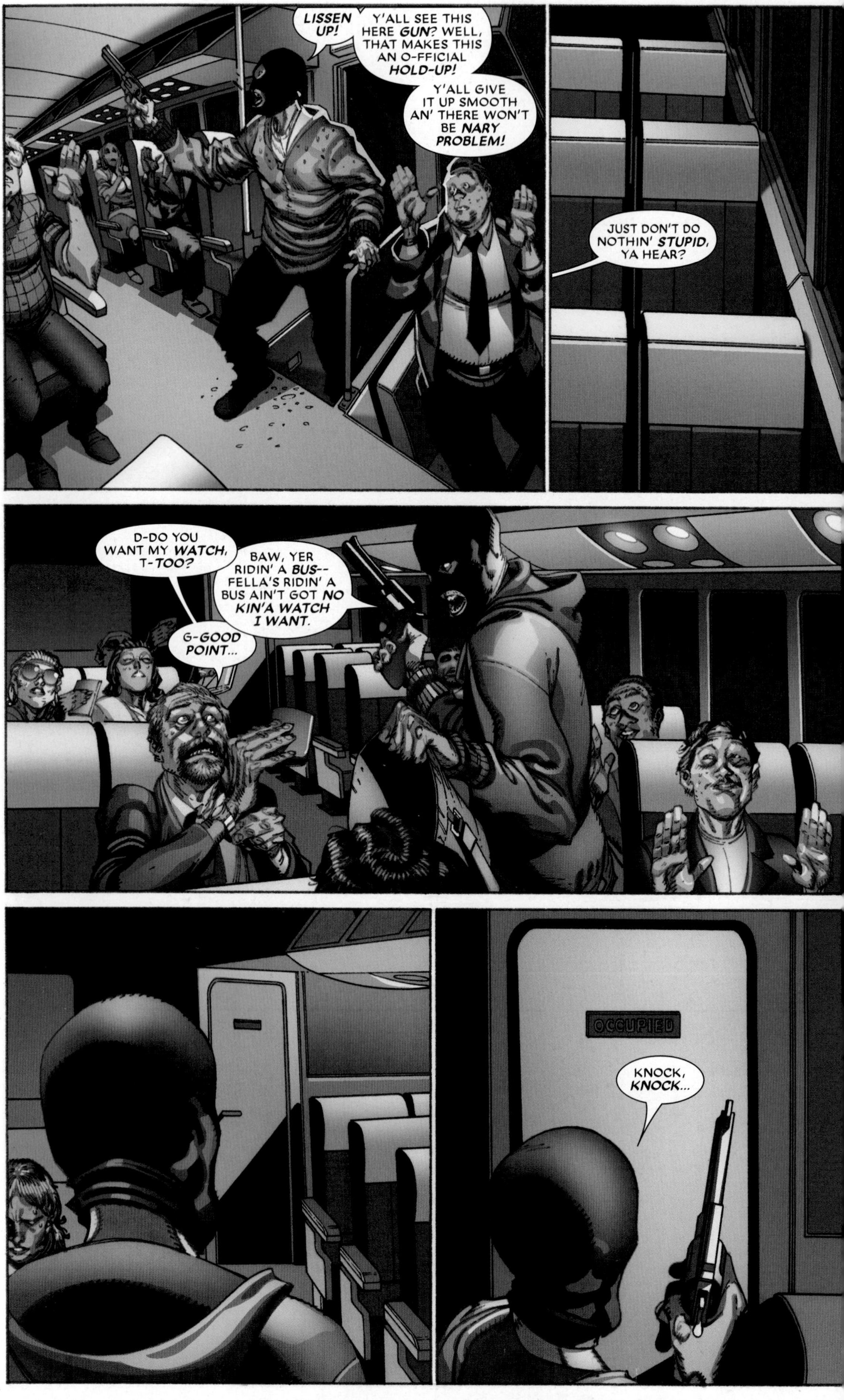
LISSEN UP!
Y'ALL SEE THIS HERE GUN? WELL, THAT MAKES THIS AN O-FFICIAL HOLD-UP!
Y'ALL GIVE IT UP SMOOTH AN' THERE WON'T BE NARY PROBLEM!
JUST DON'T DO NOTHIN' STUPID, YA HEAR?
D-DO YOU WANT MY WATCH, T-TOO?
BAW, YER RIDIN' A BUS-- FELLA'S RIDIN' A BUS AIN'T GOT NO KIN'A WATCH I WANT.
G-GOOD POINT...
OCCUPIED
KNOCK, KNOCK...

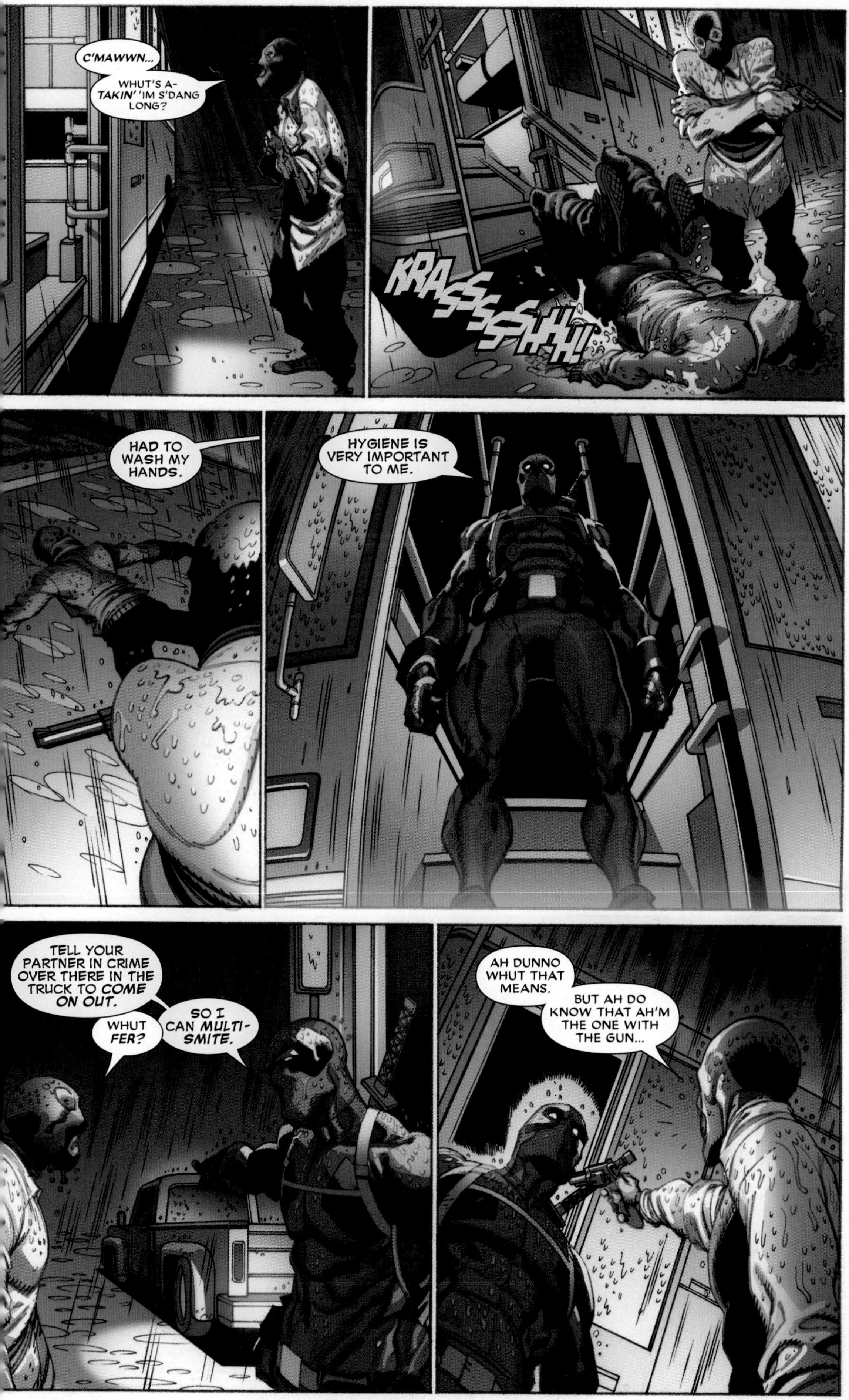
C'MAWWN...
WHUT'S A-TAKIN' 'IM S'DANG LONG?
KRASSSSSHH!
HAD TO WASH MY HANDS.
HYGIENE IS VERY IMPORTANT TO ME.
TELL YOUR PARTNER IN CRIME OVER THERE IN THE TRUCK TO COME ON OUT.
SO I CAN MULTI-SMITE.
WHUT FER?
AH DUNNO WHUT THAT MEANS.
BUT AH DO KNOW THAT AH'M THE ONE WITH THE GUN...

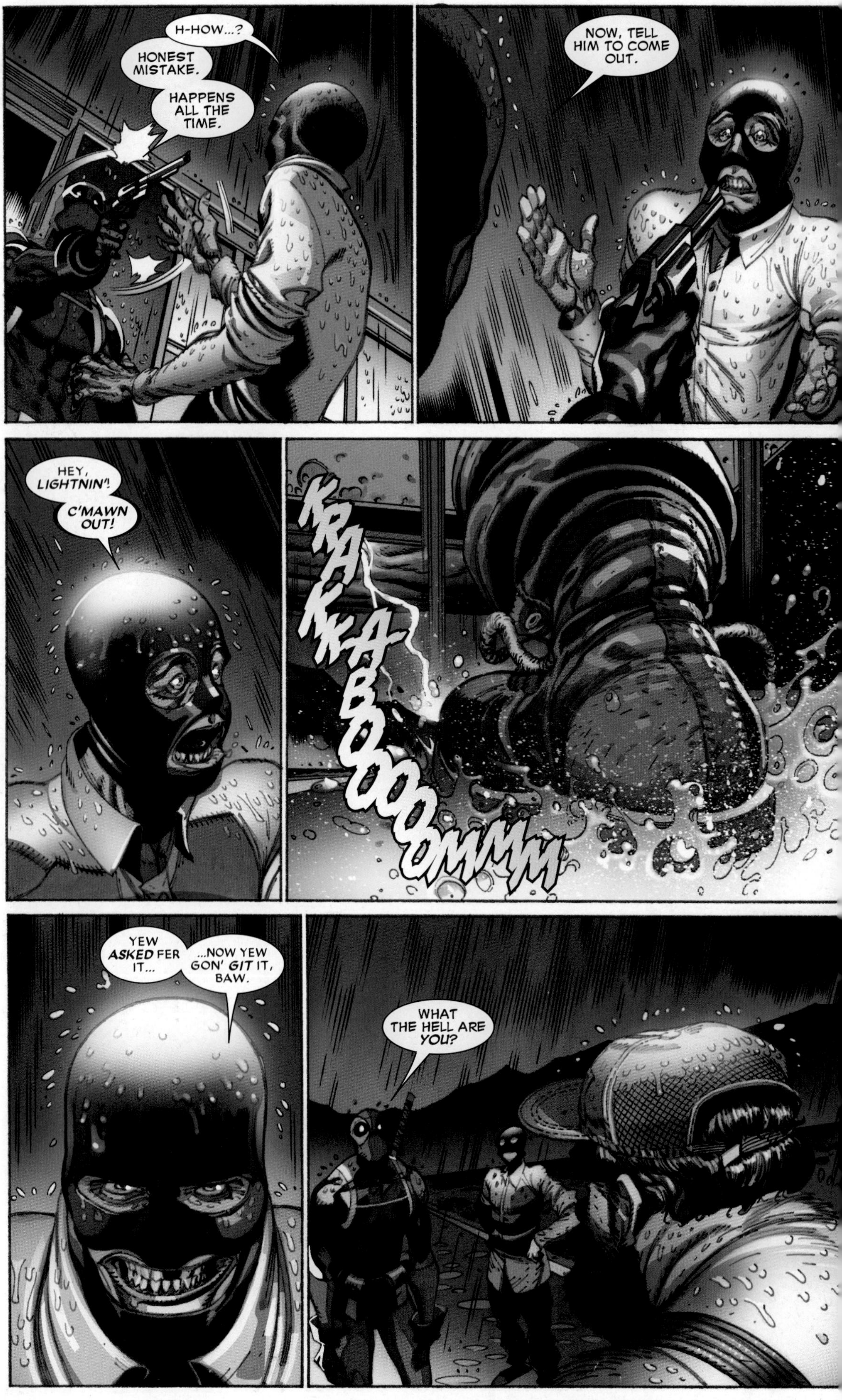
H-HOW...?
HONEST MISTAKE.
HAPPENS ALL THE TIME.
NOW, TELL HIM TO COME OUT.
HEY, LIGHTNIN'!
C'MAWN OUT!
KRAKKABOOOOOMMM
YEW ASKED FER IT...
...NOW YEW GON' GIT IT, BAW.
WHAT THE HELL ARE YOU?

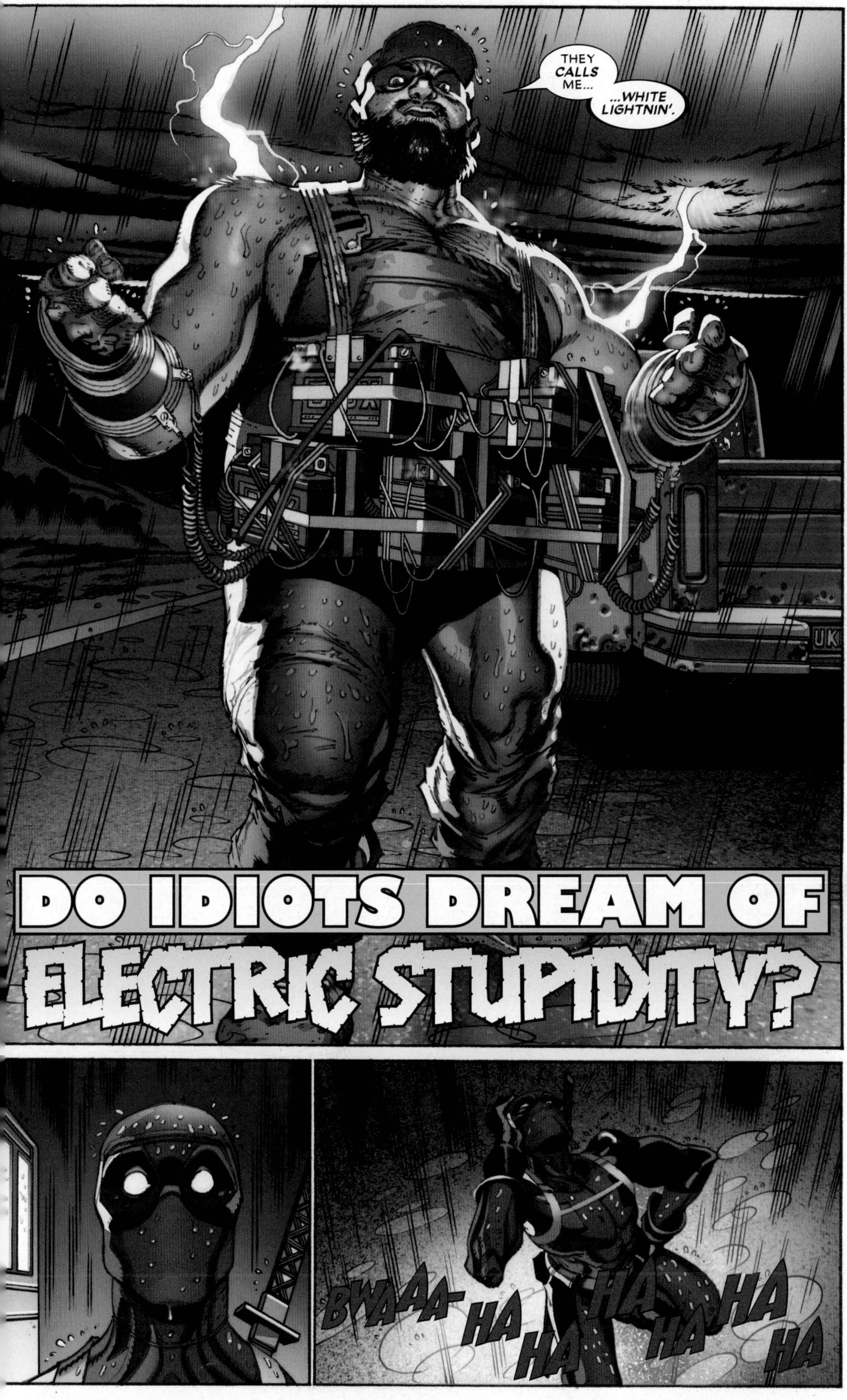
THEY CALLS ME...
...WHITE LIGHTNIN'.
UK
DO IDIOTS DREAM OF
ELECTRIC STUPIDITY?
BWAAA-HA HA HA HA HA HA HA

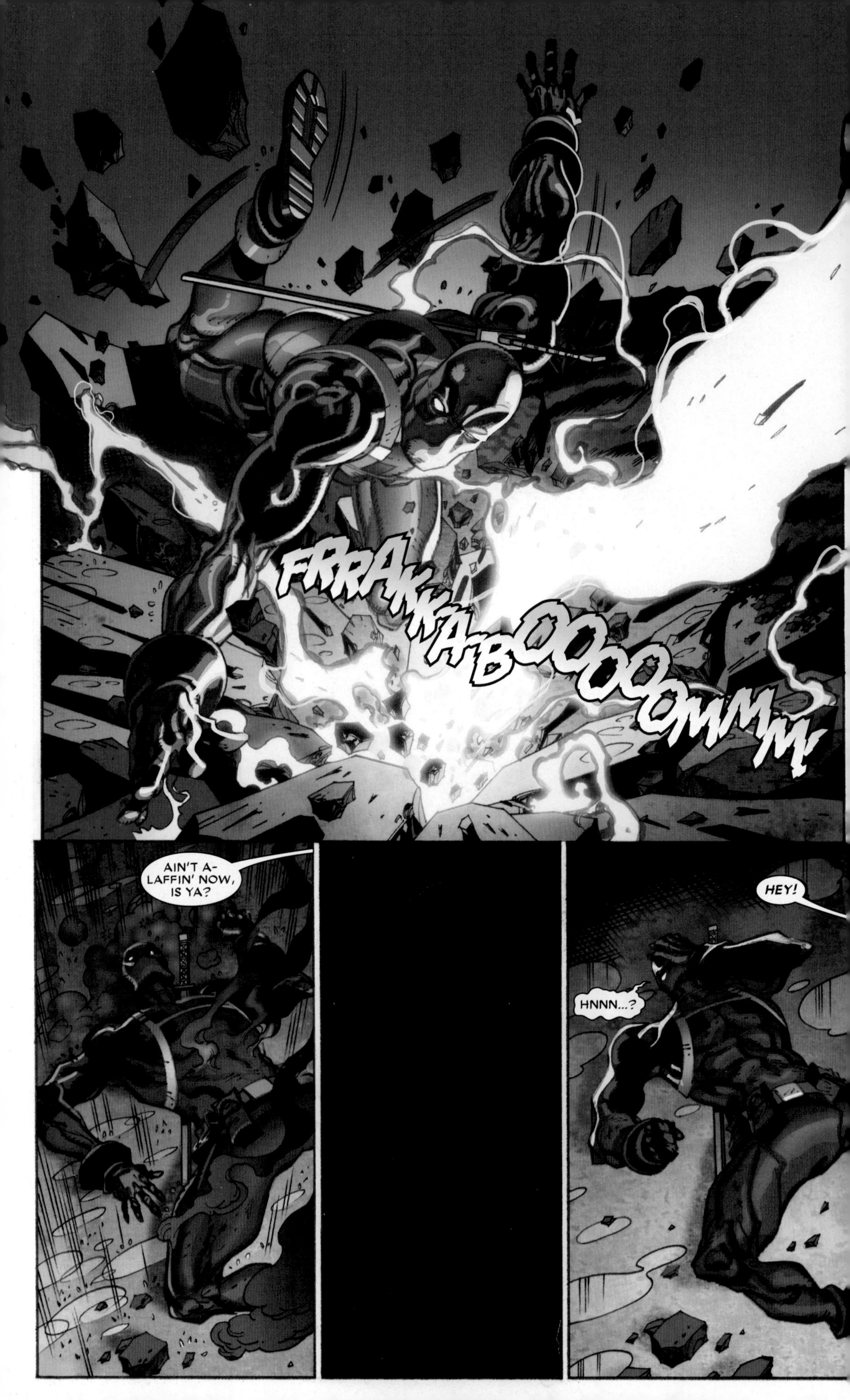
FRRAKKA-BOOOOOMMM!
AIN'T A-LAFFIN' NOW, IS YA?
HEY!
HNNN...?

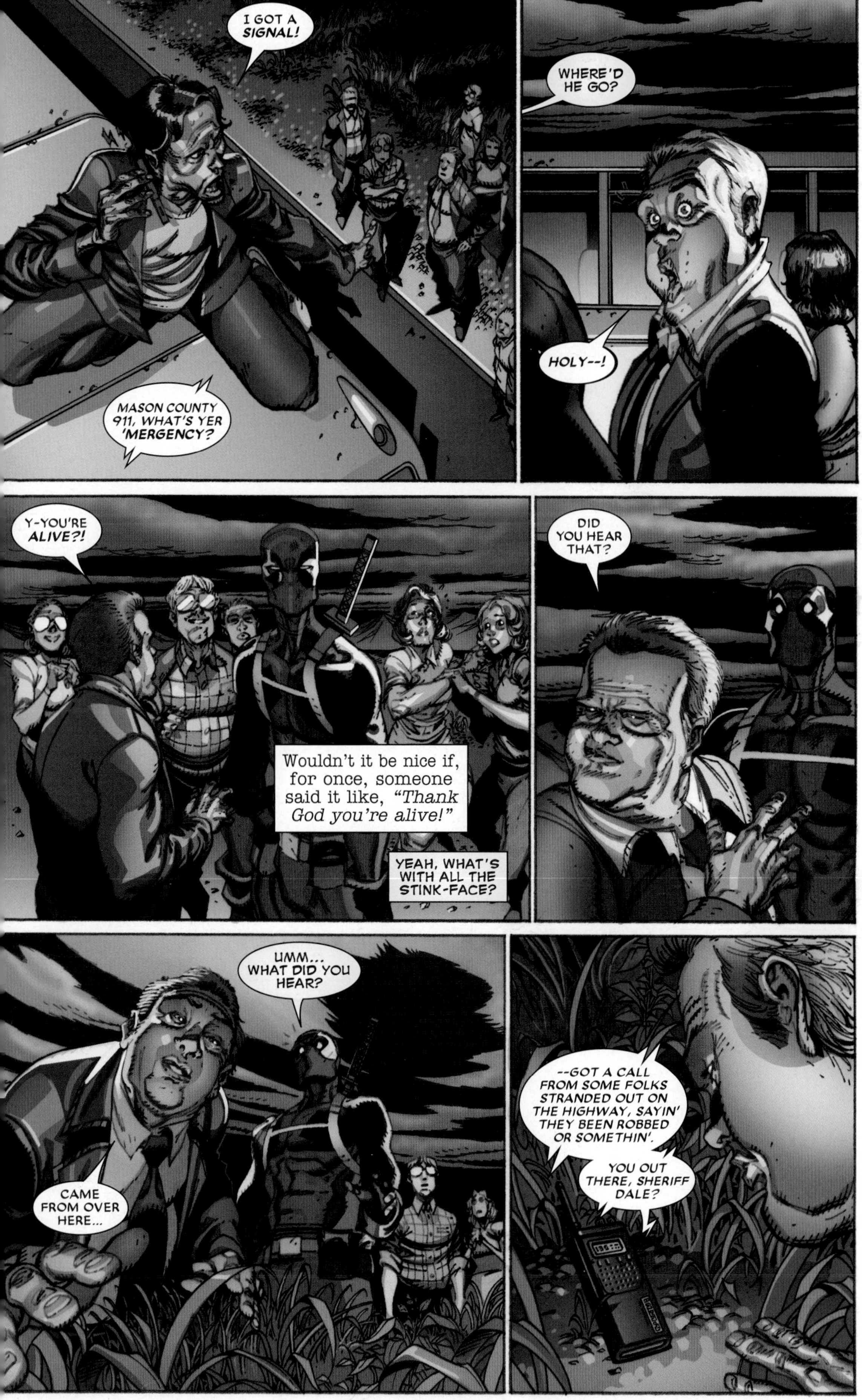
I GOT A SIGNAL!
MASON COUNTY 911, WHAT'S YER 'MERGENCY?
WHERE'D HE GO?
HOLY--!
Y-YOU'RE ALIVE?!
Wouldn't it be nice if, for once, someone said it like, "Thank God you're alive!"
YEAH, WHAT'S WITH ALL THE STINK-FACE?
DID YOU HEAR THAT?
UMM... WHAT DID YOU HEAR?
CAME FROM OVER HERE...
--GOT A CALL FROM SOME FOLKS STRANDED OUT ON THE HIGHWAY, SAYIN' THEY BEEN ROBBED OR SOMETHIN'.
YOU OUT THERE, SHERIFF DALE?

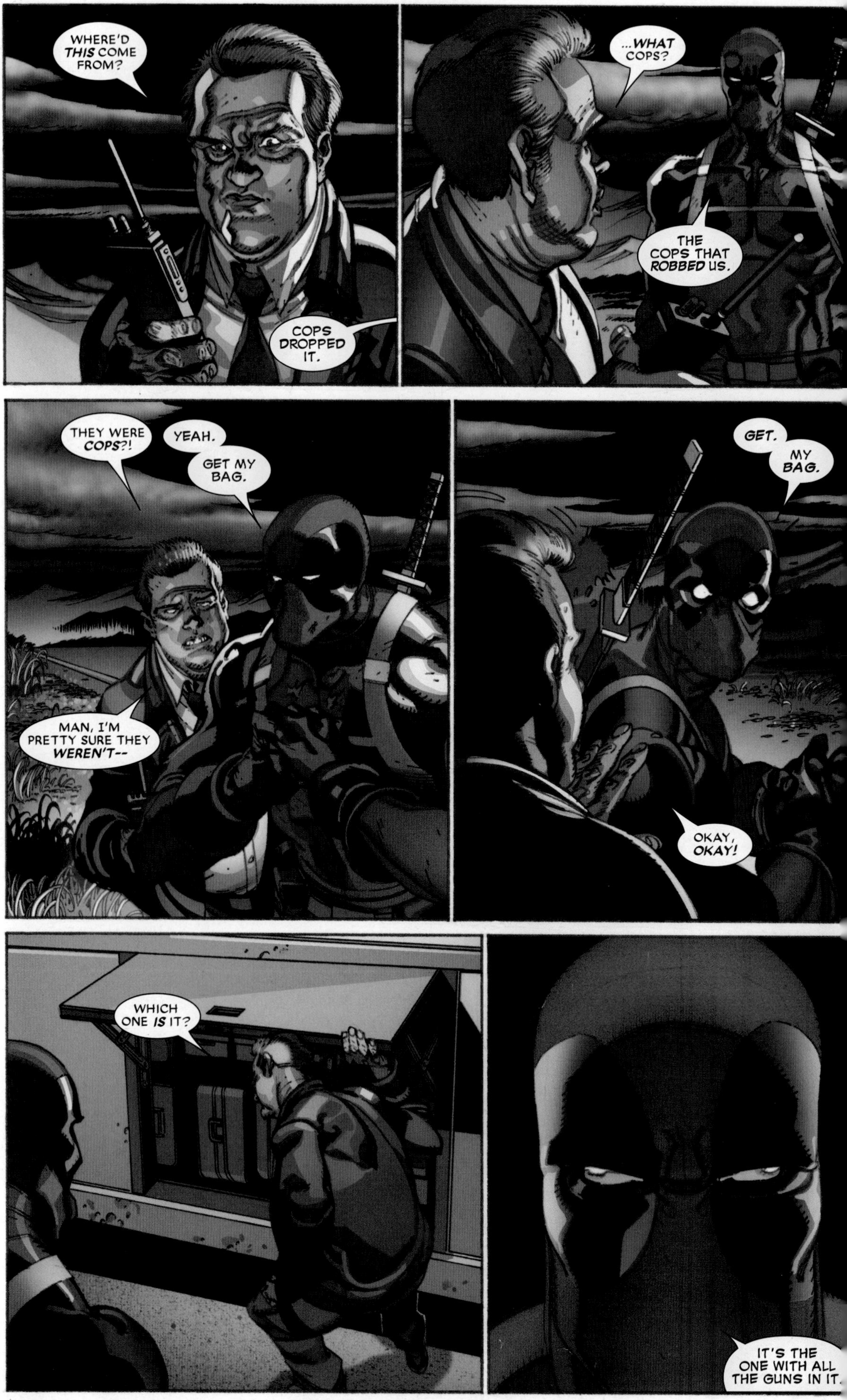

WHERE'D THIS COME FROM?
COPS DROPPED IT.
...WHAT COPS?
THE COPS THAT ROBBED US.
THEY WERE COPS?!
YEAH.
GET MY BAG.
MAN, I'M PRETTY SURE THEY WEREN'T--
GET.
MY BAG.
OKAY, OKAY!
WHICH ONE IS IT?
IT'S THE ONE WITH ALL THE GUNS IN IT.

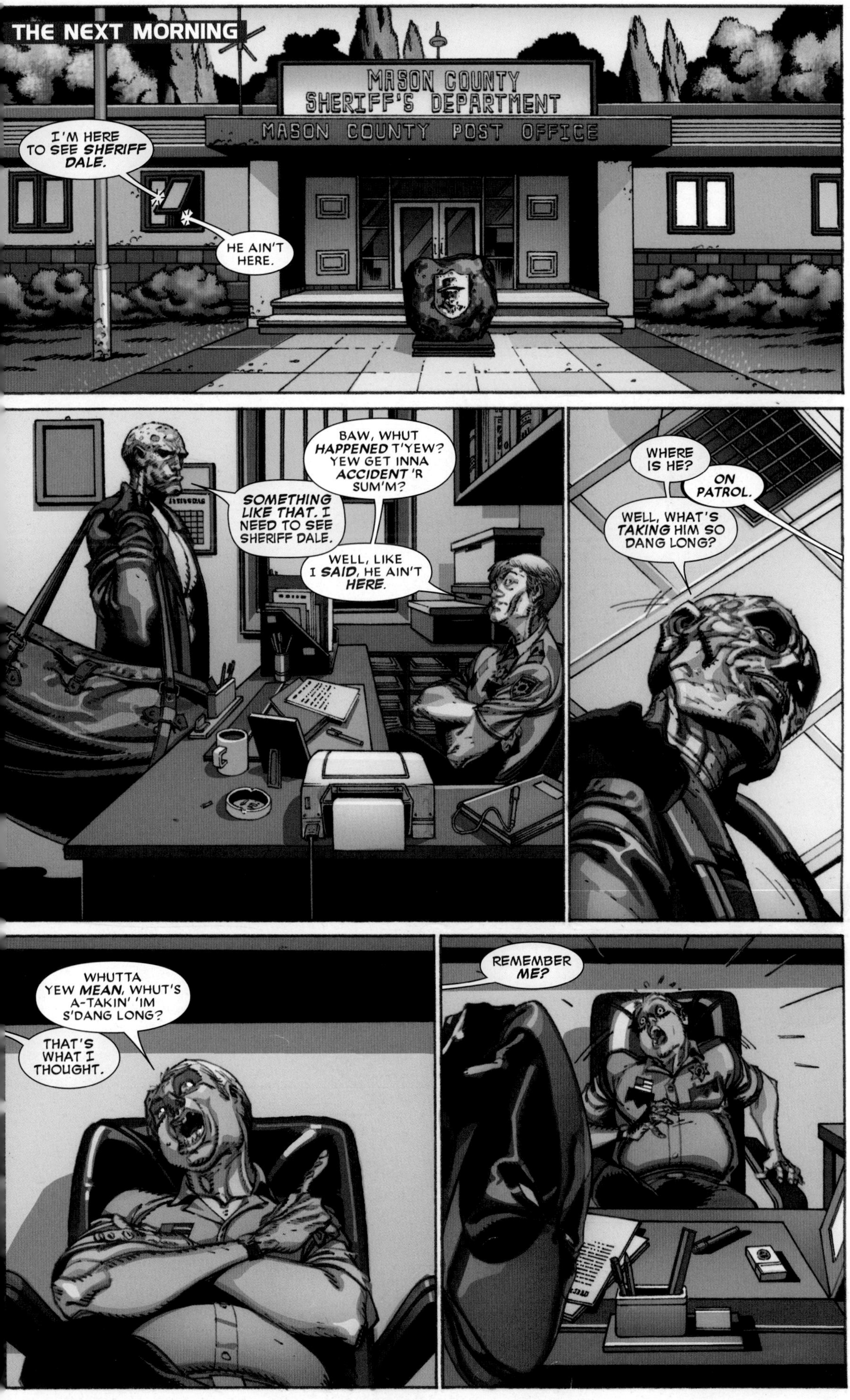
THE NEXT MORNING
MASON COUNTY SHERIFF'S DEPARTMENT
MASON COUNTY POST OFFICE
I'M HERE TO SEE SHERIFF DALE.
HE AIN'T HERE.
SOMETHING LIKE THAT. I NEED TO SEE SHERIFF DALE.
BAW, WHUT HAPPENED T'YEW? YEW GET INNA ACCIDENT 'R SUM'M?
WELL, LIKE I SAID, HE AIN'T HERE.
WHERE IS HE?
ON PATROL.
WELL, WHAT'S TAKING HIM SO DANG LONG?
WHUTTA YEW MEAN, WHUT'S A-TAKIN' 'IM S'DANG LONG?
THAT'S WHAT I THOUGHT.
REMEMBER ME?

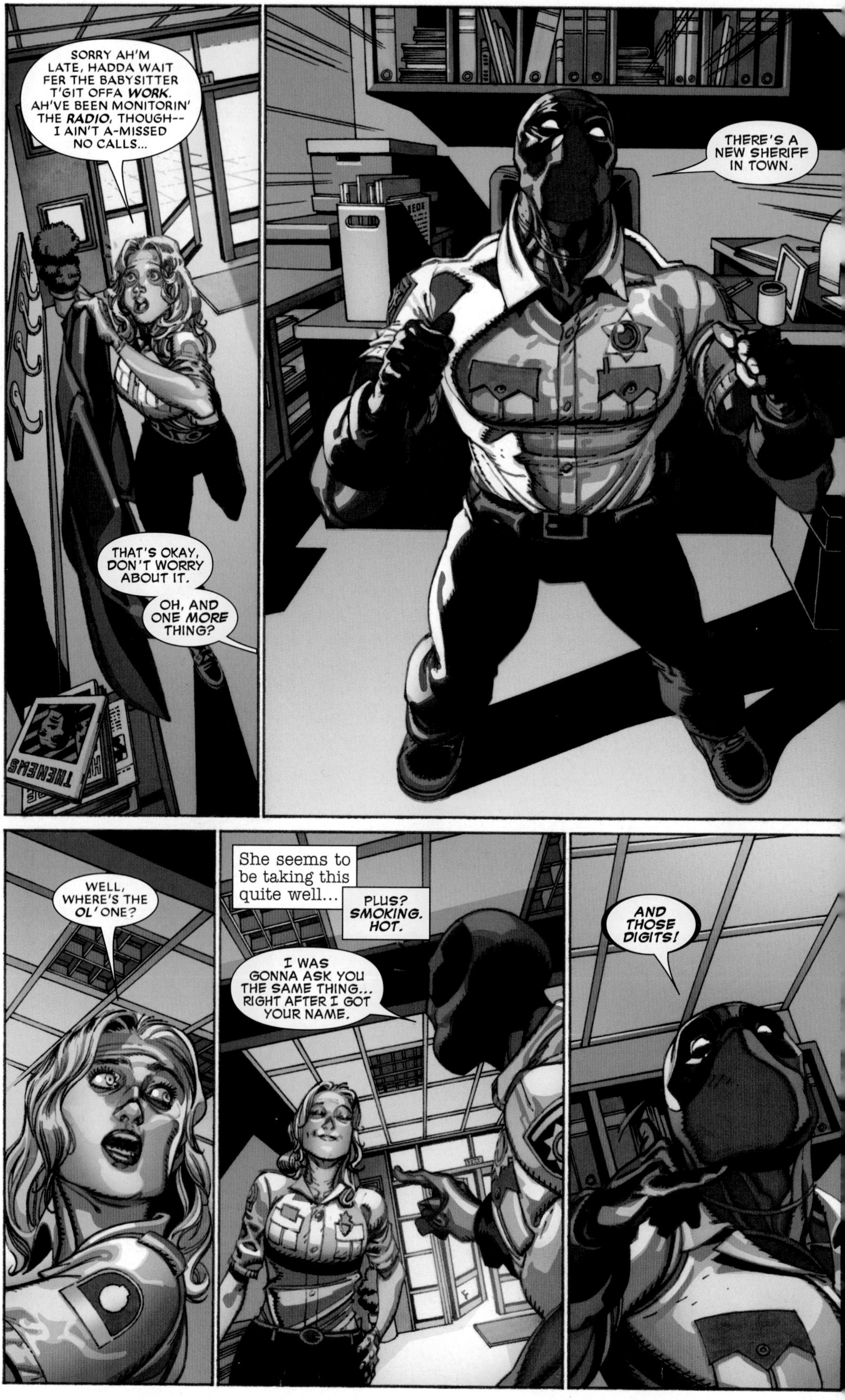
SORRY AH'M LATE, HADDA WAIT FER THE BABYSITTER T'GIT OFFA WORK. AH'VE BEEN MONITORIN' THE RADIO, THOUGH-- I AIN'T A-MISSED NO CALLS...
THAT'S OKAY, DON'T WORRY ABOUT IT.
OH, AND ONE MORE THING?
THERE'S A NEW SHERIFF IN TOWN.
THE NEWS
WELL, WHERE'S THE OL' ONE?
She seems to be taking this quite well...
PLUS? SMOKING. HOT.
I WAS GONNA ASK YOU THE SAME THING... RIGHT AFTER I GOT YOUR NAME.
AND THOSE DIGITS!

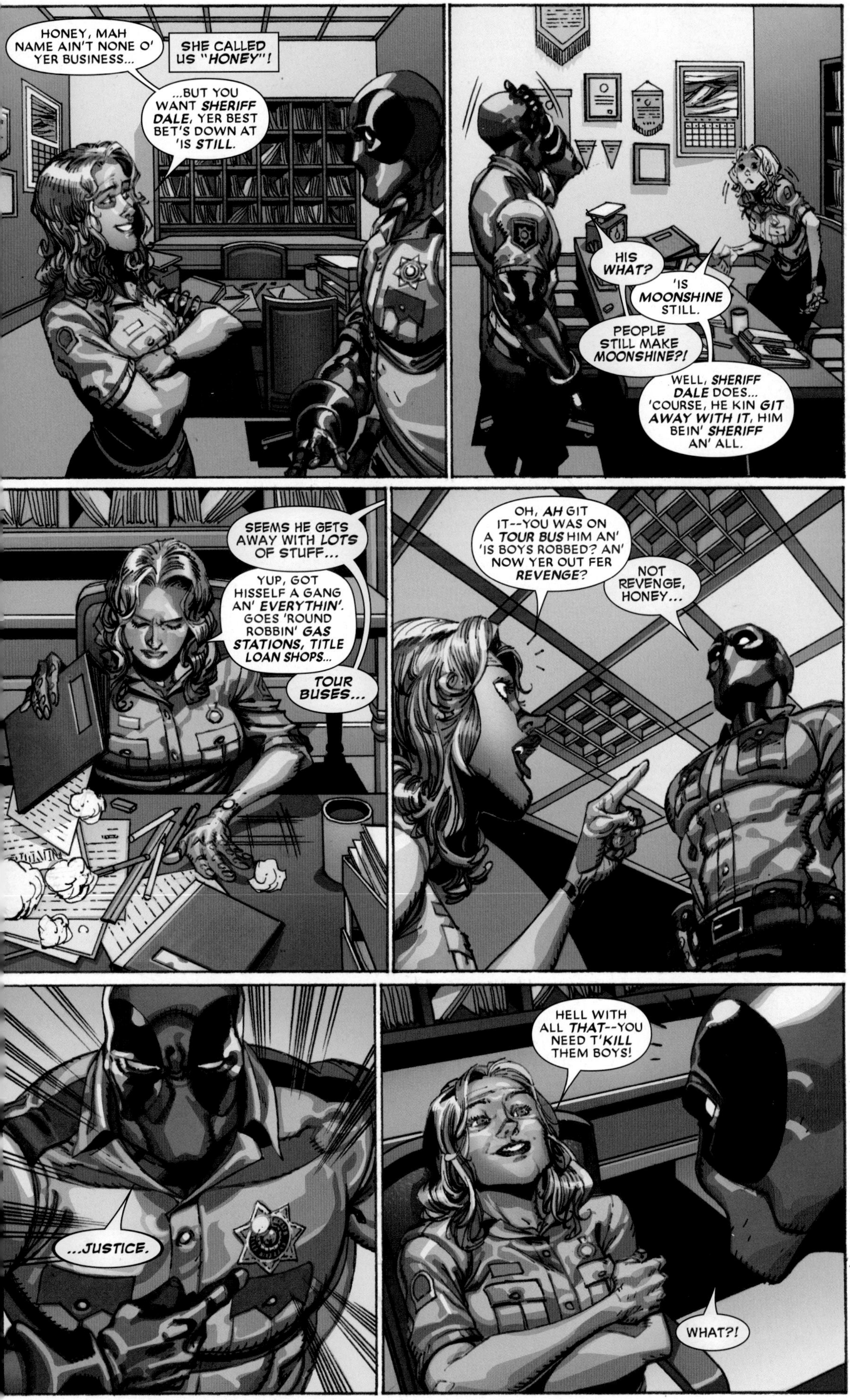

HONEY, MAH NAME AIN'T NONE O' YER BUSINESS...
SHE CALLED US "HONEY"!
...BUT YOU WANT SHERIFF DALE, YER BEST BET'S DOWN AT 'IS STILL.
HIS WHAT?
'IS MOONSHINE STILL.
PEOPLE STILL MAKE MOONSHINE?!
WELL, SHERIFF DALE DOES... 'COURSE, HE KIN GIT AWAY WITH IT, HIM BEIN' SHERIFF AN' ALL.
SEEMS HE GETS AWAY WITH LOTS OF STUFF...
YUP, GOT HISSELF A GANG AN' EVERYTHIN'. GOES 'ROUND ROBBIN' GAS STATIONS, TITLE LOAN SHOPS...
TOUR BUSES...
OH, AH GIT IT--YOU WAS ON A TOUR BUS HIM AN' 'IS BOYS ROBBED? AN' NOW YER OUT FER REVENGE?
NOT REVENGE, HONEY...
...JUSTICE.
HELL WITH ALL THAT--YOU NEED T'KILL THEM BOYS!
WHAT?!

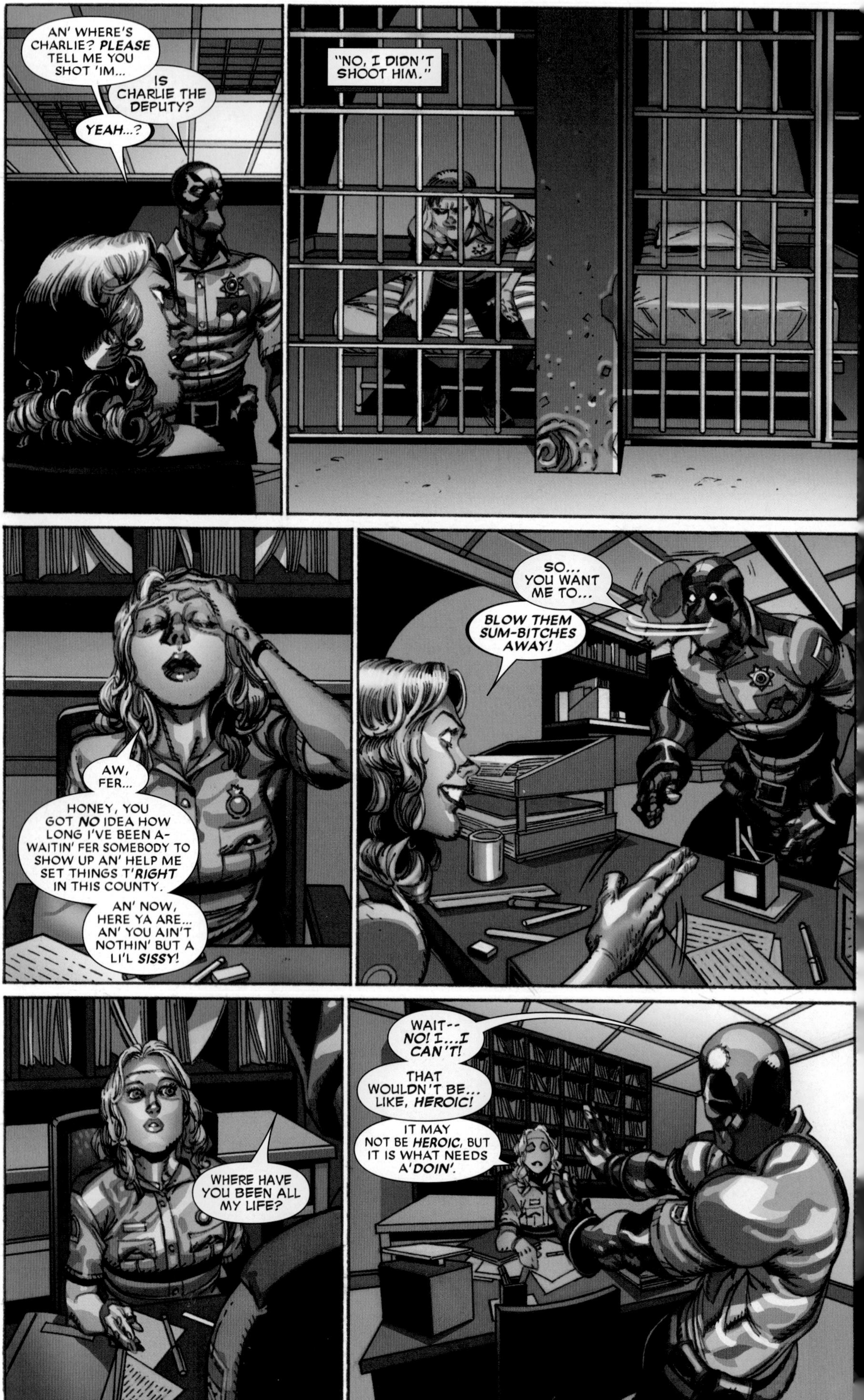
AN' WHERE'S CHARLIE? PLEASE TELL ME YOU SHOT 'IM...
IS CHARLIE THE DEPUTY?
YEAH...?
"NO, I DIDN'T SHOOT HIM."
AW, FER...
HONEY, YOU GOT NO IDEA HOW LONG I'VE BEEN A-WAITIN' FER SOMEBODY TO SHOW UP AN' HELP ME SET THINGS T'RIGHT IN THIS COUNTY.
AN' NOW, HERE YA ARE... AN' YOU AIN'T NOTHIN' BUT A LI'L SISSY!
SO... YOU WANT ME TO...
BLOW THEM SUM-BITCHES AWAY!
WHERE HAVE YOU BEEN ALL MY LIFE?
WAIT-- NO! I...I CAN'T!
THAT WOULDN'T BE... LIKE, HEROIC!
IT MAY NOT BE HEROIC, BUT IT IS WHAT NEEDS A'DOIN'.

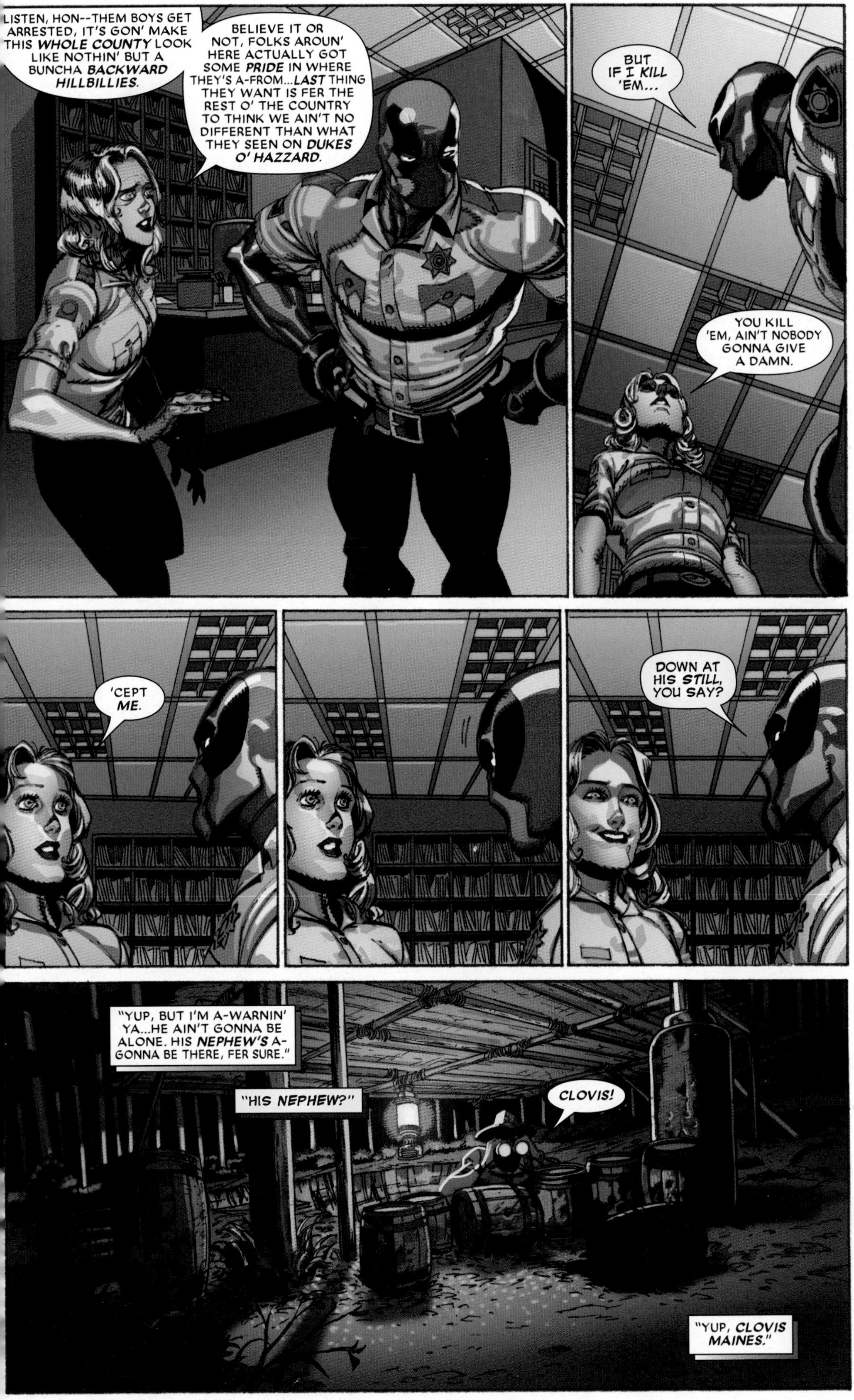
LISTEN, HON--THEM BOYS GET ARRESTED, IT'S GON' MAKE THIS WHOLE COUNTY LOOK LIKE NOTHIN' BUT A BUNCHA BACKWARD HILLBILLIES.
BELIEVE IT OR NOT, FOLKS AROUN' HERE ACTUALLY GOT SOME PRIDE IN WHERE THEY'S A-FROM...LAST THING THEY WANT IS FER THE REST O' THE COUNTRY TO THINK WE AIN'T NO DIFFERENT THAN WHAT THEY SEEN ON DUKES O' HAZZARD.
BUT IF I KILL 'EM...
YOU KILL 'EM, AIN'T NOBODY GONNA GIVE A DAMN.
'CEPT ME.
DOWN AT HIS STILL, YOU SAY?
"YUP, BUT I'M A-WARNIN' YA...HE AIN'T GONNA BE ALONE. HIS NEPHEW'S A-GONNA BE THERE, FER SURE."
"HIS NEPHEW?"
CLOVIS!
"YUP, CLOVIS MAINES."

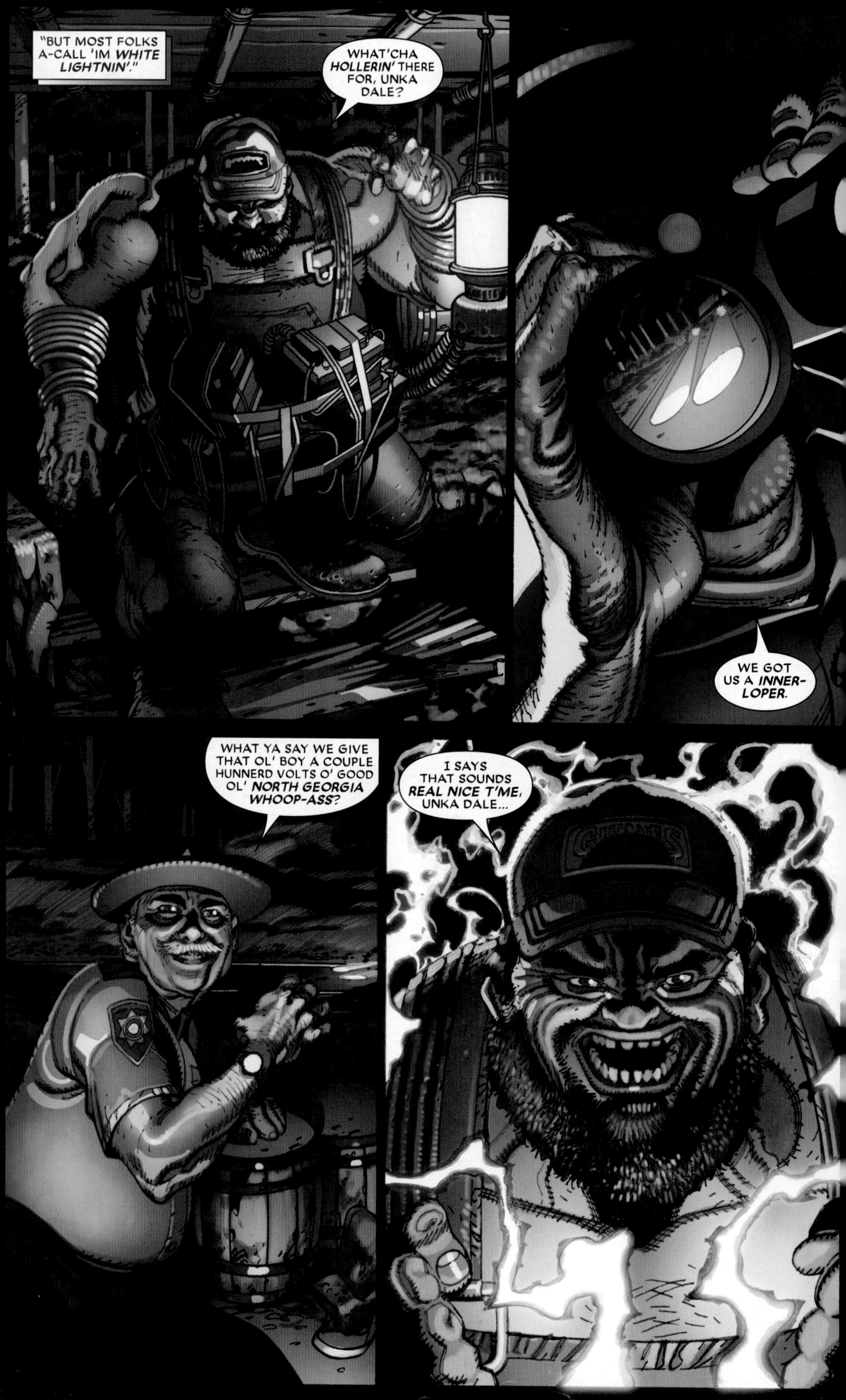
"BUT MOST FOLKS A-CALL 'IM WHITE LIGHTNIN'."
WHAT'CHA HOLLERIN' THERE FOR, UNKA DALE?
WE GOT US A INNER-LOPER.
WHAT YA SAY WE GIVE THAT OL' BOY A COUPLE HUNNERD VOLTS O' GOOD OL' NORTH GEORGIA WHOOP-ASS?
I SAYS THAT SOUNDS REAL NICE T'ME, UNKA DALE...

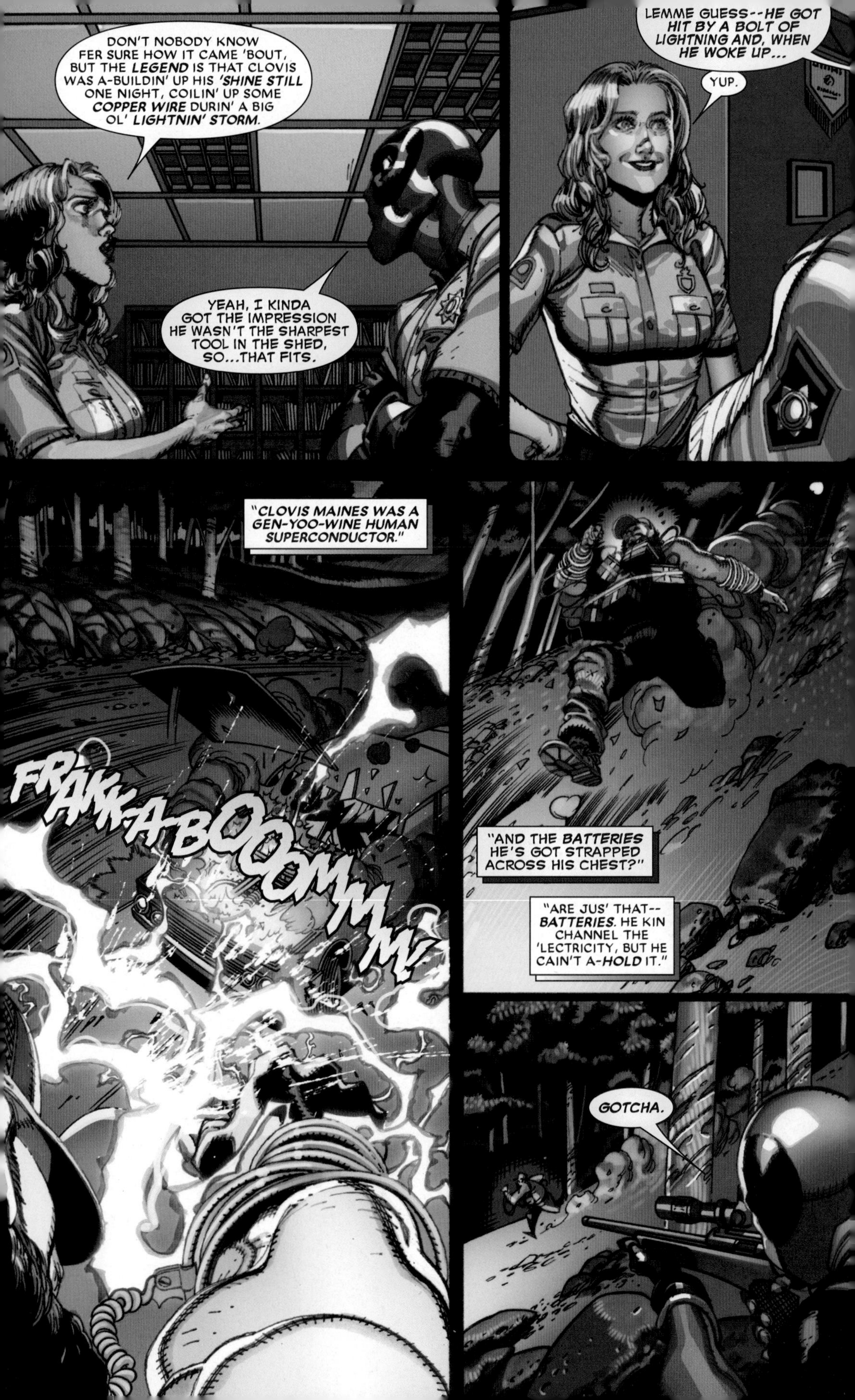
DON'T NOBODY KNOW FER SURE HOW IT CAME 'BOUT, BUT THE LEGEND IS THAT CLOVIS WAS A-BUILDIN' UP HIS 'SHINE STILL ONE NIGHT, COILIN' UP SOME COPPER WIRE DURIN' A BIG OL' LIGHTNIN' STORM.
YEAH, I KINDA GOT THE IMPRESSION HE WASN'T THE SHARPEST TOOL IN THE SHED, SO...THAT FITS.
LEMME GUESS--HE GOT HIT BY A BOLT OF LIGHTNING AND, WHEN HE WOKE UP...
YUP.
"CLOVIS MAINES WAS A GEN-YOO-WINE HUMAN SUPERCONDUCTOR."
FRAKK-A-BOOOMMM!
"AND THE BATTERIES HE'S GOT STRAPPED ACROSS HIS CHEST?"
"ARE JUS' THAT-- BATTERIES. HE KIN CHANNEL THE 'LECTRICITY, BUT HE CAIN'T A-HOLD IT."
GOTCHA.

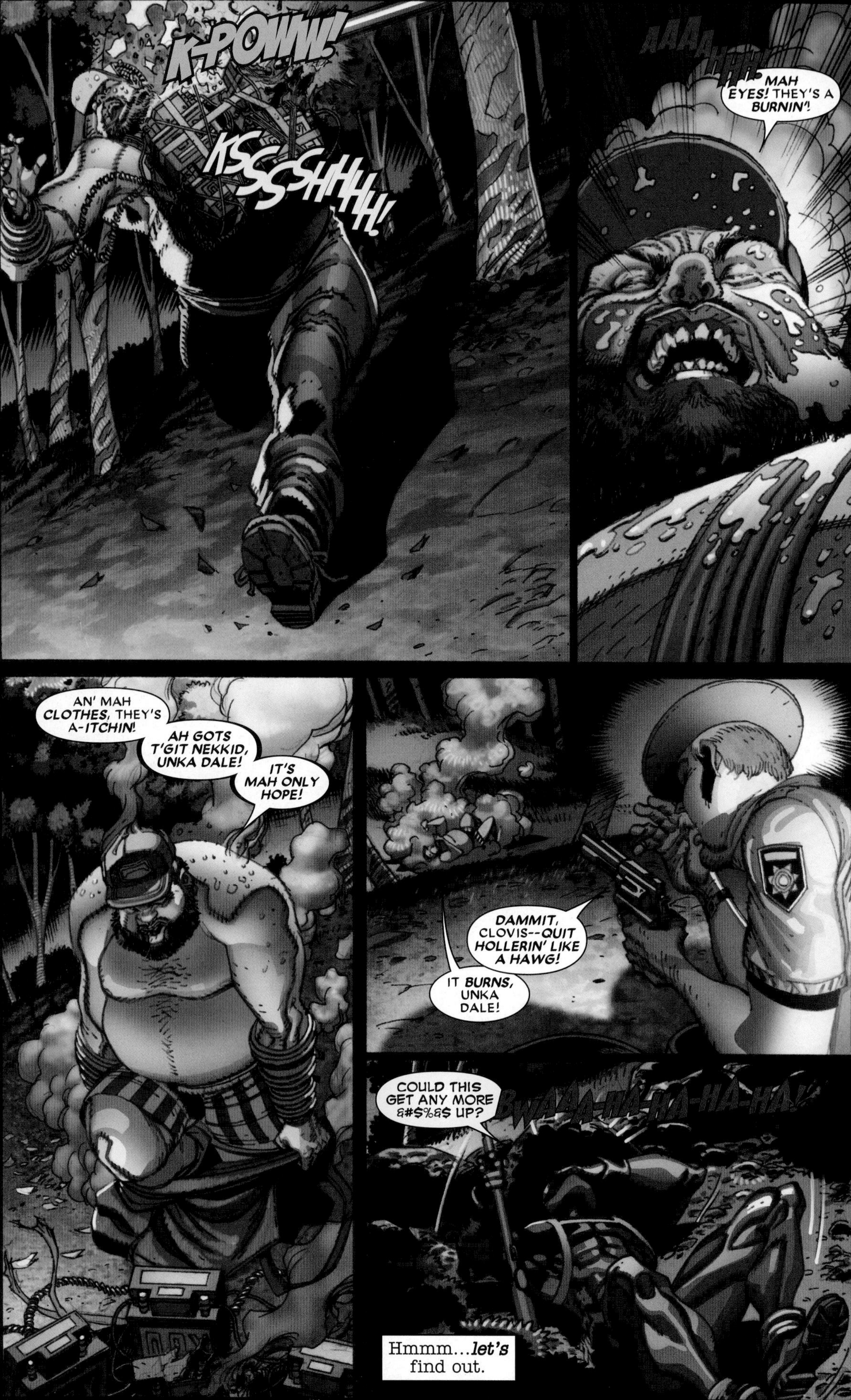
K-POWW!
KSSSHHHH!
AAAAHHH!
MAH EYES! THEY'S A BURNIN'!
AN' MAH CLOTHES, THEY'S A-ITCHIN!
AH GOTS T'GIT NEKKID, UNKA DALE!
IT'S MAH ONLY HOPE!
DAMMIT, CLOVIS--QUIT HOLLERIN' LIKE A HAWG!
IT BURNS, UNKA DALE!
COULD THIS GET ANY MORE &#$%&$ UP?
BWAAA-HA-HA-HA-HA!
Hmmm...let's find out.

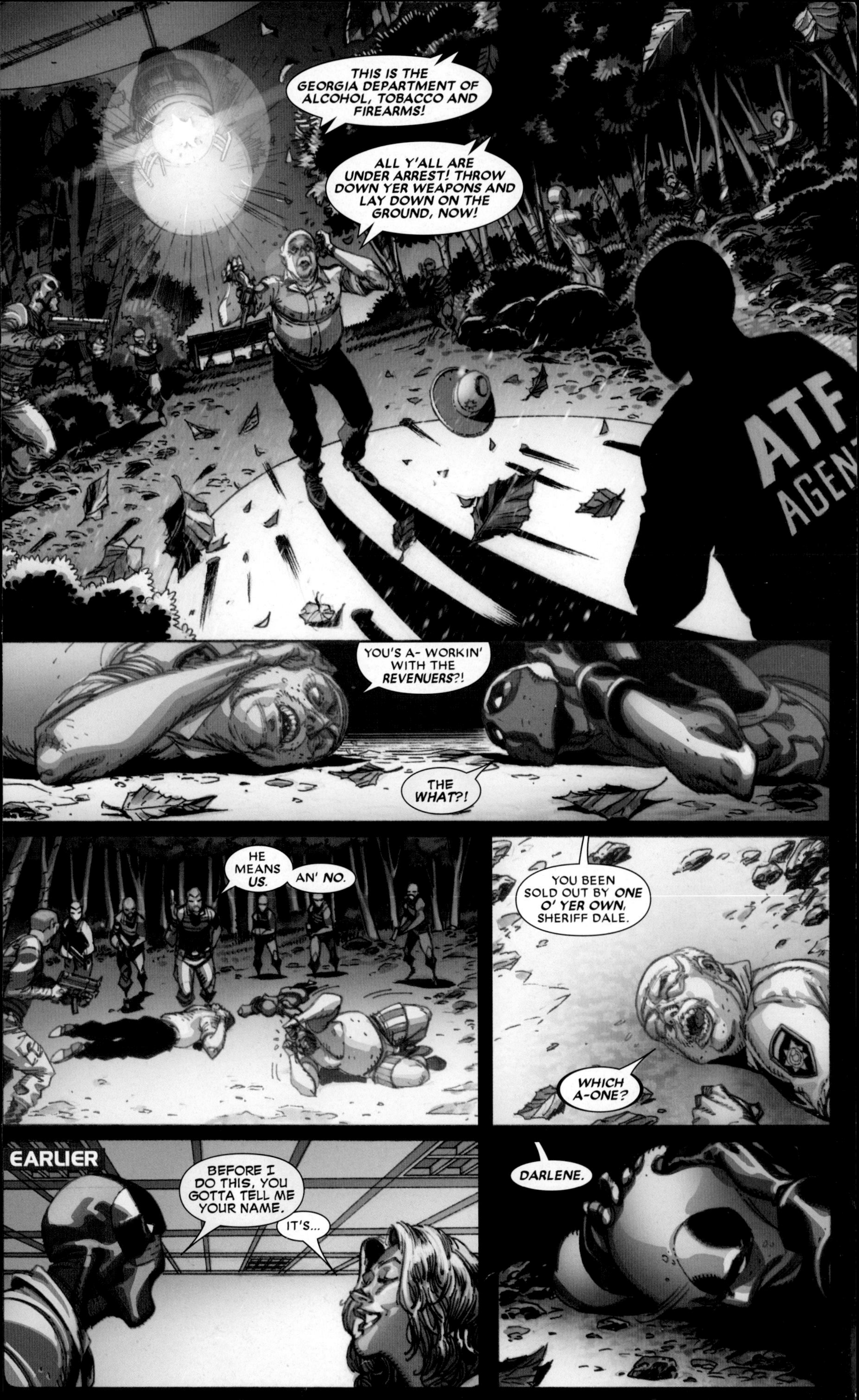

THIS IS THE GEORGIA DEPARTMENT OF ALCOHOL, TOBACCO AND FIREARMS!
ALL Y'ALL ARE UNDER ARREST! THROW DOWN YER WEAPONS AND LAY DOWN ON THE GROUND, NOW!
ATF AGENT
YOU'S A- WORKIN' WITH THE REVENUERS?!
THE WHAT?!
HE MEANS US.
AN' NO.
YOU BEEN SOLD OUT BY ONE O' YER OWN, SHERIFF DALE.
WHICH A-ONE?
EARLIER
BEFORE I DO THIS, YOU GOTTA TELL ME YOUR NAME.
IT'S...
DARLENE.

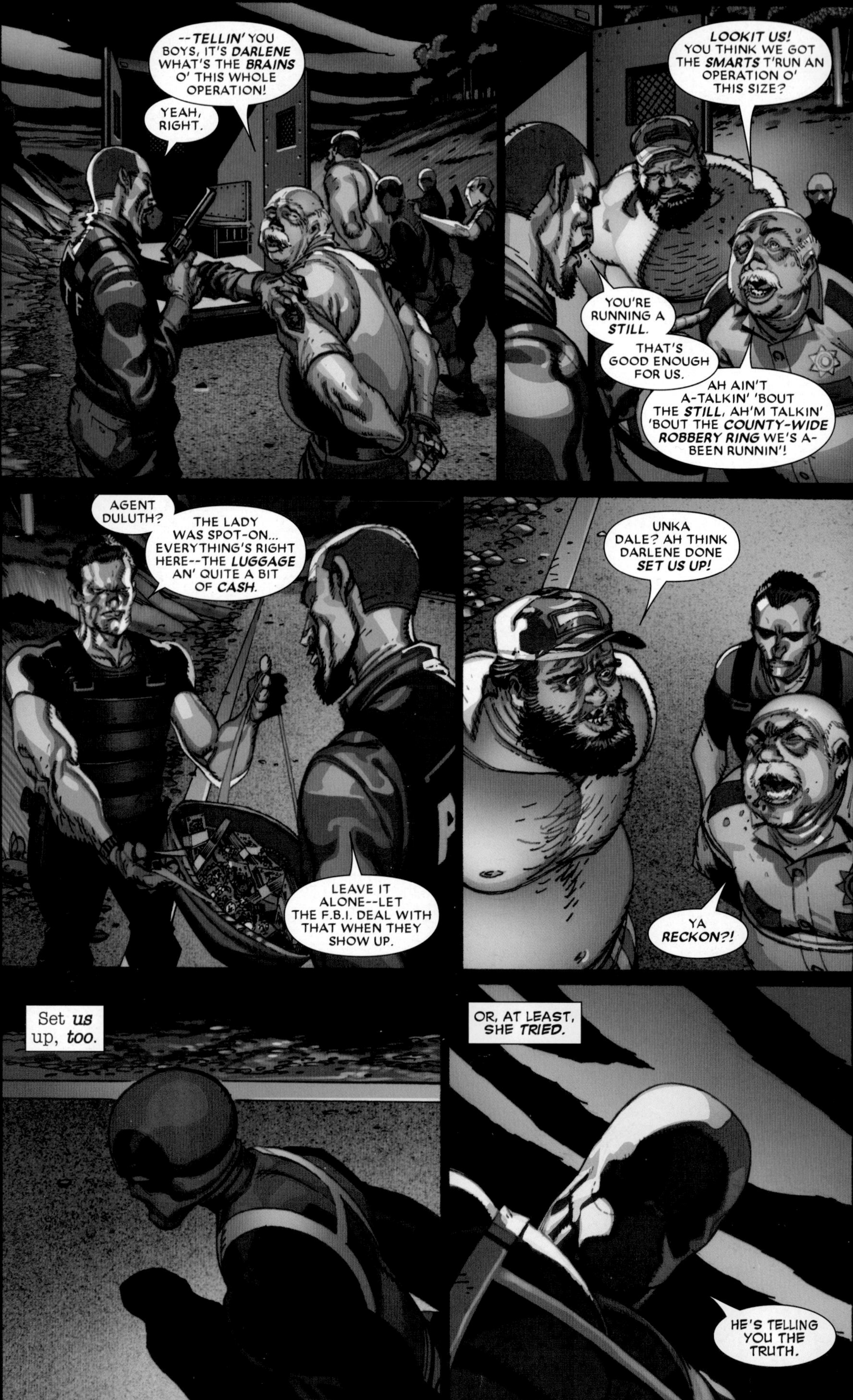
--TELLIN' YOU BOYS, IT'S DARLENE WHAT'S THE BRAINS O' THIS WHOLE OPERATION!
YEAH, RIGHT.
LOOKIT US! YOU THINK WE GOT THE SMARTS T'RUN AN OPERATION O' THIS SIZE?
YOU'RE RUNNING A STILL.
THAT'S GOOD ENOUGH FOR US.
AH AIN'T A-TALKIN' 'BOUT THE STILL, AH'M TALKIN' 'BOUT THE COUNTY-WIDE ROBBERY RING WE'S A-BEEN RUNNIN'!
AGENT DULUTH?
THE LADY WAS SPOT-ON... EVERYTHING'S RIGHT HERE--THE LUGGAGE AN' QUITE A BIT OF CASH.
LEAVE IT ALONE--LET THE F.B.I. DEAL WITH THAT WHEN THEY SHOW UP.
UNKA DALE? AH THINK DARLENE DONE SET US UP!
YA RECKON?!
Set us up, too.
OR, AT LEAST, SHE TRIED.
HE'S TELLING YOU THE TRUTH.

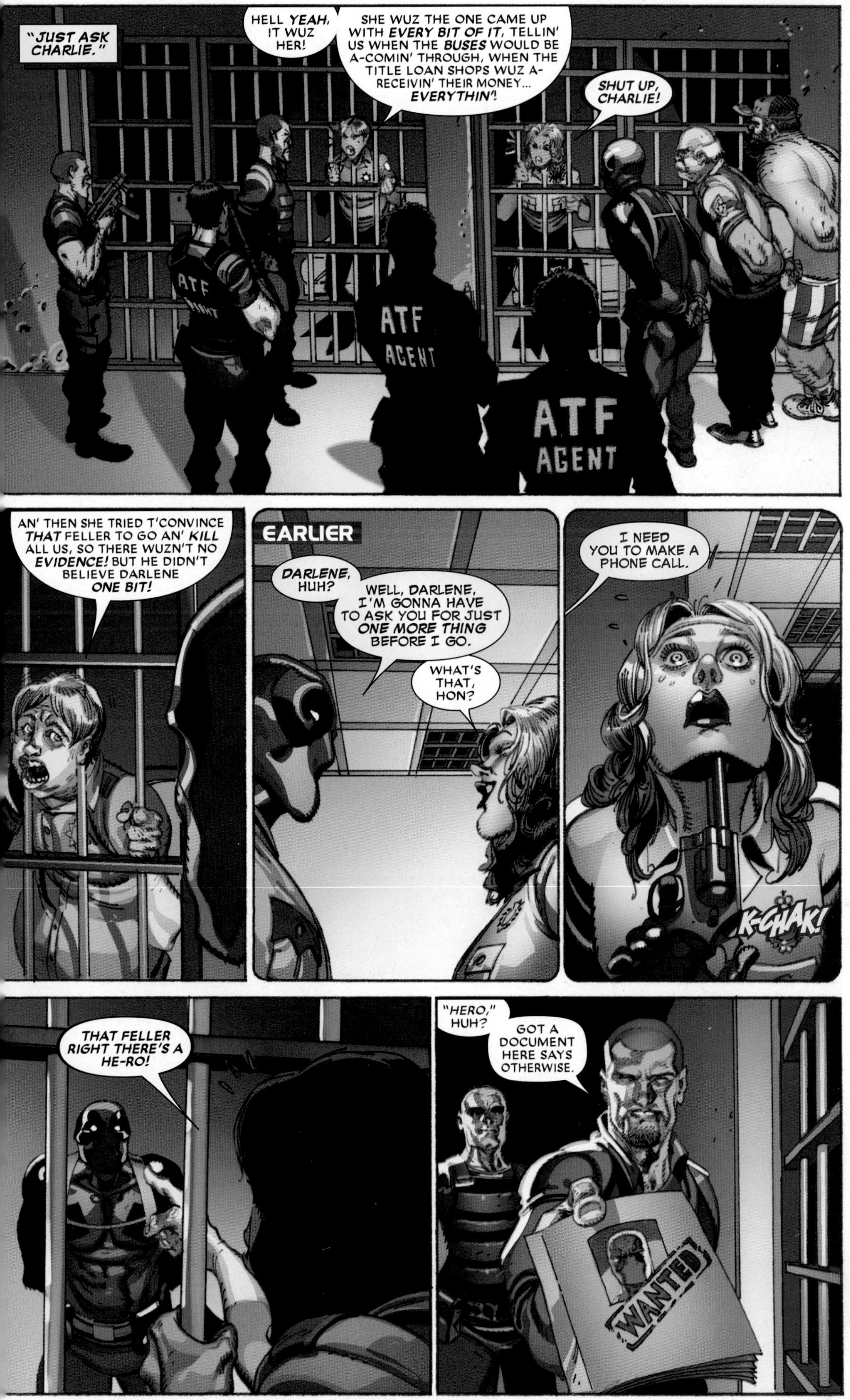
"JUST ASK CHARLIE."
HELL YEAH, IT WUZ HER!
SHE WUZ THE ONE CAME UP WITH EVERY BIT OF IT, TELLIN' US WHEN THE BUSES WOULD BE A-COMIN' THROUGH, WHEN THE TITLE LOAN SHOPS WUZ A-RECEIVIN' THEIR MONEY... EVERYTHIN'!
SHUT UP, CHARLIE!
ATF AGENT
ATF AGENT
AN' THEN SHE TRIED T'CONVINCE THAT FELLER TO GO AN' KILL ALL US, SO THERE WUZN'T NO EVIDENCE! BUT HE DIDN'T BELIEVE DARLENE ONE BIT!
EARLIER
DARLENE, HUH?
WELL, DARLENE, I'M GONNA HAVE TO ASK YOU FOR JUST ONE MORE THING BEFORE I GO.
WHAT'S THAT, HON?
I NEED YOU TO MAKE A PHONE CALL.
K-CHAK!
THAT FELLER RIGHT THERE'S A HE-RO!
"HERO," HUH?
GOT A DOCUMENT HERE SAYS OTHERWISE.
WANTED

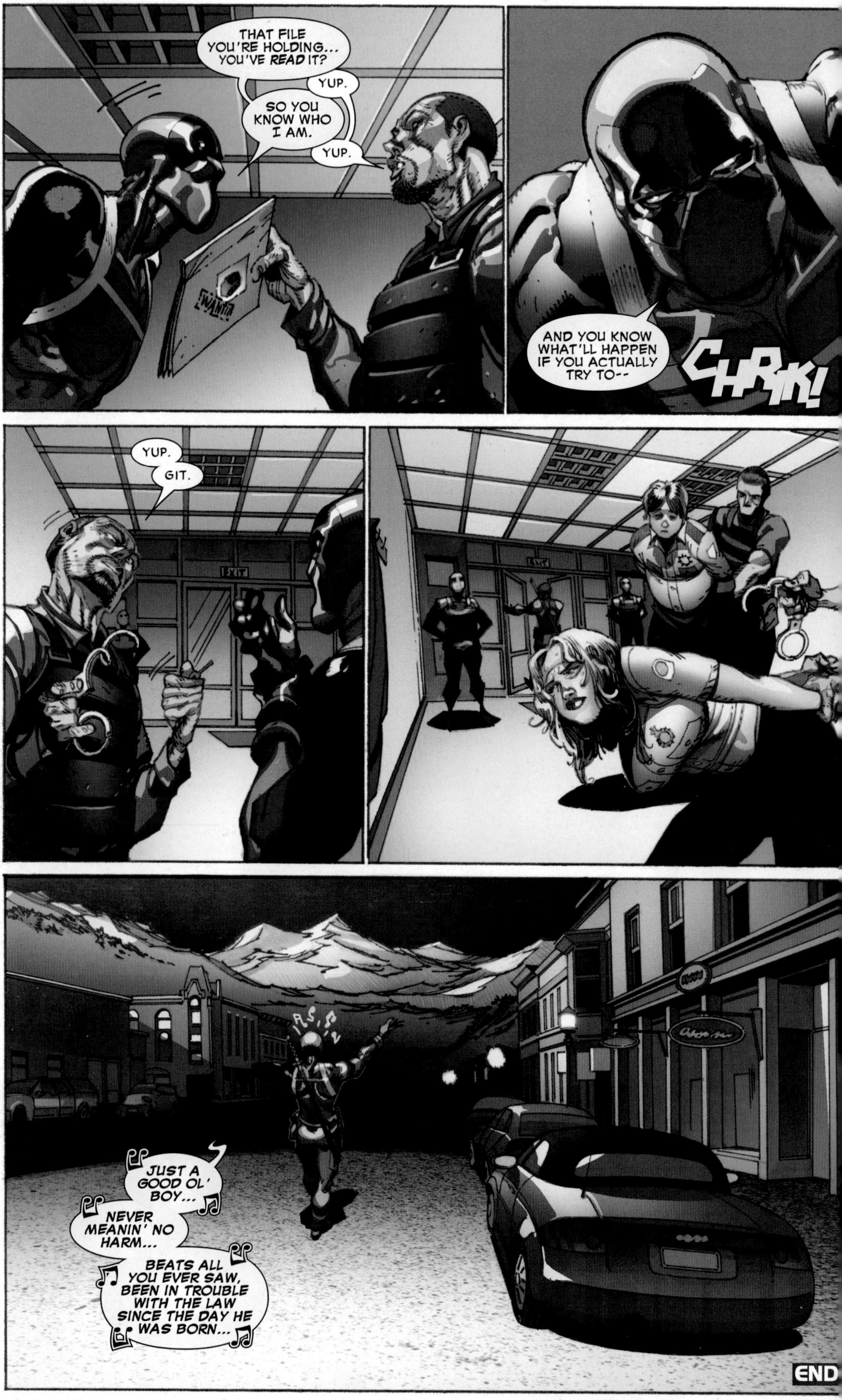
THAT FILE YOU'RE HOLDING... YOU'VE *READ* IT?
YUP.
SO YOU KNOW WHO I AM.
YUP.
AND YOU KNOW WHAT'LL HAPPEN IF YOU ACTUALLY TRY TO--
CHRIK!
YUP.
GIT.
JUST A GOOD OL' BOY...
NEVER MEANIN' NO HARM...
BEATS ALL YOU EVER SAW, BEEN IN TROUBLE WITH THE LAW SINCE THE DAY HE WAS BORN...
END

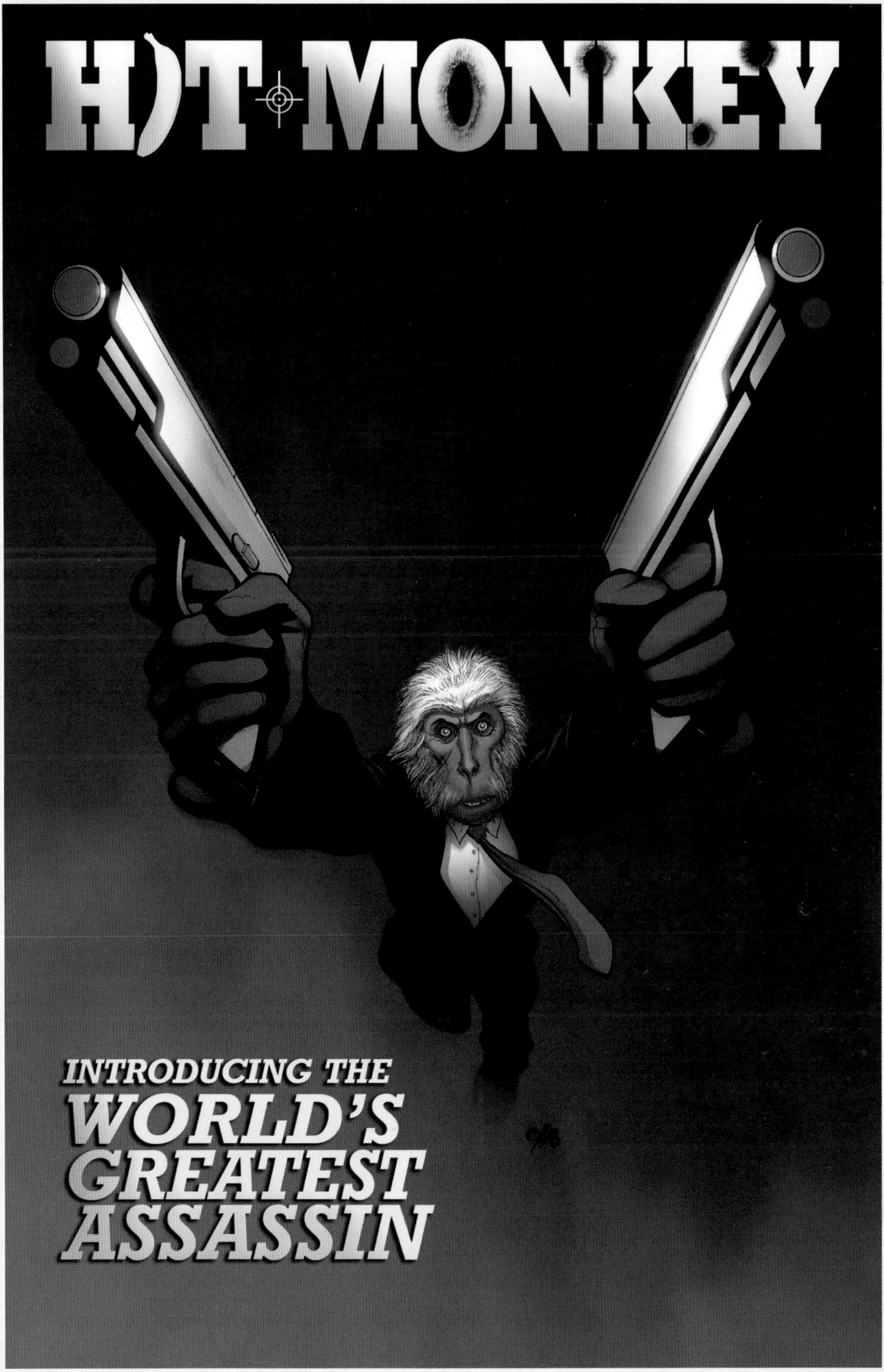
HIT MONKEY
INTRODUCING THE
WORLD'S
GREATEST
ASSASSIN

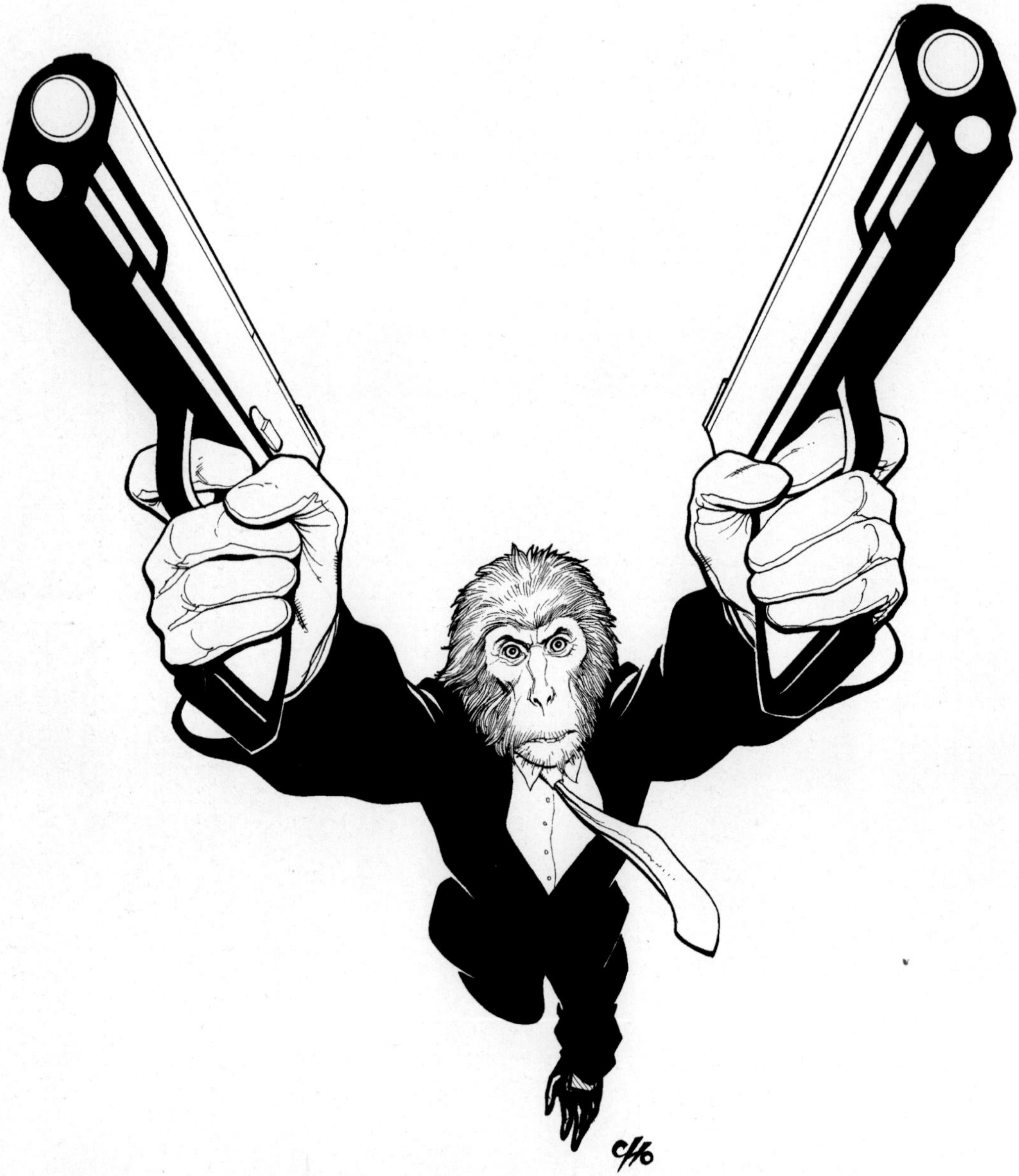

HIT-MONKEY #1 SECOND PRINTING VARIANT

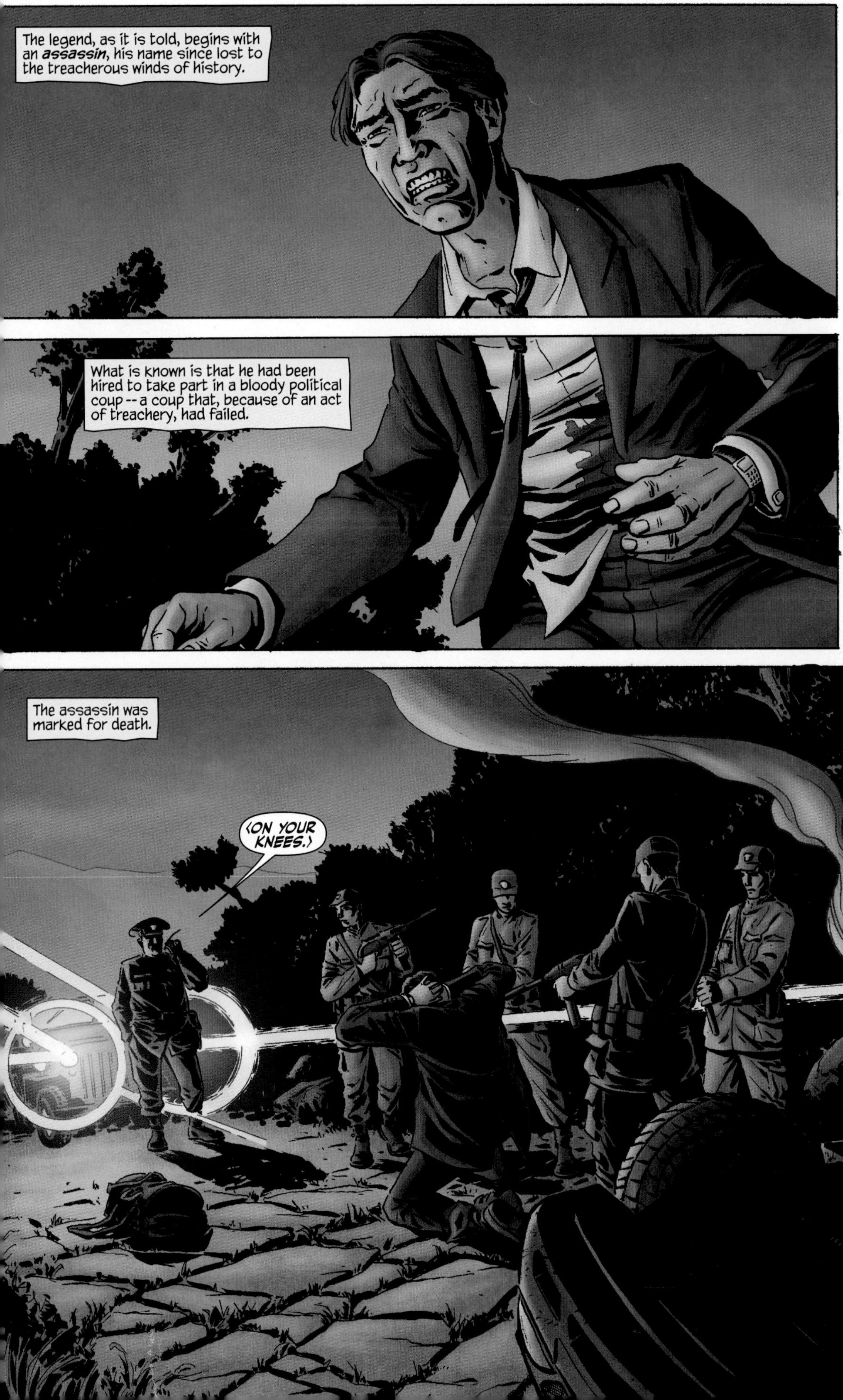
The legend, as it is told, begins with an *assassin*, his name since lost to the treacherous winds of history.
What is known is that he had been hired to take part in a bloody political coup -- a coup that, because of an act of treachery, had failed.
The assassin was marked for death.
‹ON YOUR KNEES.›

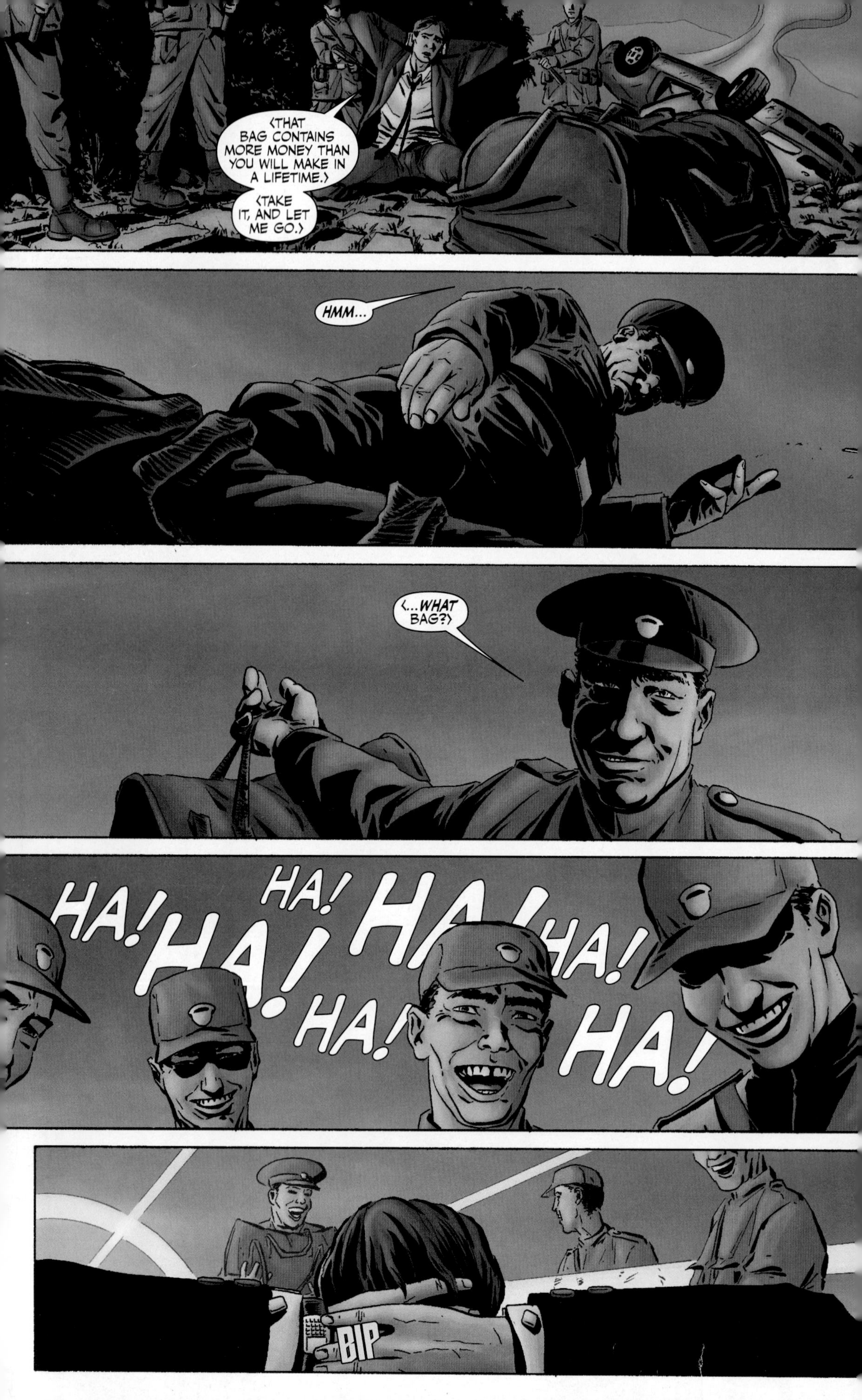
‹THAT BAG CONTAINS MORE MONEY THAN YOU WILL MAKE IN A LIFETIME.›
‹TAKE IT, AND LET ME GO.›
HMM...
‹...WHAT BAG?›
HA! HA! HA! HA! HA! HA! HA!
BIP

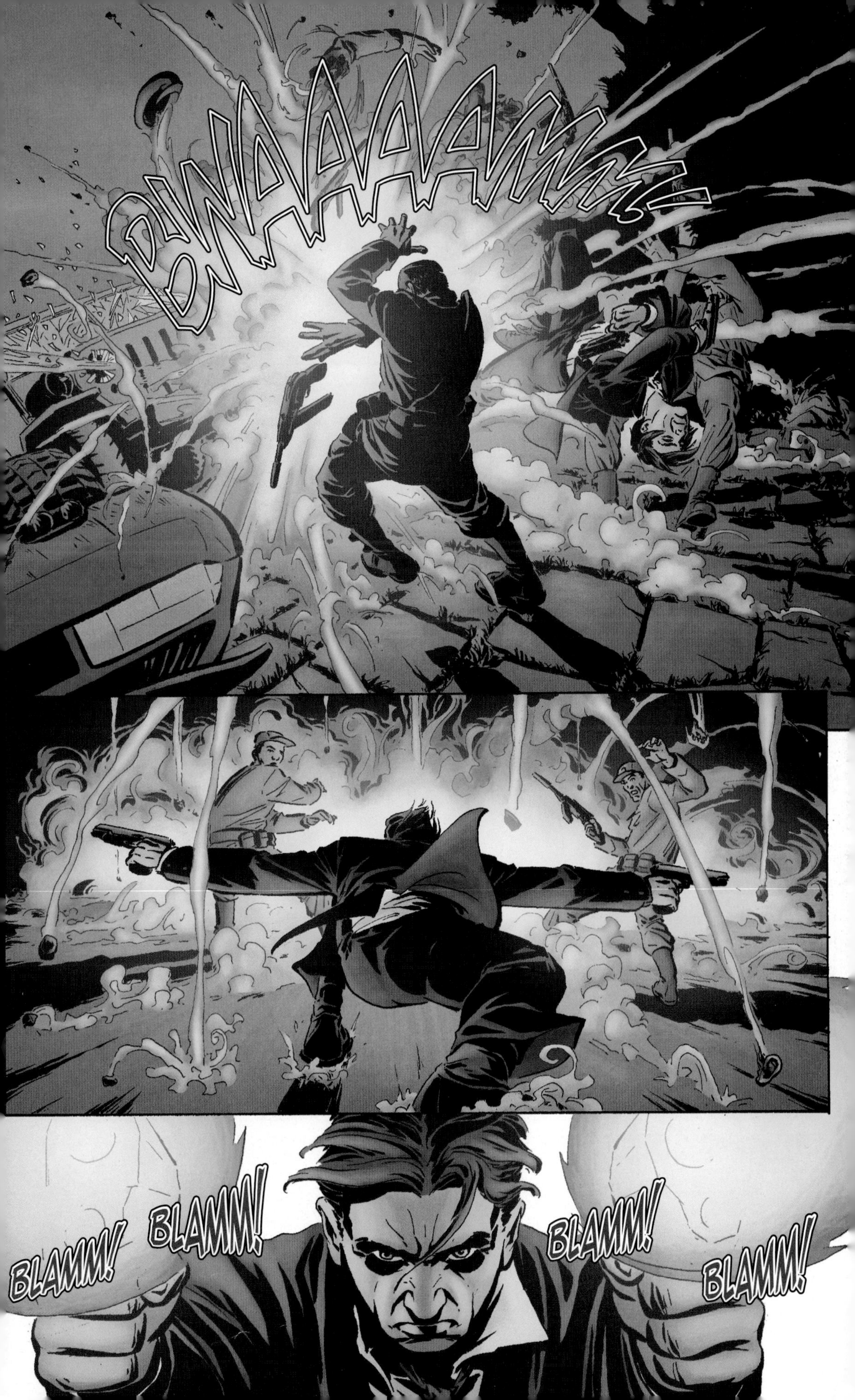
BWAAAAMM!
BLAMM!
BLAMM!
BLAMM!
BLAMM!

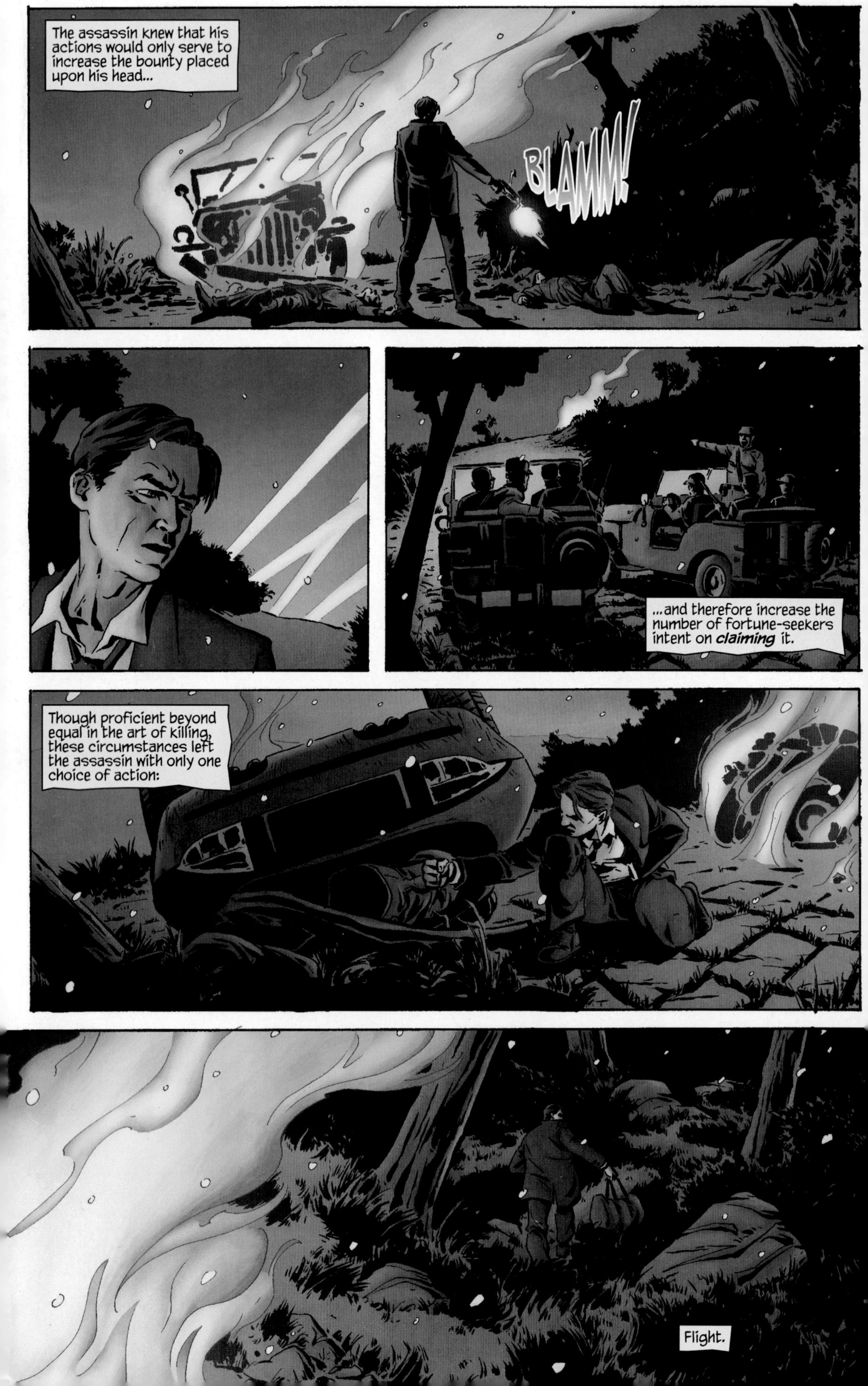
The assassin knew that his actions would only serve to increase the bounty placed upon his head...
BLAMM!
...and therefore increase the number of fortune-seekers intent on *claiming* it.
Though proficient beyond equal in the art of killing, these circumstances left the assassin with only one choice of action:
Flight.

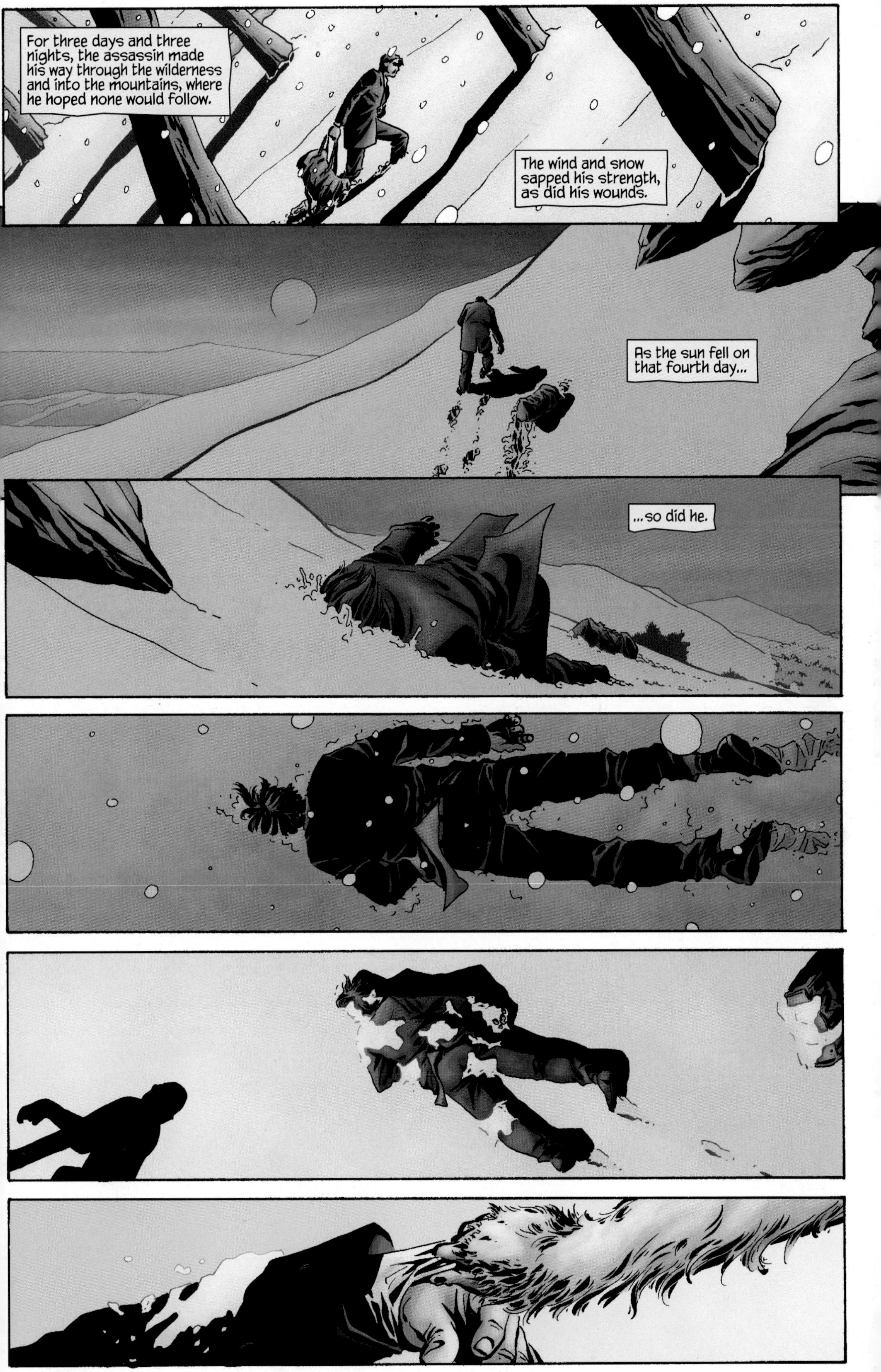
For three days and three nights, the assassin made his way through the wilderness and into the mountains, where he hoped none would follow.
The wind and snow sapped his strength, as did his wounds.
As the sun fell on that fourth day...
...so did he.

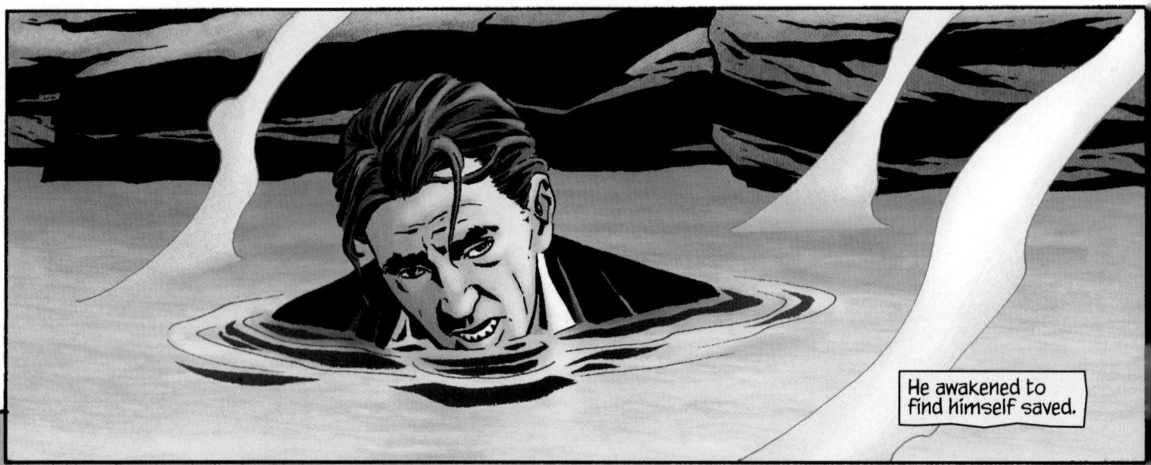
He awakened to
find himself saved.

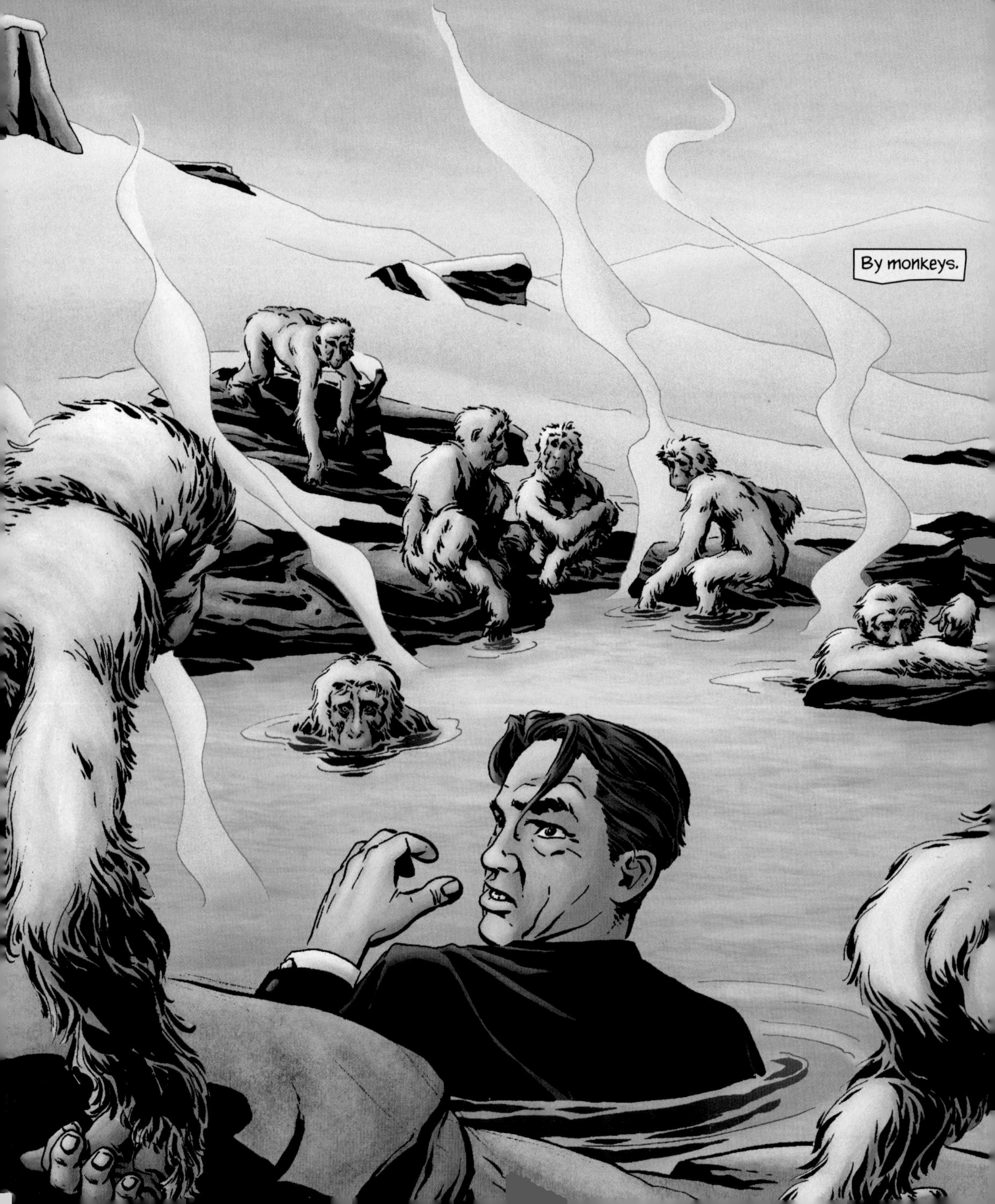
By monkeys.

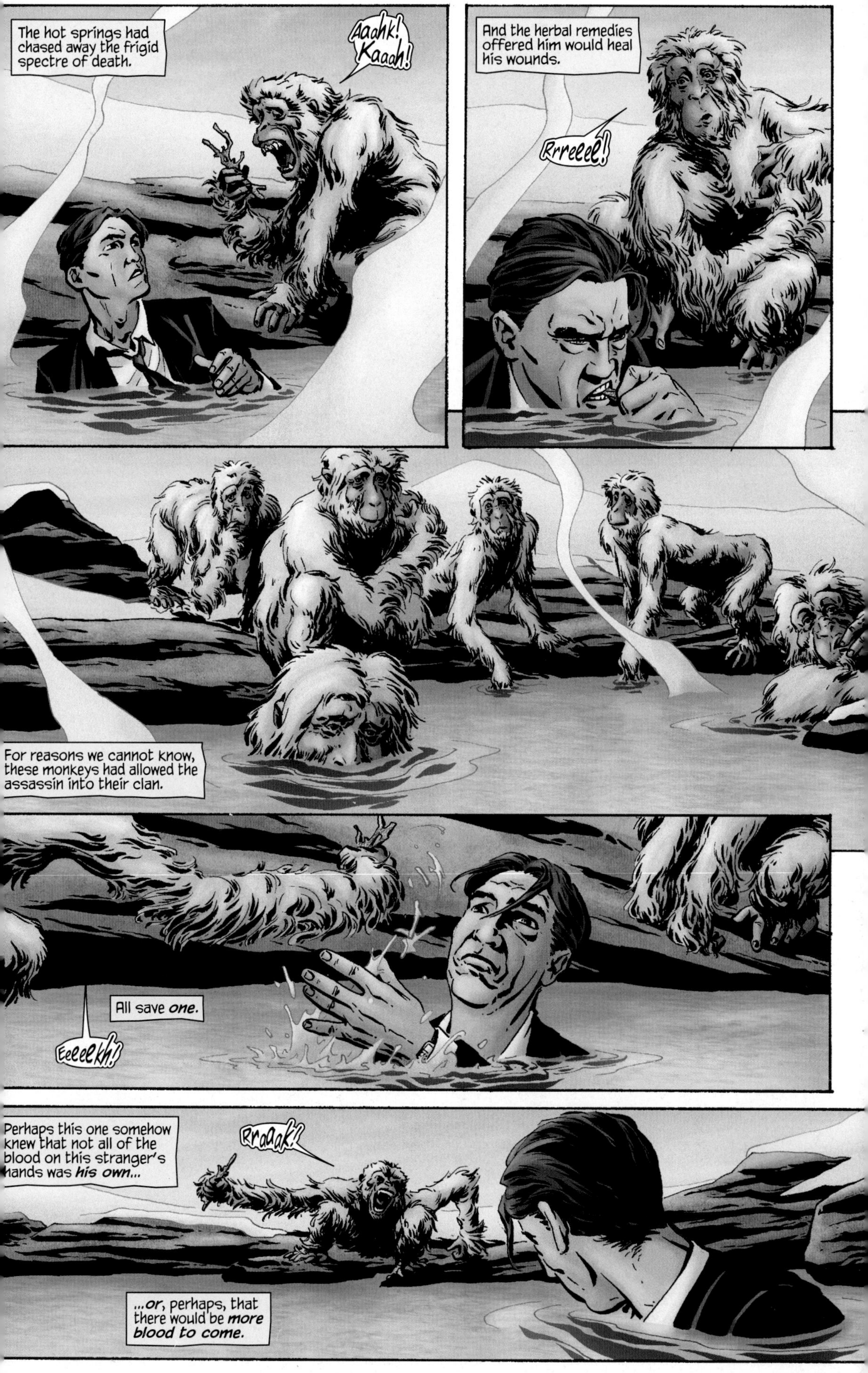

The hot springs had chased away the frigid spectre of death.
Aaahk! Kaaah!
And the herbal remedies offered him would heal his wounds.
Rrreeee!
For reasons we cannot know, these monkeys had allowed the assassin into their clan.
All save one.
Eeeeekh!
Perhaps this one somehow knew that not all of the blood on this stranger's hands was his own...
Rraaak!
...or, perhaps, that there would be more blood to come.

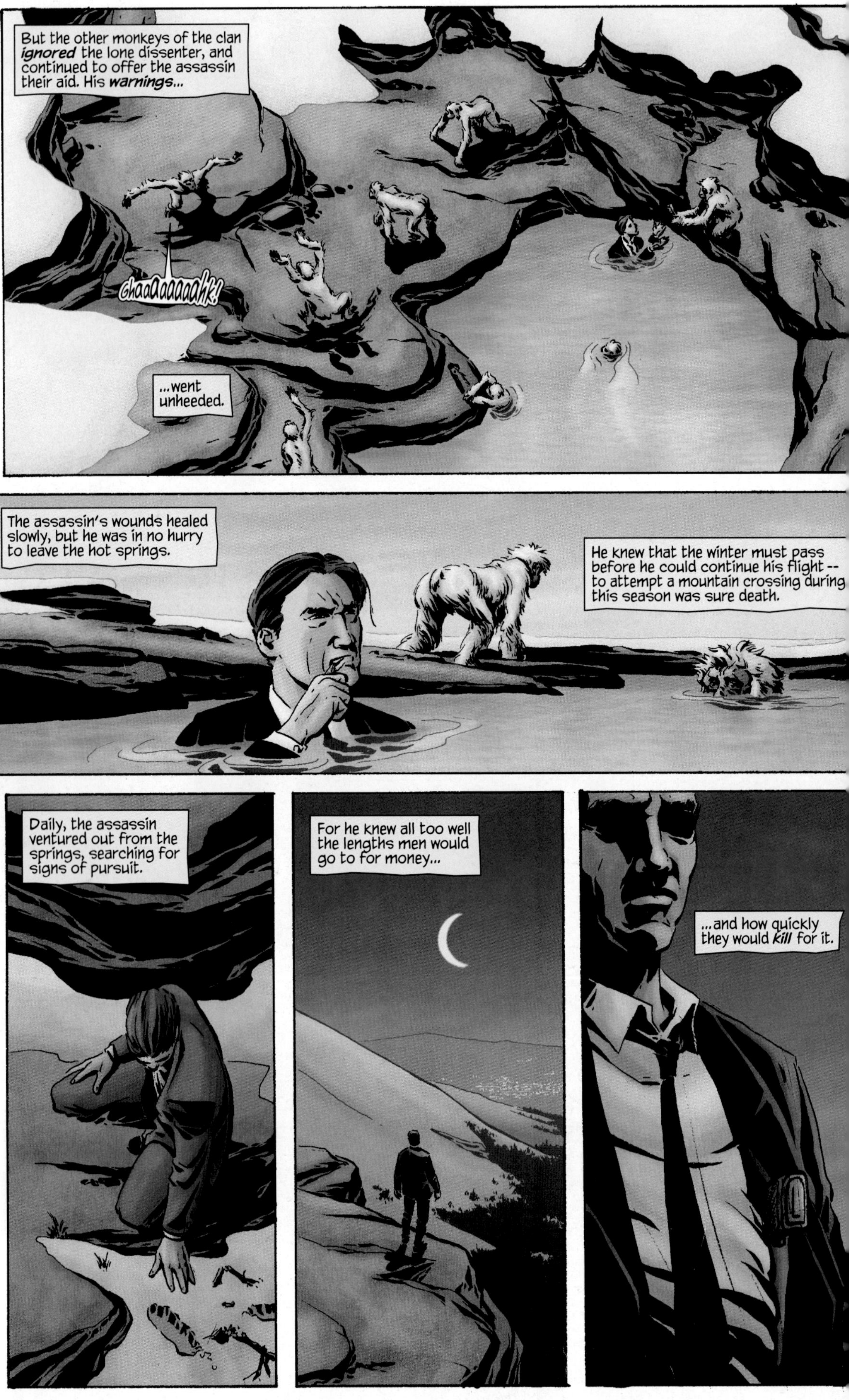
But the other monkeys of the clan *ignored* the lone dissenter, and continued to offer the assassin their aid. His *warnings*...
Ghaaaaaaaahk!
...went unheeded.
The assassin's wounds healed slowly, but he was in no hurry to leave the hot springs.
He knew that the winter must pass before he could continue his flight -- to attempt a mountain crossing during this season was sure death.
Daily, the assassin ventured out from the springs, searching for signs of pursuit.
For he knew all too well the lengths men would go to for money...
...and how quickly they would *kill* for it.

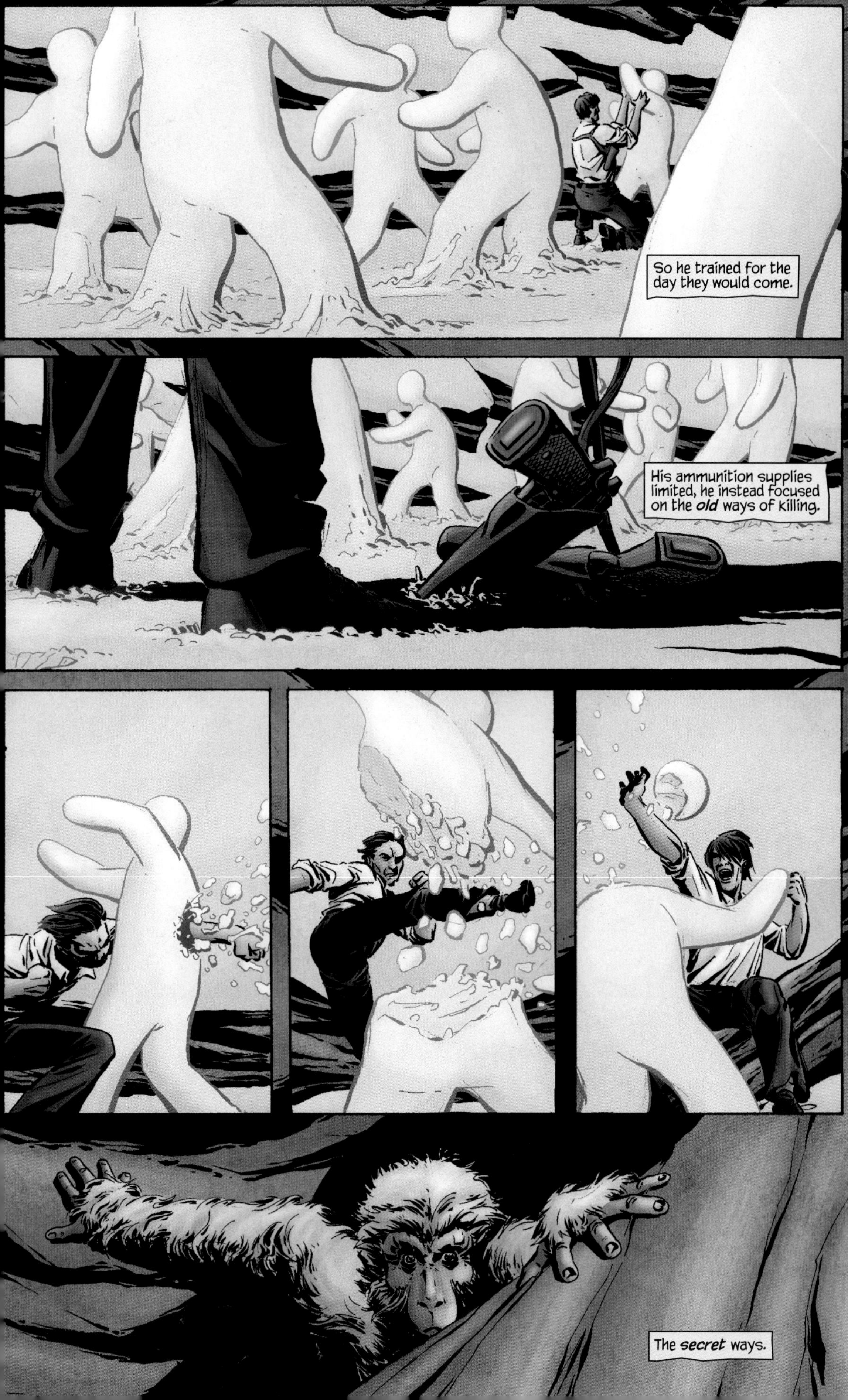
So he trained for the day they would come.
His ammunition supplies limited, he instead focused on the *old* ways of killing.
The *secret* ways.

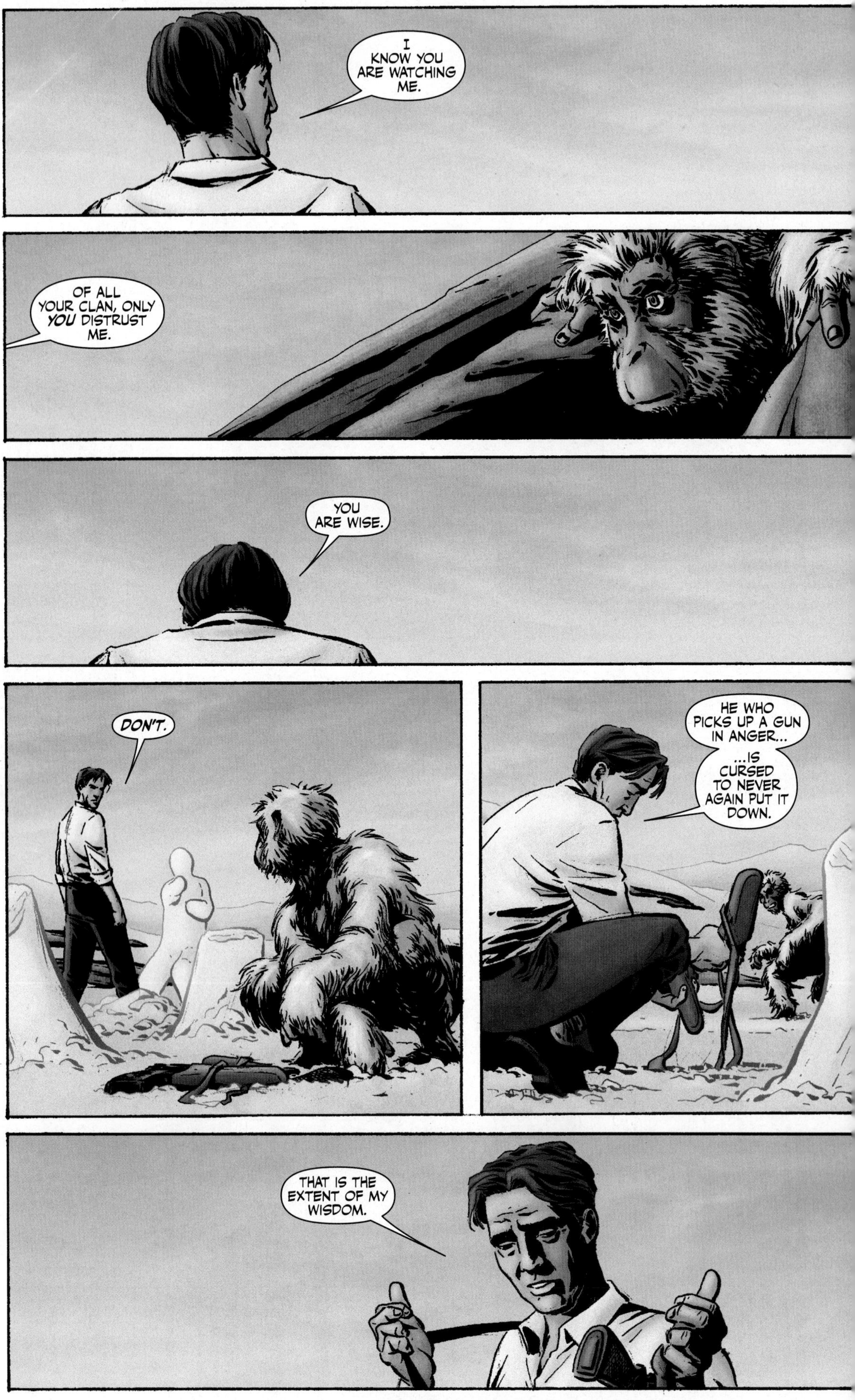
I KNOW YOU ARE WATCHING ME.
OF ALL YOUR CLAN, ONLY *YOU* DISTRUST ME.
YOU ARE WISE.
DON'T.
HE WHO PICKS UP A GUN IN ANGER...
...IS CURSED TO NEVER AGAIN PUT IT DOWN.
THAT IS THE EXTENT OF MY WISDOM.

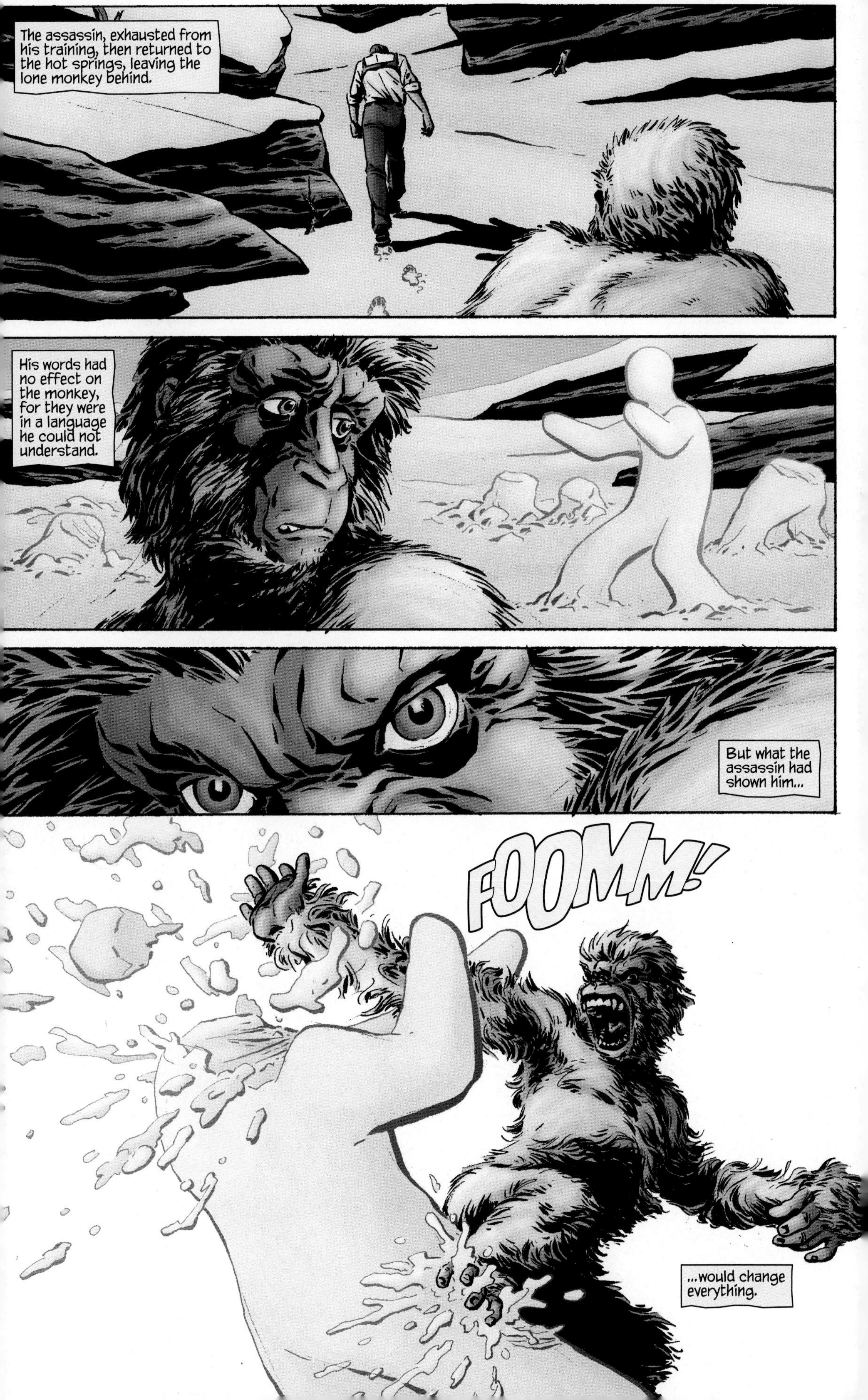
The assassin, exhausted from his training, then returned to the hot springs, leaving the lone monkey behind.
His words had no effect on the monkey, for they were in a language he could not understand.
But what the assassin had shown him...
FOOMM!
...would change everything.

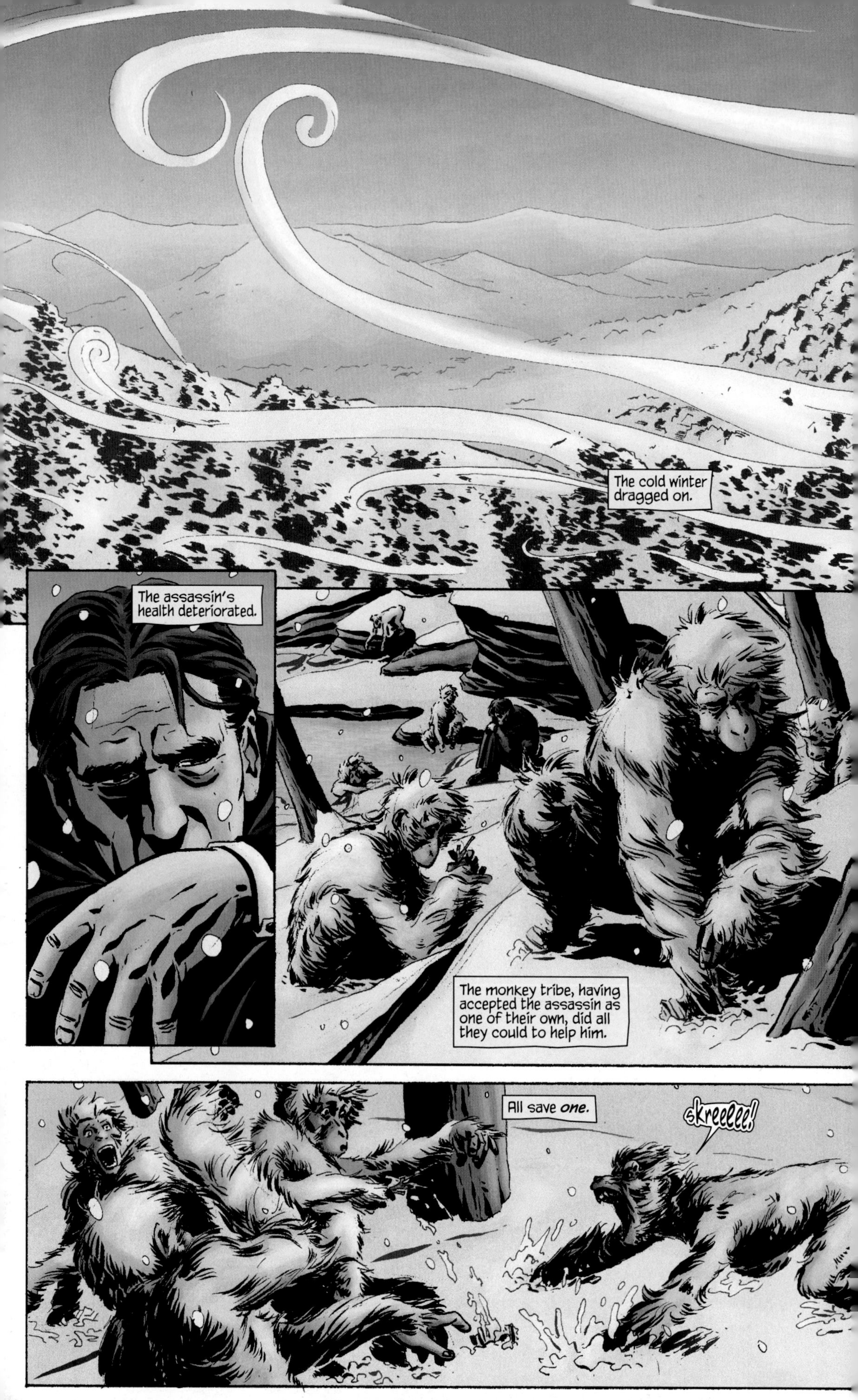
The cold winter dragged on.
The assassin's health deteriorated.
The monkey tribe, having accepted the assassin as one of their own, did all they could to help him.
All save *one.*
skreeeee!

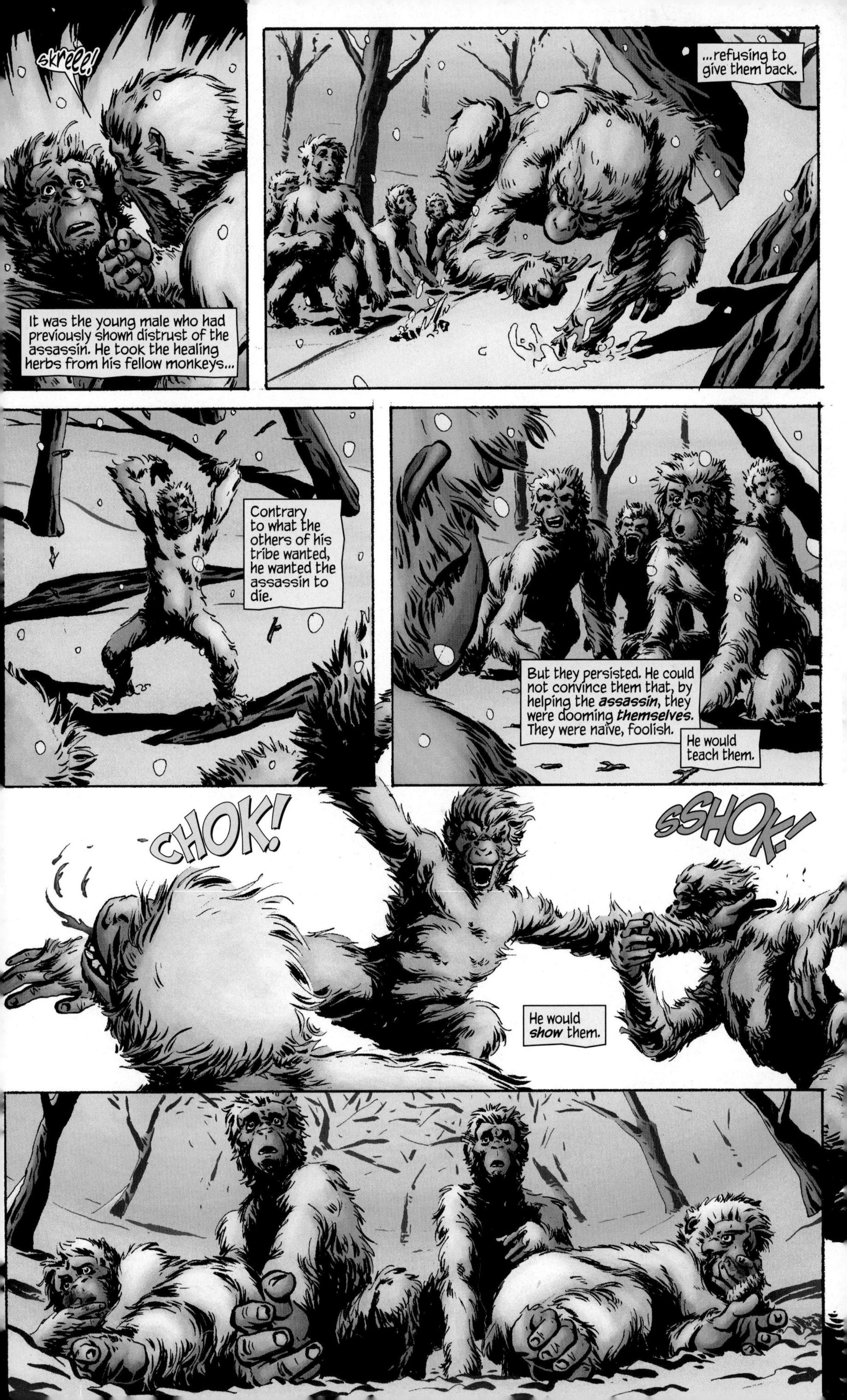

skreee!
It was the young male who had previously shown distrust of the assassin. He took the healing herbs from his fellow monkeys...
...refusing to give them back.
Contrary to what the others of his tribe wanted, he wanted the assassin to die.
But they persisted. He could not convince them that, by helping the *assassin*, they were dooming *themselves*. They were naive, foolish.
He would teach them.
CHOK!
SSHOK!
He would *show* them.

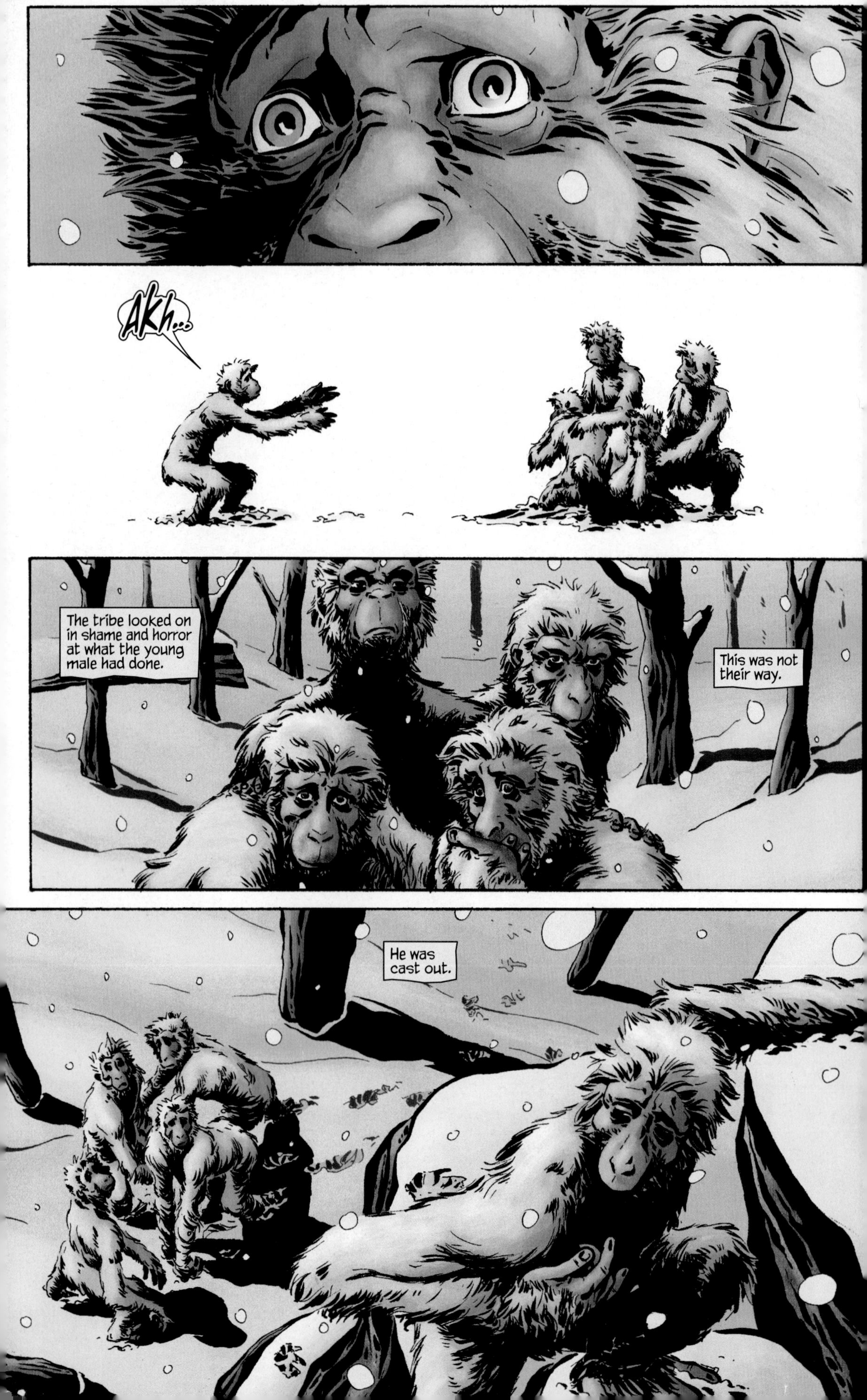
AKH...
The tribe looked on in shame and horror at what the young male had done.
This was not their way.
He was cast out.

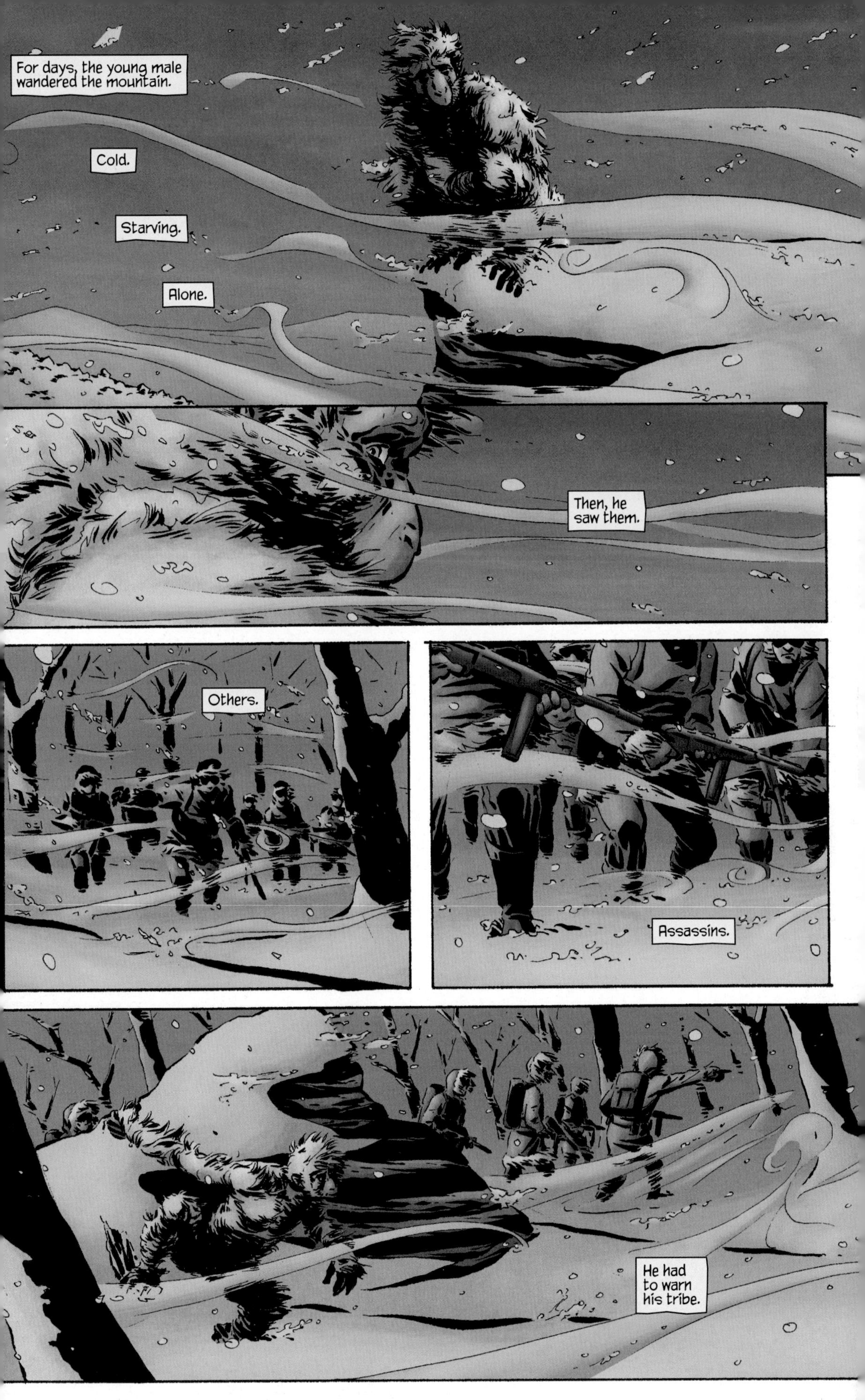
For days, the young male wandered the mountain.
Cold.
Starving.
Alone.
Then, he saw them.
Others.
Assassins.
He had to warn his tribe.

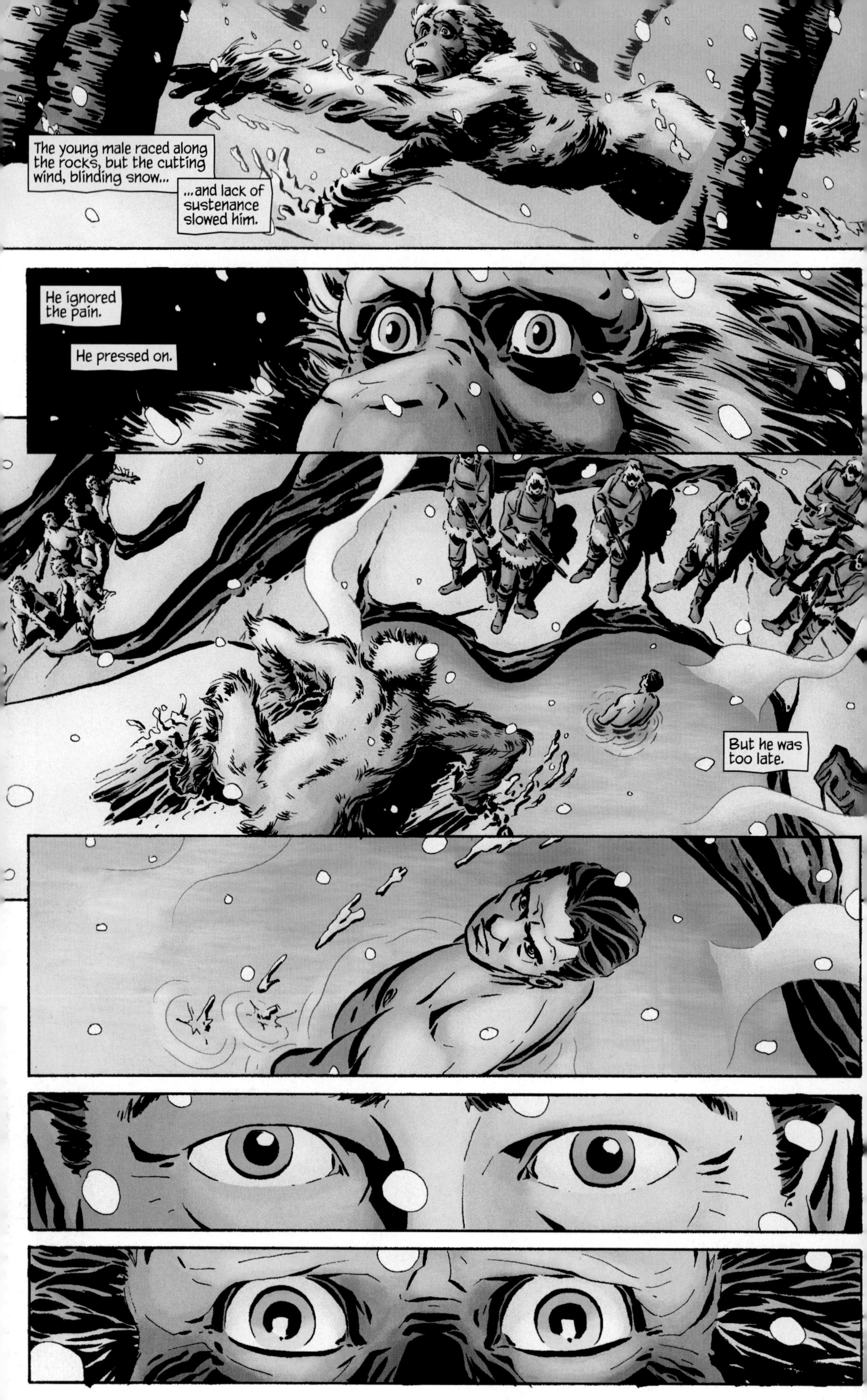
The young male raced along the rocks, but the cutting wind, blinding snow...
...and lack of sustenance slowed him.
He ignored the pain.
He pressed on.
But he was too late.

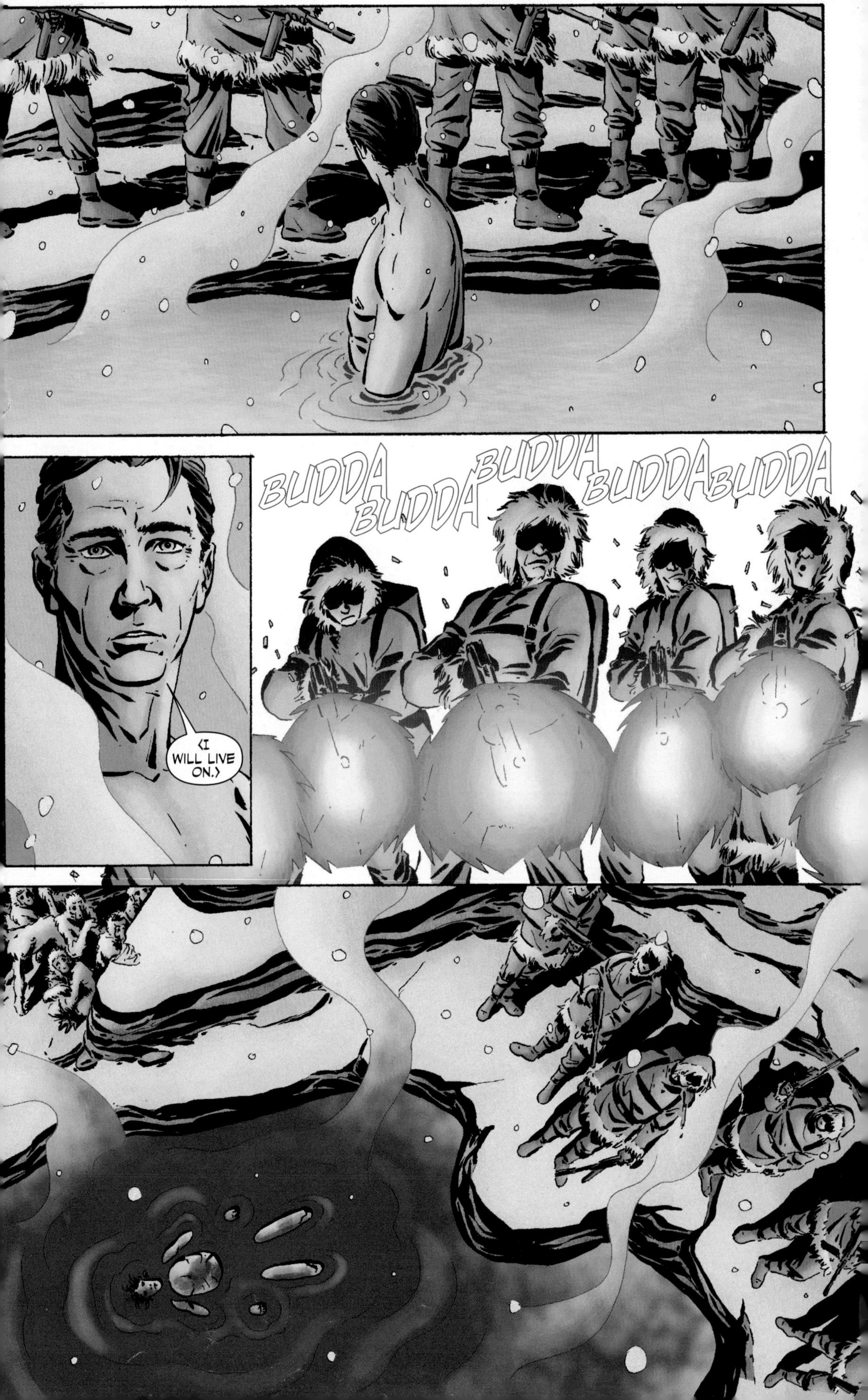

‹I WILL LIVE ON.›
BUDDA BUDDA BUDDA BUDDA BUDDA

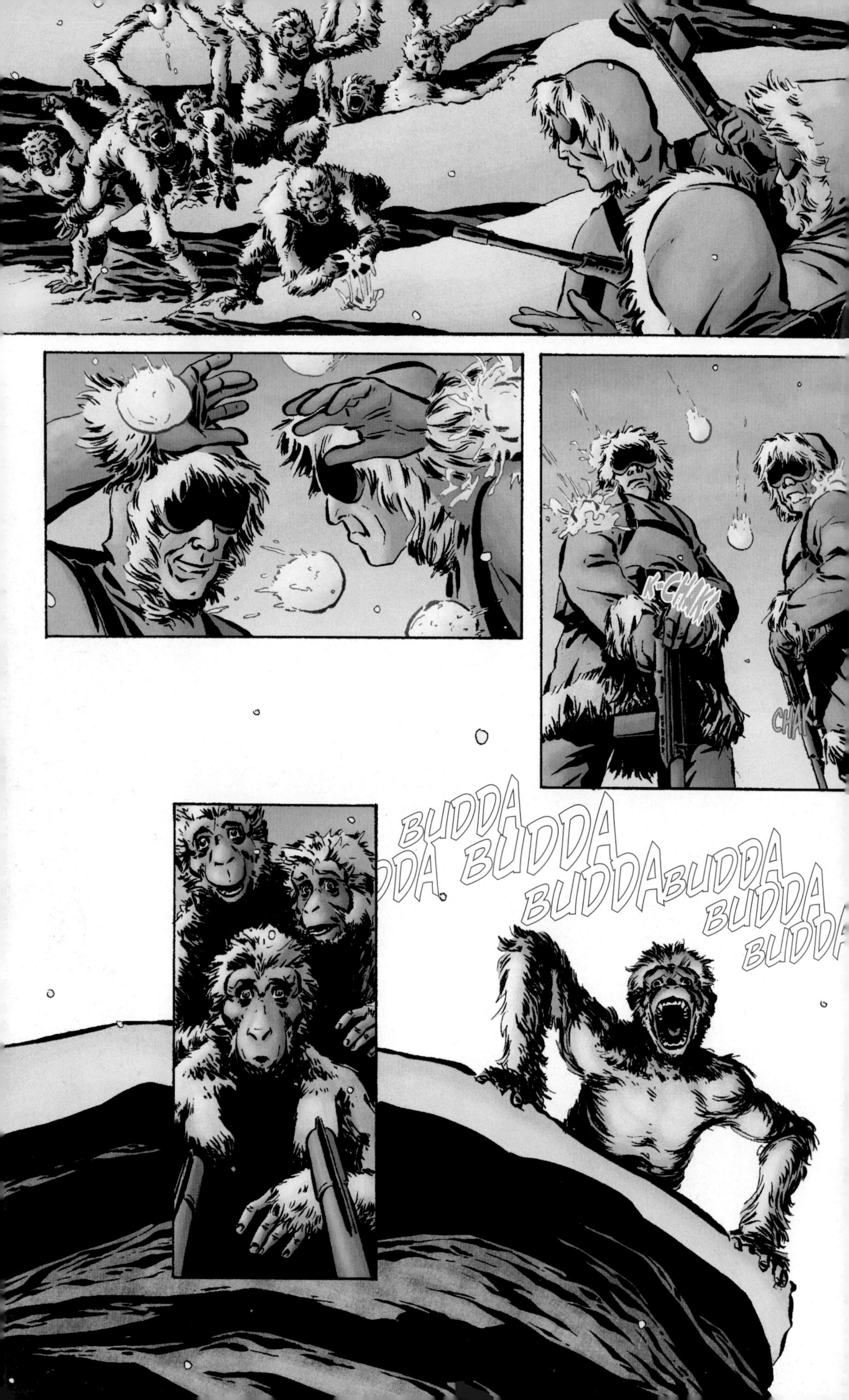
K-CHAK!
CHAK!
BUDDA
BUDDA
BUDDA
BUDDA
BUDDA

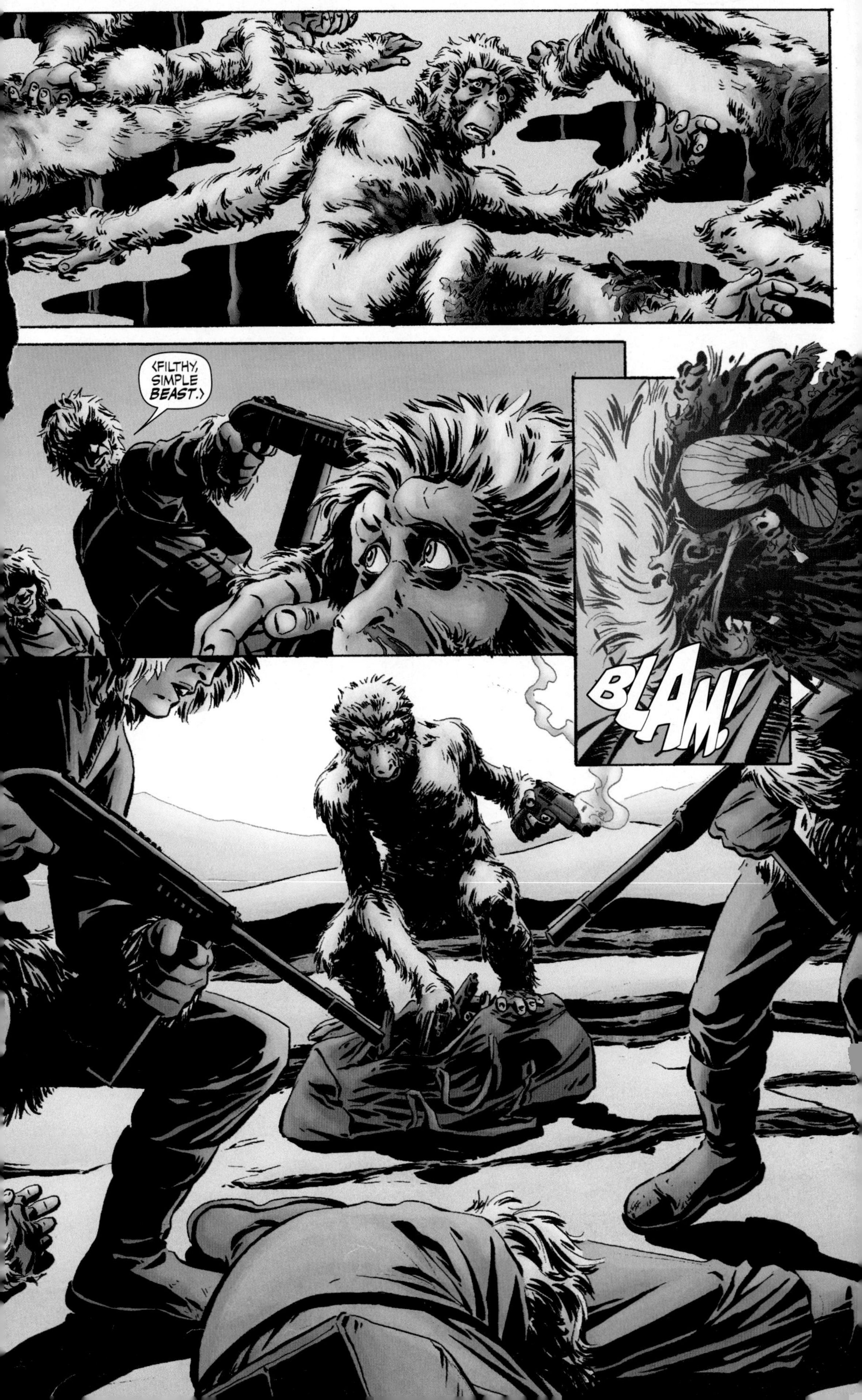

‹FILTHY, SIMPLE BEAST.›
BLAM!

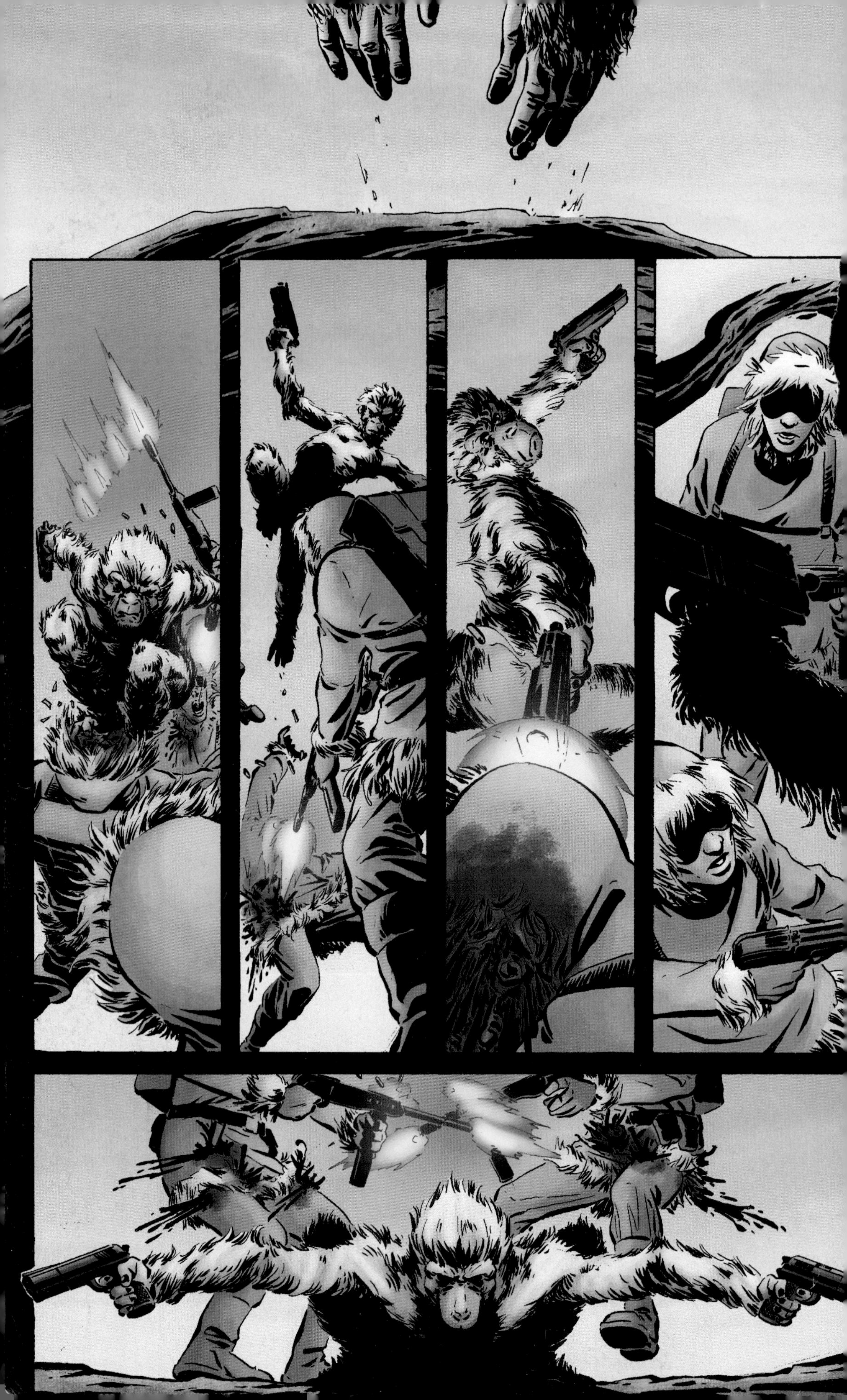

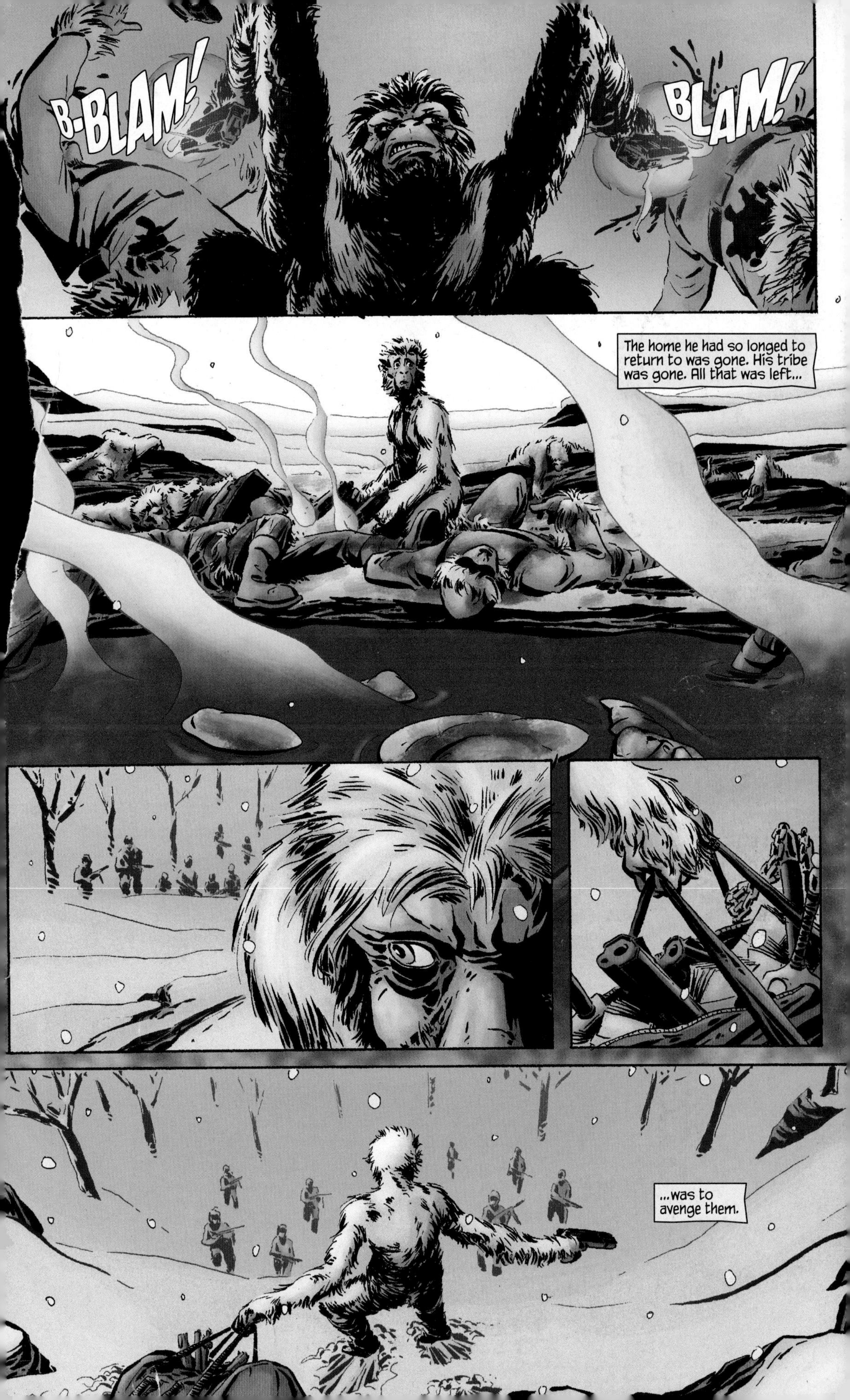
B-BLAM!
BLAM!
The home he had so longed to return to was gone. His tribe was gone. All that was left...
...was to avenge them.

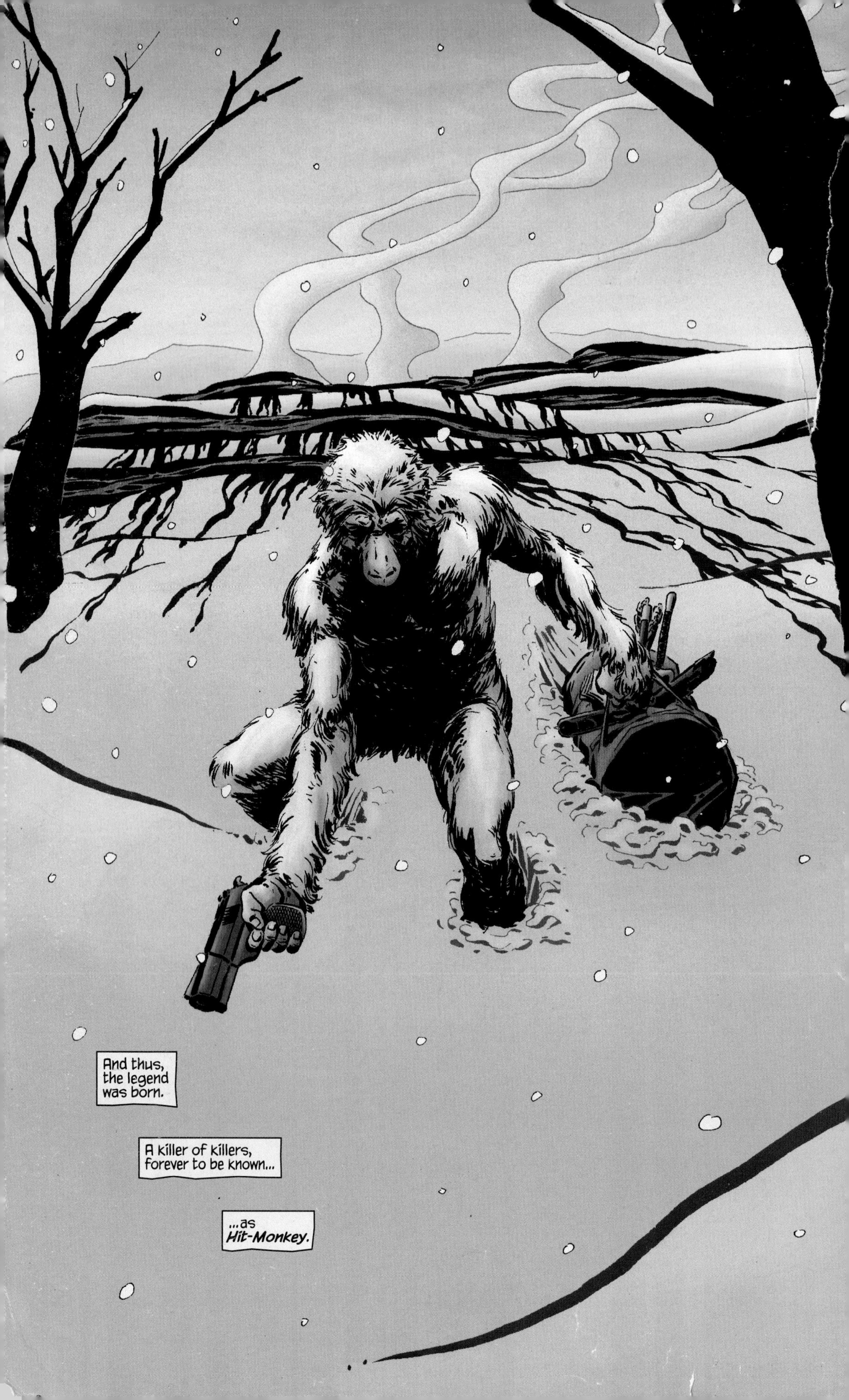
And thus, the legend was born.
A killer of killers, forever to be known...
...as *Hit-Monkey.*